Also By _The A.V. Club_

_Inventory: 16 Films Featuring Manic Pixie Dream Girls, 10 Great
Songs Nearly Ruined By Saxophone, And 100 More Obsessively Specific
Pop-Culture Lists_

_The Tenacity Of The Cockroach: Conversations With
Entertainment's Most Enduring Outsiders_

Also By Nathan Rabin

The Big Rewind: A Memoir Brought To You By Pop Culture

MY YEAR

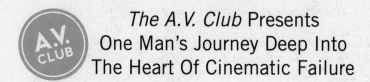

OF

FLOPS

The A.V. Club Presents
One Man's Journey Deep Into
The Heart Of Cinematic Failure

Nathan Rabin

Scribner

New York   London   Toronto   Sydney

SCRIBNER
A Division of Simon & Schuster, Inc.
1230 Avenue of the Americas
New York, NY 10020

First Scribner trade paperback edition October 2010

SCRIBNER and design are registered trademarks of The Gale Group, Inc., used under
license by Simon & Schuster, Inc., the publisher of this work.

For information about special discounts for bulk purchases,
please contact Simon & Schuster Special Sales at
1-866-506-1949 or business@simonandschuster.com.

The Simon & Schuster Speakers Bureau can bring authors to your live event. For more
information or to book an event contact the Simon & Schuster Speakers Bureau at
1-866-248-3049 or visit our website at www.simonspeakers.com.

Designed by Carla Jayne Jones
Interior illustrations by Danny Hellman

Manufactured in the United States of America

3   5   7   9   10   8   6   4   2

Library of Congress Control Number: 2010018224

ISBN 978-1-4391-5312-3
ISBN 978-1-4391-6031-2 (ebook)

For Danya, who loves movies and books
and has taught me all about joy

Contents

My Year Of Flops: An Introduction   xv

Chapter 1: Disastrous Dramas   1

Bataan Death March Of Whimsy Case File #1: *Elizabethtown*   1

Book-Exclusive Savage In Its Barbaric Intensity Case File:
The Conqueror   6

Upside Down And Starting To Like It That Way Case File #58:
The End Of Violence   11

Misunderestimated Book-Exclusive Case File: *W.*   14

Book-Exclusive Patented, Pain-Free Case File:
The Great Moment   21

Testifying Book-Exclusive Case File: *Gospel Road:*
A Story Of Jesus   27

Chapter 2: Calamitous Comedies   33

Tenacious Teen Terrors Case File #54: *O.C. And Stiggs*   33

Woody/Not Woody Case File #57: *Scenes From A Mall*   37

Contents

Book-Exclusive $20 Million Case File: *The Cable Guy*   40

Fun With Animals Case File #61: *Freddy Got Fingered*   46

Hippified Book-Exclusive Case File: *Skidoo*   48

Good-bye Blue Monday Case File #88:
   Breakfast Of Champions   57

Hickory Dickory Dock, George H. W. Bush–Era Playground
   Shock Book-Exclusive Case Files: *Dice Rules* And
   The Adventures Of Ford Fairlane   61

Trigger-Happy Teutonic Book-Exclusive Case File: *Postal*   69

Kicking A Man While He's Down Case File #132:
   The Love Guru   76

Chapter 3: Musical Misfires And Misunderstood Masterpieces   **82**

Beatles Smile-Time Variety Hour Without The Beatles
   Case File #51: *Sgt. Pepper's Lonely Hearts Club Band*   82

Madcap Musical Miserablism Case File #59:
   Pennies From Heaven   86

Biblical Disco Freak-Out Case File #79: *The Apple*   90

Seven-Octave Butterfly-Shaped Case File #90: *Glitter*   93

Seasons Of Cynicism Case File #98: *Rent*   96

Let's Go Crazy Case File #102: *Under The Cherry Moon*   100

All-Singing, All-Dancing Book-Exclusive Case File:
   The Musical Version Of *I'll Do Anything*   105

It Ain't Over 'Til The Old Lady Sings Book-Exclusive
   Case File: *Mame*   109

Chapter 4: It's A Bird! It's A Plane! It's A Flop! Superheroes, Science Fiction, And Action   **114**

Lady And Gentleman, You Are Now Floating In The
   Floposphere Case File #46: *It's All About Love*   114

Mad Mutated Case File #64: *The Island Of Dr. Moreau*   117

Spaced-Out Oddity Case File #91: *Southland Tales*   121

Big Green Brooding Case File #100: *Hulk*   127

All-Time Action-Comedy Classic Book-Exclusive Case File:
  Last Action Hero   129
Disgustingly Patriotic Case File #122: *The Rocketeer*   134

Chapter 5: Unsexy Sexy Films   **140**
Reality Bites Case File #56: *The Real Cancun*   140
Book-Exclusive, Freely Adapted Case File: *The Scarlet Letter* 142
Desperotica Case File #86: *Body Of Evidence*   147
Sex-Fantasy Island Case File #97: *Exit To Eden*   150
Maniacal Death-Orgy Case File #107: *Tough Guys Don't Dance* 155
Dominant-Paradigm-Subverting Case File #137:
  Even Cowgirls Get The Blues   160
How Do You Solve A Problem Like *Lolita*? Book-Exclusive
  Case File: *Lolita*   165

Chapter 6: My Year Of Flops Jr.: "You Know, For Kids!" **175**
When Middle-Aged Puppet-Men Attack! Case File #78:
  Pinocchio   175
Fuck You, Jew Case File #96: *Santa Claus: The Movie*   182
Totally Tween Case File #118: *Bratz: The Movie*   185

Chapter 7: The Floppiest Flops   **191**
Honestly Unpopular Case File #3: *Ishtar*   191
How The West Was Sung Case File #50: *Paint Your Wagon*   197
Fucking Original Straight First Foremost Pimp Mack
  Fucking Hustler Original Gangster's Gangster
  Case File #52: *Gigli*   200
Bicurious, Hankie-Waving Case File #63: *Cruising*   207
Rat-Brained, Man-Animal-Friendly Case File #66:
  Battlefield Earth   211
Animal-Abusing, Studio-Wrecking, Career-Killing Case
  File #81: *Heaven's Gate*   214
Trapped In A World It Never Made Case File #94:
  Howard The Duck   221

Pointlessly Postmodern Case File #103: *Psycho*   224

Epic, Extravagant, Excruciating Book-Exclusive Case File:

     Cleopatra   229

Chapter 8: A Fairy-Tale Ending; Or, Manic Pixie Dream Girls I Have Known   **235**

Constant, Total Amazement Case File #40: *Joe Versus The Volcano*   235

Full Circle Case File #1, Take 2: *Elizabethtown*   244

Death Is Not The End: An Afterword   **250**

Appendix: *Waterworld*: Director's Cut, Minute-By-Minute   **253**

Acknowledgments   **263**

If He made me in his image, then He's a failure too.

—Laura Marling, "Failure"

My Year Of Flops: An Introduction

From an early age, I learned to stop worrying and love the bombs. I've always been a failure junkie. I get giddy over toxic buzz, noxious press, and scathing reviews. I'm fascinated by the art and sociology of flops. You can learn a lot about society by the pop culture it embraces, and just as much by what it angrily rejects. As parents are keen to remind their children, there's no shame in failure, only in not trying. The biggest, most notorious flops generally fail because they try too hard, not because they lack ambition or audacity.

My solidarity with misfits, outsiders, and underachievers helped define my professional development. I began my film-reviewing career happily critiquing the dregs of cinema, forgotten ephemera like *Chill Factor* and *Gone Fishing*. As the first head writer of *The A.V. Club*, the entertainment section of *The Onion*, I've immersed myself in the dark, shadowy corners of the entertainment universe, where saner folks fear to tread: direct-to-video movies (for a column called Dispatches From Direct-To-DVD Purgatory), cheaply produced books by C-listers and hangers-on (for Silly Little Show-Biz Book Club), the *NOW That's What I Call Music!* series (for THEN That's What They Called

Music!), and audio commentaries on terrible films (for Commentary Tracks Of The Damned).

In *The A.V. Club*, I found a home and an audience willing to indulge my pop-culture masochism. Ah, but maybe "masochism" isn't the right word, because I love what I do; a trip to the multiplex to see the latest Tyler Perry movie or not-screened-for-critics dancesploitation cheapie fills me with anticipation rather than dread. Thirteen years on, I still sometimes can't believe I make my living writing about pop culture.

So when I decided to embark on a twice-weekly yearlong blog project in early 2007, I naturally gravitated toward an in-depth exploration of the biggest failures in cinematic history. I called the column My Year Of Flops. To qualify for My Year Of Flops, a film had to meet three unyielding/slippery criteria. It had to be a critical and commercial failure upon its release (domestically, at least). It had to have, at best, a marginal cult following. And it had to facilitate an endless procession of facile observations and labored one-liners.

Along with providing a forum for jokes, japes, and jests, My Year Of Flops had a serious goal. I wanted to fight our cultural tendency to associate commercial failure with artistic bankruptcy. I wanted to give flops something everyone deserves but precious few ever receive: a second chance. When I look at failures, cinematic and otherwise, I see myself. I welcomed the opportunity to provide a sympathetic reappraisal of some of the most reviled films of all time.

During the first year of My Year Of Flops, I found acceptance and validation from readers who cheered me on throughout my quixotic quest. Internet commenters, those nattering nabobs of negativism, transformed into perspicacious proponents of positivity. An online community that all too often resembles an easily agitated lynch mob turned into a band of angels. For I had created not just a blog project but an entire weird world of failure, regret, and bad ideas: a floposphere for pop-culture rubberneckers and schadenfreude enthusiasts. Fulfilling my wildest dreams, My Year Of Flops steadily grew to become that rarest and most wondrous of creatures: a moderately popular ongoing online feature. It was such a surprising success that readers wouldn't let go after the initial year was over, so I was "persuaded" to continue it indefinitely as a twice-monthly feature at avclub.com. At gunpoint.

Then My Year Of Flops became something even more rare and more wonderfultastic: a book. Not just any book—the book you currently hold in your hands! That you bought! With money you earned doing chores and robbing student nurses! And are going to read! Using your brain bone and imagination!

After much consideration, consultation with our pastors, and several rolls of the 12-sided die, we here at *The A.V. Club* have decided to augment 35 of what *SCTV*'s Guy Caballero would call My Year Of Flops' "Golden Classics" (which is to say, columns, aka Case Files, that already ran online in some form) with 15 brand-spanking-new Case Files of films too explosively floptastical for the Internet. But that isn't all! In a bid to break up the oppressive tyranny of my literary voice, we've included mini-interviews with some of the people involved in the flops I've covered. You angrily demanded Austin Pendleton's wry recollections of the making of *Skidoo*. We happily acquiesced.

The flops have been grouped according to genre, beginning with the first Case File, on *Elizabethtown*, which also provided the series with a ratings system dividing all films into three nebulous categories: Failure, Fiasco, and Secret Success. As Orlando Bloom stiffly declaims at the start of *Elizabethtown*, anyone can achieve failure, but a fiasco requires mad-prophet ambition and woeful miscalculation. At the top of the scale lie Secret Successes, films that have been slandered by history yet remain worthy of critical rehabilitation.

After chapters devoted to drama, comedy, superhero/science fiction/action films, musicals, the unsexiest sex films ever made, and family films that qualify as child abuse under the Geneva Conventions, we have a murderer's row of the most notorious flops ever made. Even a book about flops needs a happy ending and redemptive arc, so I conclude with the fairy-tale ending that fate wouldn't grant the films I've documented. There's an entry on *Joe Versus The Volcano*, a life-affirming fable about a miserable Failure who becomes a Secret Success because of a Fiasco. And I close with a reconsideration of the film that began it all—*Elizabethtown*—and then a blow-by-blow account of the three-hour-long director's cut of *Waterworld*.

I never intended *My Year Of Flops* to be a book about the 50 biggest flops or worst films of all time. There are plenty of books like that. This is not one of them. Rather, it's a deeply personal, deeply idiosyncratic journey through the history of cinematic failure populated both by the usual suspects (*Gigli, Battlefield Earth, Ishtar*) and intriguing semi-obscurities like Johnny Cash's *Gospel Road* and Thomas Vinterberg's *It's All About Love*.

I chose many of these flops not because their failure casts a huge shadow over pop culture but because they reflect the mythology of their creators and the cultural epoch they inhabited in fascinating and revealing ways. With each Case File, I set out to write about much more than the film addressed, to use an entry to explore, for example, the curious communion of Otto Preminger and the free-love movement in *Skidoo* or the perils and limitations of literary adaptations epitomized by *The Scarlet Letter, Breakfast of Champions,* and Adrian Lyne's *Lolita*.

Welcome to my wonderful world of flops. I'm psyched to explore the curious geography of celluloid bombs with you. It's a colorful realm of pee-drinking man-fish, inexplicably floating Africans, psychedelic disco/biblical freak-outs, time-traveling action heroes, an effeminate green alien only Fred Flintstone and Marlon Brando can see, and Rosie O'Donnell in leather bondage gear. Ignore all the road signs warning you to stay away. You're in Failure Country now, with me as your disreputable guide. Enjoy the ride.

MY YEAR

~ OF ~

FLOPS

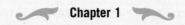 **Chapter 1**

Disastrous Dramas

Bataan Death March Of Whimsy Case File #1: *Elizabethtown*
Originally Posted January 25, 2007

> *As somebody once said, there's a difference between a failure and a fiasco. A failure is simply the non-presence of success. Any fool can accomplish failure. But a fee-ass-scoe, a fiasco is a disaster of mythic proportions. A fiasco is a folktale told to others that makes other people feel more alive because. It. Didn't. Happen. To. Them.*
> —*Drew Baylor,* Elizabethtown

After that opening piece of voice-over narration, Cameron Crowe's 2005 flop *Elizabethtown* goes on to illustrate by example just what a fiasco looks and feels like. *Elizabethtown* was cursed from its inception. Crowe cast, then uncast, Ashton Kutcher (in the role eventually played by Orlando Bloom) and Jane Fonda (in the role Susan Sarandon ultimately played) in the lead roles: Kutcher as a soulful superstar-shoe-designer-turned-suicidal-pariah who travels to Ken-

1

tucky to bury his dead father, and Fonda as his mother, an eccentric who spirals into impish lunacy once she's widowed. Like Crowe's *Jerry Maguire, Elizabethtown* is a populist morality play about a cocky young man humanized by failure who becomes a success in life only after failing spectacularly in business. After a disastrous early screening at the Toronto Film Festival, the film was drastically shortened and its ending altered.

So by the time *Elizabethtown* arrived in theaters, it was already a wounded duck. Going into the film, I thought, "How bad can a Cameron Crowe movie be?" Before *Elizabethtown*, I could say without reservation that Crowe was one of my favorite filmmakers. I don't just love his movies, I want to live in his world. The universe of *Almost Famous, Jerry Maguire,* and *Say Anything* is an infinitely humane realm ruled by an endlessly benevolent deity: Crowe himself. It's a world where no existential quandary is so great that it can't be solved by the perfect combination of classic rock song and dream girl. It's a world of happy pop epiphanies and gentle humanism, bravely devoid of protective irony or sneering cynicism.

In *Elizabethtown*, all Crowe's formidable virtues as a filmmaker betray him. His palpable affection for his characters devolves into pathological emotional neediness. Every frame and character screams, "Love me, love me, love me!" *Elizabethtown* feels like an X-ray of Crowe's soul set to the soundtrack of his life.

Crowe has never been afraid to go for big, pop-operatic moments that bound past realism in their quest for immortality. There's nothing naturalistic about lines like *Jerry Maguire*'s "You complete me," "You had me at hello," and "Show me the money," or John Cusack playing "In Your Eyes" on a boombox outside Ione Skye's window in *Say Anything*. Yet they spoke to moviegoers' deep, unfulfilled hunger for grand theatrical gestures and outsized declarations of love.

With *Elizabethtown*, Crowe subscribes to the logic that it's never enough merely to try; no, one must try way too fucking hard. It isn't enough that Drew is the corporate pariah behind a failed shoe; no, he has to be the man behind the greatest athletic-shoe debacle of all time, a nearly billion-dollar fuckup. Similarly, Crowe can't just have Drew contemplate suicide; he has to have his sad-sack protagonist create a homemade suicide machine with knives affixed to the handlebars that's 90 percent exercise bike, 10 percent gimmicky instrument of permanent self-negation. It's like the secret love child of Dr. Kevorkian and Rube Goldberg. In *Elizabethtown*'s universe, even suicide can be oppressively whimsical.

And he can't just have Drew's mom go a little loopy following her beloved husband's death. No, Crowe has Drew's mom use her late husband's memorial to introduce the world's first You-might-be-a-widow-manic-and-raw-with-grief-if . . . stand-up comedy routine. For example:

> *If the bank teller looks at you funny because you forgot to rinse off a green facial mask before leaving home . . . You might be a manic widow raw with grief!*

> *If you think a memorial for your dead husband is the appropriate place to launch your stand-up comedy and tap-dancing careers . . . You might be a manic widow raw with grief!*

> *If you think it's appropriate to tell the audience at your husband's memorial that your next-door neighbor got a massive boner while trying to console you, then repeat the word "boner" over and over as the crowd of mourners goes into red-faced hysterics . . . You might be a manic widow raw with grief!*

In writing and directing *Elizabethtown*, Crowe somehow managed to silence his inner censor and cynic, the naysayer in each of us that implores, "Don't write that. People will make fun of you. Do you really expect a line like, 'This loss will be met by a hurricane of love,' to be met with anything other than a tornado of derisive snickers?" That's both admirable and insane. Crowe never lets audiences forget that they're watching not just a Cameron Crowe film but the Cameron Croweiest film in existence, a movie so poignantly personal it makes even the autobiographical *Almost Famous* look like cynical work-for-hire.

But the purest manifestation of Crowe's need to afflict audiences with a two-hour-long hurricane of self-love lies in the unbearably twee conception of Drew's love interest, Claire (Kirsten Dunst). Claire embodies a character type I call the Manic Pixie Dream Girl. (See Natalie Portman in *Garden State* for another prime example.) The Manic Pixie Dream Girl exists solely in the fevered imaginations of sensitive writer-directors, who use them to teach broodingly soulful young men to embrace life. The Manic Pixie Dream Girl serves as a means to an end, not a flesh-and-blood human being. Once life lessons have been imparted, the Manic Pixie Dream Girl might as well disappear in a *poof!* for her life's work is done.

The Manic Pixie Dream Girl is an all-or-nothing proposition. Audiences either want to marry her, or commit grievous bodily harm upon her and her immediate family. Claire, for all her overly caffeinated joie de vivre, falls on the wrong side of that divide. She is a prolific disseminator of Crowe's patented big pop-operatic moments, whether she's keeping Drew awake and giddy during an all-night cell-phone verbal duet, or sending him on an intricately mapped-out road trip that ends the film on a note of delirious excess.

I once had a Manic Pixie Dream Girlfriend who induced terrifying *Elizabethtown* flashbacks. We even bonded over a marathon phone call that left us exhausted and exhilarated in equal measure. Not long after we started dating, she began asking if I was falling in love with her, over and over. At the risk of waxing hyperbolic, it was the single most annoying thing in the history of the universe. It was as if she was trying to bully me into falling in love. That's the essence of the Manic Pixie Dream Girl: She doesn't ask for our love, she demands it. But love isn't enough. She also needs to be romanticized, idealized, fetishized, worshipped, and adored. You know, all the stupid shit young men do. She glares impishly in our direction menacingly with a look that says, "You better fall in love with me, fuckface, or I will open up a big can of joy on that ass."

Elizabethtown shows what happens when a gifted writer-director lets his heart do his brain's work for him. Yet the film stuck with me in ways genuinely successful films haven't. I still talk and think about it all the time. The origins of My Year Of Flops began with *Elizabethtown*. By the time Drew embarked on a Claire-orchestrated road trip set to a mixtape of Crowe's favorite songs, *Elizabethtown* was starting to barrel through my formidable defenses. [So I vowed to rewatch it later in the project, to see if another viewing would win me over. Did it? Find out later, when I revisit *Elizabethtown* as the very last Case File in this here book.]

Failure, Fiasco, Or Secret Success? *Fiasco*

Book-Exclusive Savage In Its Barbaric Intensity Case File: *The Conqueror*

In his book *Citizen Hughes: The Power, The Money, And The Madness*, Michael Drosnin quotes extensively from a memo the reclusive billionaire Howard Hughes fired off to top aide Robert Maheu, chronicling a glimpse of hell he'd spied on television. Claiming the sight "literally and actually physically made me nauseated," Hughes goes on to describe the nightmare vision of "the biggest, ugliest negro you ever saw in your life . . . covered—literally [*sic*] covered from head to foot with Vaseline almost ¼ of an inch thick."

That image alone was enough to fuel Hughes' nightmares, but what happened next sent him into a rage. The Vaseline-smeared man-beast lurched savagely over to what Hughes describes as "an immaculately dressed white woman—sort of an English noblewoman type" and subjected her to an obscene, endless open-mouthed kiss with the power to single-handedly destroy civilization and usher in a hellscape of raging, open miscegenation.

The "biggest, ugliest negro you ever saw in your life" in question was James Earl Jones. The "English noblewoman type" was Jane Alexander. And the film was 1970's *The Great White Hope*. It wasn't the only time the terrifying prospect of miscegenation threw the easily excited tycoon into a tizzy. Hughes was so horrified at what he saw as a "sinful interracial assignation" (it was actually a light-skinned black woman dating a darker-skinned black man) on *The Dating Game* that he fired off another enraged memo to Maheu and put the kibosh on plans to spend $200 million to buy ABC, the network that ran *The Dating Game*.

What does Howard Hughes' profound discomfort at a young James Earl Jones fiendishly rubbing his Vaseline-coated body all over the delicate ladyparts of proper white women have to do with My Year Of Flops? Judging by 1956's *The Conqueror*, which Hughes produced through his RKO studio, miscegenation obsessed him well before he traded in the high life for television, solitude, and insanity.

One of the biggest, ugliest epics you never saw in your life, *The Conqueror* is only slightly less obsessed with the carnal possibilities of folks from different ethnicities getting it on than *Interracial Gang Bang Sluts Volume 7*. *The Conqueror* offers a mind-bending act of interracial minstrelsy, as supercracker John Wayne fused DNA with the great Asian conqueror eventually known as Genghis Khan but known as Temujin here to become an odd creature known, to me at least, as John Wayneghis Khan. Marvel at this strange beast, neither Caucasian nor Asian! Gawk at the unconvincing makeup and silly Fu Manchu designed to transform a top American movie star into the living personification of what old-time folks called the Yellow Peril!

While Wayneghis Khan is not quite white and not quite Asian, the object of his intense erotic fascination, Bortai (Susan Hayward), a goddess with skin the color of bone china, is ostensibly the daughter of a Tatar leader. Yet she's codified unmistakably as a cross between an icy Southern belle and what Hughes would describe approvingly as an "English noblewoman type."

Hayward plays her haughty empress of the desert as the Scarlett O'Hara of Central Asia, an ice queen who must be tamed by the calloused hands and hot breath of the right savage. The film's first half is one long intimation of sexual violence, as Wayneghis Khan violates Bortai with his eyes and defiles her with his crude words before bludgeoning his way into her heart and loins through sheer force.

In that respect, the philosophy of Wayneghis Khan echoes the personal ethos of Hughes, who didn't court women so much as conquer them. Hughes undoubtedly saw an awful lot of himself in Genghis. Hughes was a fascinating contradiction: He was simultaneously a superhero and a supervillain, Tony Stark as Iron Man and the Mandarin, a comic-book nemesis descended, appropriately enough, from Genghis Khan. Hughes seduced movie stars and crashed experimental planes for fun and profit. It makes sense that he would be drawn to figures as outsized as Wayne and Genghis.

What did Hughes see when he looked at Wayneghis Khan in *The Conqueror*? Did he see a surrogate for his own boundless ambition and unrelenting determination? Or did he see a terrifying Other that would not rest until it transformed the raging hatred of an idealized White Woman into sweaty, uncontrollable lust? Did he see Genghis as a threat, or as a figure of wish fulfillment? That ambiguity is a big part of what makes *The Conqueror* equal parts compelling and repellent.

Actor-turned-director William Powell makes the regressive racial politics of his Far East Western apparent in an opening crawl that ushers audiences into a 12th-century Gobi desert that "seethed with unrest," as "petty chieftains pursued their small ambitions with cunning and wanton cruelty. Plunder and rapine were a way of life, and no man trusted his brother." Other than that, though, it was pretty chill.

The filmmakers weren't kidding about rapine and plunder being a way of life. From the moment Wayneghis Khan spies Bortai—who's reclining languidly atop a yak-pulled caravan with a bored look that says, "Calgon or a fiery yellow brute, take me away!"—he's intent on having her, preferably by force.

Thus begins one of cinema's most rapecentric romances. The purple dialogue is riddled with references to sexual assault. When Wayneghis Khan brings Bortai to meet his hunched-over crone of a mother, she counsels, "Let your slaves have their sport with her!" When Wayneghis Khan checks his internal moral compass/circulatory system to decide whether rape is the right choice for him, he reports back, "My blood says 'take her.'" He threatens Bortai's father by vowing, "Your treacherous head is not safe on your shoulders, nor [Bortai] in her bed!" He also warns, "While I live, while my blood burns hot, your daughter is not safe in her tent."

"He took what he wanted, when he wanted it!" screams the film's trailer before tastefully promising "Barbaric passions!" and "Savage conquests!" Sure enough, Wayneghis Khan expresses his fondness for Bortai by ripping off her dressing gown and vowing to soil her lady virtue.

The Conqueror's violence isn't limited to constant references to rape. At one point, a chieftain describes, with altogether too much relish, what is referred to as the "slow death": "Joint by joint, from the toe and fingertip upwards, shall you be cut to pieces, and each carrion piece, hour by hour and day by day, shall be cast to the dogs before your very eyes, until they, too, shall be plucked out as morsels for the vultures!" This is seriously nasty stuff, an ungodly cross between a lurid paperback novel (*Her Savage Love!*) and a porn film with the sex removed.

Powell and Hughes' film feels dirty and borderline pornographic, and not just because of its loathsome racial politics, its rape-happy hero in yellowface, and its looming threat of sexual violence. Hughes' millions could buy big stars and big production values, but it couldn't buy taste or professionalism. Accordingly, an air of amateurishness hangs heavy over the film. Some of the dialogue is so unwieldy it appears to be poorly translated from Cantonese. You have to really ponder a line like, "You know ill the son of Yessugai!" (which is Wayneghis Khan's convoluted way of saying, "Y'all don't know me, dog!"), and you have to keep the right punctuation in mind just for it to make sense. Otherwise, it could easily be mistaken for, "You know Ill, the son of Yessugai? He just purchased a lovely new tent! He's quite the macher, that Ill! Yessugai must be proud!"

Wayne shouts every line through clenched teeth, like an actor in a fifth-grade production whose ambition begins and ends with making sure his parents in the back row can hear him. What Wayne's acting lacks in competence, it makes up for in volume: He doesn't deliver his lines so much as declaim them to the heavens.

Wayneghis eventually succeeds in wearing down Bortai's defenses. But first, they enter into an endless dance of seduction and repulsion, love and hate. In the film's most memorable sequence, he takes Bortai to a palace where they watch exotic Mongol dancers writhe with sensual abandon. When one of their hosts inquires why Bortai seethes with such barely restrained animosity, Wayneghis Khan jokes, "Lacking the talents of these women, the sight of them irks her."

Eager to prove him wrong, Bortai indulges in an erotic dance of her own. The untouchable ice princess is revealed to be a carnal creature after all. The sword she flings at him as a crowning gesture is *The Conqueror*'s idea of foreplay. Bortai can't resist much longer. She tells his brother, "Tell me of Temujin. I know of him only that on a sudden, my hatred for him could not withstand my love."

The Conqueror loses much of its creepy power in its second half, as the train-wreck fascination of dialogue like "Not even the mighty Kasar bends iron forged by Sorgan. There's a secret in the dipping of it" gives way to a bloody, simple-minded, fairly conventional B-Western with Eastern epic trappings.

The Conqueror's legacy is only partly rooted in the surreal incongruity of John Wayne turning Genghis Khan into a shit-kicking cowboy with ridiculous facial hair and its abhorrent racial/sexual politics. Much of the debacle's infamy stems from Hughes' decision to film the movie downwind from a nuclear testing site, a decision that might have contributed to the cancer deaths of Powell, Wayne, Hayward, and costar Agnes Moorehead.

Hughes reportedly felt so guilty about the film and the death of many of its principals that he paid $12 million for every existing print and didn't allow it to be seen on television until 1974. *The Conqueror* marked the end of Hughes' dalliance with filmmaking; he'd never produce another film (RKO put out *Jet Pilot* in 1957, but it was completed in 1949). The film was predictably eviscerated by critics and ignored by audiences before being embraced as übercamp by bad-movie aficionados.

It could be argued that God delivered a final punishment to the makers of *The Conqueror* for their transgressions against cinema. But no one deserves to die for making a bad movie, even a film as egregiously awful as *The Conqueror.* Hughes was lucky enough to avoid cancer. Instead, obsessive-compulsive disorder hastened his descent into madness and paranoia. According to show-business legend, he rewatched *The Conqueror* repeatedly during the grim final years of his life, dreaming in the dark about a world waiting to be conquered and a legendary warrior whose savage lust for power, women, and glory must have struck him as terrifying yet familiar.

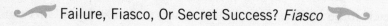 Failure, Fiasco, Or Secret Success? *Fiasco*

Upside Down And Starting To Like It That Way Case File #58: *The End Of Violence*
Originally Posted August 14, 2007

Wim Wenders' 1997 muddle *The End Of Violence* surveys a United States where the government covertly spies on its own people in the name of protecting them. It anticipates a paranoid national climate of free-floating dread, where citizens are willing to sacrifice liberty for security. The attacks of September 11 and the rise of the U.S.A. PATRIOT Act should lend the film an air of uncanny prescience. So why does Wenders' moody meditation on violence feel more like the paranoid ravings of a street-corner lunatic than like a profound act of pop-art prophecy? Probably because while Wenders gets a few crucial things right, he gets nearly everything else hilariously, unbelievably, almost inconceivably wrong—particularly violence, movies, American culture, human psychology, and (oh, dear Lord) gangsta rap. Sometimes it takes foreign eyes to discern great truths about our country that are invisible to natives, like when Vladimir Nabokov wrote *Lolita*. (I discuss that book and its second film adaptation in a later chapter.) And sometimes it takes a foreigner to craft a portrayal of our culture so bizarrely off base that it borders on bad science fiction. *The End Of Violence* holds a funhouse mirror up to our culture's obsession with violence, and the result is a portrait of God's own USA that's distorted, grotesque, and borderline unrecognizable.

Wenders' film asks what it imagines is a deep, relevant question: How do violence merchants like Jerry Bruckheimer and Joel Silver sleep at night? I'm guessing the answer is, "Soundly, and with high-priced, 19-year-old call girls on either side of them."

The End Of Violence centers on gruff, well-compensated Hollywood superproducer Mike Max (Bill Pullman), who decides he needs to be less like Don Simpson and more like Jesus Christ after a pair of sloppy contract killers nearly murder him. In pretentious death-of-the-soul movies like this, there's a direct correlation between spiritual emptiness and technology usage. So it's telling that Mike's high-powered vulgarian is introduced alternately communicating through video conferencing, a headset, a cell phone, and a football-sized mobile phone. If Mike were even slightly more removed from nature, his feelings, and his family, he'd also be manning a CB radio ("Ten-four, good buddy, looks like the missus got herself a killer case a that, whaddyacallit, existential ennui!").

While manning his interpersonal battle station, Mike gets distressing news from one of his underlings: Someone has dropped a 400-page file in his e-mail! On the Intern-nets! Using various tubes! Shortly thereafter, a pair of goons nearly murder Mike, and he goes on the lam as an anonymous everyman. After surviving his close call with death, he begins behaving like a hard-boiled gumshoe in a Mickey Spillane paperback. While recuperating, Mike rasps, "There's nothing quite like a couple of killers with a shotgun to your head to make you pay attention." So Mike gives up the Hollywood good life to toil as a humble gardener in a Latino neighborhood. He's like a Hollywood Jesus who came back from the dead solely to finish his work as a carpenter.

Mike continues to dispense bite-sized nuggets of hard-boiled wisdom throughout the film. Here are some other choice selections from my forthcoming book, *All I Really Need To Know I Learned From The Narration In* The End Of Violence: "There are no enemies or strangers. Just a strange world." "'Perversely': That's one thing I think I can define now. It's when things are upside down and you start to like them that way." "The thing about a sudden attack is, you never know where it's coming from." (Also, it happens suddenly, and involves an attack.) "I guess sometimes your friends are really your enemies. Sometimes your enemies are your friends. Sometimes they're one and the same. Who can you trust? Reminds me of what a prick I was."

So anyway. The botched Mike assassination is linked to a mysterious FBI program run by sad-eyed ex–NASA man Ray Bering (Gabriel Byrne), who spies furtively on the citizens of Los Angeles from countless unseen electronic eyes scattered throughout the city.

Even before Mike's mysterious disappearance, his wife, Page (Andie MacDowell), seems to be suffering a terminal case of art-film ennui, a condition she expresses by lurching about in a depressed, vaguely narcotized haze and babbling spacily about how being married to Mike is like being a sentient rocketship with him at the controls. Page stares vacantly into space, mopes, and cries—first a single perfect tear, then a whole stream of them. This is somehow supposed to be distinguishable from MacDowell's usual performances. *The End Of Violence* affords ample time to contemplate the enigma that is Andie MacDowell's face: perfect, icy, remote, empty.

In *Violence*, people constantly undergo astonishing transformations. Mike impulsively decides that fame, riches, and power are no substitute for poverty and anonymity. Page undergoes a similarly dramatic transformation. In Mike's absence, she morphs from a powerless Ophelia into a cold-blooded, iron-willed Lady Macbeth eager to assume leadership of her missing husband's empire.

But these transformations pale in comparison to the spiritual metamorphosis of the film's most deliciously ridiculous, wonderfully implausible character, a mustachioed gangsta-rap mogul, producer, and rapper named Six O One played by K. Todd Freeman, a respected theater director and actor woefully ill equipped to play a sneering studio gangsta. Six O One is clearly modeled on Dr. Dre, yet he looks and dresses like a smooth-jazz musician, is clearly pushing 40, employs slang that hasn't been current since they stopped making breakdancing exploitation movies, and says things like, "You know my shit is phat. It's hot, man. You gonna be using it? Or are you going to be losing it?"

After Six receives a prank call urging him to abandon violence in his lyrics, he experiences a profound existential crisis (which seems to be sweeping the greater Los Angeles area) and delivers a patchouli-scented spoken-word piece about how, like, violence is played out and wack, and being peaceful is where it's at.

The End Of Violence is about the emptiness of popular culture from a filmmaker who apparently hasn't picked up a magazine or listened to the radio in 15 years. As an allegorical, downbeat mood piece, the film has a certain power. As usual with Wenders' films, it features an elegant soundtrack and superb cinematography. Narratively and psychologically, the film is so perversely upside down that I almost began to like it that way. But its singular fusion of arthouse pretension and hard-boiled posturing seems completely removed from the world on which it's supposed to be commenting. "Why do I make films in America? I should have stayed in Europe," frustrated filmmaker/Wenders surrogate Zoltan Kovacs (Udo Kier) muses late in the film. In spite of Wenders' scattered successes on this side of the pond, that's the one line in *Violence* that rings absolutely true.

Failure, Fiasco, Or Secret Success? *Fiasco*

Misunderestimated Book-Exclusive Case File: *W.*

All cinephiles reach a moment in their intellectual development when they realize that Oliver Stone is full of shit. I experienced that epiphany at 15 while watching *The Doors*. Suddenly everything about Stone and his aesthetic seemed patently ridiculous: the peyote-soaked pseudo-mysticism, the laughable pretension, the stylistic excess, the self-aggrandizing idealization of the '60s counterculture, and the exhausting, empty hedonism. It was as if a Native American spirit guide appeared to me in the bathroom of the Lincoln Village Theater in the form of a majestic eagle and uttered the magical words, "You know this guy's a fucking hack, don't you? Major, major tool. The path to wisdom begins with that understanding."

I'd grown up seeing Oliver Stone as the archetypal Serious Art-ist. Turns out he was simultaneously more and less than that: He was an outsized caricature of a Serious Artist. He made Important Films about Important Subjects that demanded to be capitalized, including War (*Platoon*), the Antiwar Movement (*Born On The Fourth Of July*), Business (*Wall Street*), The Kennedy Assassination (*JFK*), Violence in the Media (*Natural Born Killers*), and Presidential Politics (*Nixon*). He was nominated for 11 Oscars, and won three.

Stone's Very Important Films about Very Important Issues both reflected and affected the zeitgeist. For almost a decade, an intense culture-wide conversation accompanied almost every Stone film. After *Platoon*, no one could shut the fuck up about Vietnam. *Wall Street* unleashed a wave of editorial hand-wringing about the excesses of capitalism. *JFK* incited a firestorm of controversy about the Kennedy assassination. *Nixon* proved that, to borrow William Faulkner's famous line (and mix it with some Gerald Ford), the long national nightmare of Watergate is never dead; it's not even past. *Natural Born Killers* gave thousands of freelance writers permission to pitch stories about the desensitizing effects of violence in the media.

Where other major filmmakers trafficked in irony and ambiguity, Stone was considerate enough to tell audiences how they should feel and think. Around the time I was visited by the Native American spirit guide, I came to realize that great art doesn't tell you what to think—that's propaganda's job. Great art respects audiences enough not to bombard them with heavy-handed messages. To paraphrase the theme song to *Skidoo*, Stone forgot about the color that's between the black and white, the groovy little in-between.

During his 1986 to 1994 heyday, Stone couldn't be denied. After that, it became prohibitively difficult to take him seriously. Stone had a remarkable eight-year run as our most controversial, talked-about filmmaker, but then began a long, seemingly permanent slide into irrelevance. After his long stint as American film's reigning enfant terrible, everyone seemed to realize he was just plain terrible.

After the failure of 2004's *Alexander*, Stone delivered his most conventional film in 2006's tastefully dull *World Trade Center*. Stone surprised his detractors by releasing a film about 9/11 that conservatives could embrace. He'd gotten boring and safe in his old age. With his next project, he looked to reestablish his maverick reputation by setting his sights on the most famous, controversial man in the world at the time: George W. Bush.

Stone wasn't going to wait for history to render its verdict on Bush's legacy. Like Haskell Wexler with *Medium Cool*, Stone was going to capture history as it was being written. 2008's *W.* was rushed into production and filmed in just 46 days so it could hit theaters at the tail end of the presidential election. From the beginning, an air of instant obsolescence hung over the film. By October 17, 2008, the film's release date, even George W. Bush had come to think of George W. Bush as history's greatest monster; that "Worst. President. Ever." bumper sticker on the back of the presidential limousine was a dead giveaway.

So I entered the preview screening of *W.* with mixed emotions. The 12-year-old in me that bought the media's spin on Oliver Stone as the only filmmaker who mattered looked forward to a Bold Statement from an Important Filmmaker. The 32-year-old me dreaded a desperate stunt from an increasingly irrelevant provocateur.

The early buzz on *W.* was that it was both a raucous comedy and a surprisingly empathetic depiction of the man progressives loved to hate. In the spirit of *Nixon*, Stone was going to elicit sympathy for a preeminent political devil. Reduced to its broad outlines, *W.* certainly suggests a rowdy slobs-vs.-snobs farce: underachieving, hard-partying, malapropism-prone son of an uptight New England blueblood raises hell and runs amok for four solid decades before somehow ending up as the most powerful man in the world during a crucial period in the nation's history. Then he ends up nearly destroying the planet in a desperate attempt to impress Dad. Think of it as a real-life *King Ralph* mixed with a Shakespearean tragedy and a soupçon of *Being There*.

W. leapfrogs back and forth in time between Bush's stint as the wildly improbable leader of the free world and his far more plausible wild years as a booze-addled fuckup. Shifting easily between a simian smirk and a grimace of sober contemplation, Josh Brolin plays W. as an idiot man-child whose life and career are defined by his relationship with his wealthy, powerful father, George H. W. Bush (James Cromwell). In an acting choice as daring as it is distracting, Cromwell makes no effort to talk or act like Bush Senior, aka "Poppy." He merely functions as an exemplar of chilly aristocratic reserve who loudly broadcasts his disappointment with W. and expresses his preference for W.'s brother Jeb at every opportunity.

Bush Senior's face is permanently fixed in a scowl when dealing with W., but he talks about the bottomless potential and genius of Jeb with a gleam in his eye that implicitly says, "Why, if I weren't straight and he weren't my son, I would so go gay for Jeb. Those big, soulful eyes; those strong, masculine hands; that devastating wit . . . It would just be heaven spooning with him for hours and hours and hours. What's that, shit for brains? You just got elected governor of Texas? Good for you, though I doubt you'll do a tenth as good a job as that wonderful Jeb Bush would."

Before he essentially begins his life over at 40, W. lurches drunkenly from one low to another. He's arrested for shenanigans at a football game. He drunk-drives onto Poppy's lawn. He's a failure as an oilman and as a candidate for the House of Representatives. Just about the only thing he succeeds in is pissing off Dad and drinking his weight in liquor every night.

Then he turns 40. The rich, they are different from you and me. For example, they get a big do-over if they've wasted the first four decades of their lives. W. is born again in the truest sense: He gets smashed at his 40th birthday party and falls to the ground while running. He collapses into a fetal heap and gives his life over to Jesus.

Perhaps the ultimate tragedy of W.'s life is that the humility of an alcoholic prostrating himself before God and conceding his power-lessness before his addiction morphed into the tragic arrogance of a leader behaving as if the Lord acted directly through him. After being born again, W. acts with absolute moral certainty. He's the decider, but the Heavenly Father calls the shots.

W. clumsily acknowledges this by interminably dragging out the moment when, late in his presidency, W. is asked during a press con-ference what mistakes he's made since 9/11, and what he's learned from them. It's a major, if not definitive, moment in the man's life, as W. stumbles and bumbles and wastes a lot of words saying nothing. A man incapable of acknowledging mistakes and learning from them is a man incapable of grasping the complexities of the world, but the scene would be more resonant if Stone didn't lay on the sorrowful strings and concerned reaction shots that add exclamation points to a theme he's already spelling out in capital letters.

Once W. sets his sights first on the Texas governorship and then on the White House, the film turns into a Cliffs Notes version of his presidency, hitting all the expected notes with no poetry or grace. When Donald Rumsfeld (Scott Glenn) tells W., "You know I don't do nuance. It's just not my thing," he could be channeling Stone. Every-thing in *W.* is condensed and simplified.

Why let themes and conflicts emerge organically when you can foreground them in the dialogue? Why establish through subtext the widespread perception of Desert Storm as the antidote to our crushing defeat in Southeast Asia, when you can simply have George H. W. grin big and volunteer, "I guess we finally kicked that Vietnam Syndrome"? Why subtly hint that W.'s popularity was largely attributable to his reputation as the working man's fantasy drinking buddy, when you can simply have Karl Rove (Toby Jones) tell him, "What it all comes down to is who Joe Voter wants to sit down and have a beer with. And guess who that is?" before shooting an approving finger in W.'s direction.

Stone assembled an impressive array of ringers to round out the supporting cast, though the result plays, to borrow Woodrow Wilson's alleged praise of *Birth Of A Nation,* less like history written with lightning than like a *Saturday Night Live* sketch in which familiar faces have a go at playing top political figures. Thandie Newton decides to give her Condoleezza Rice the excitable nasal whine and demeanor of Olive Oyl, while the brilliant Jeffrey Wright gives us the Colin Powell of liberal daydreams, the noble voice of reason and restraint, a good man in an impossible situation. He's the angel on Bush's shoulder, overruled by thousands of neocon devils on the other side, baying for blood and oil.

In its painful last act, *W.* is as lost as its subject during the final years of his presidency. *W.* lacks both righteous indignation and sympathy. Stone's attitude toward his subject isn't rage or empathy so much as passive aggression. Its attempts to generate sympathy for its subject are compromised by its reliance on clunky dumb-guy humor and an unfortunate need to shoehorn W.'s greatest verbal gaffes into strange, inaccurate contexts, like having W. deliver the famous "misunderestimating" line in a strategy meeting about the Middle East.

When considering what Stone set out to do with *W.*—the first and hopefully last lame-duck presidential biopic—it's instructive to think of what *Fahrenheit 9/11,* another manifesto by a loud, divisive, self-publicizing lefty blowhard, actually accomplished. *Fahrenheit 9/11* received the reception *W.* was denied. Even before its release, *9/11* transcended film and became not just a pop-culture phenomenon but also a cultural phenomenon. It was big news.

Moore chronicled the tragicomic 2000 election with a visceral intensity that felt like an old wound being ripped open. Watching *Fahrenheit 9/11* was like reliving a national trauma. When Stone just barely dramatizes the run-up to the Iraq War, it feels like a rerun. Stone's films have always been wildly, even irritatingly cinematic, but *W.* feels like a television movie shot on the cheap.

Stone saves his worst crimes against subtlety for the very end, during a pair of fantasy sequences. In one, George H. W. decries W.'s presidency as nothing short of a "goddamned fiasco" and bitches him out for ruining things for H. W.'s beloved, beautiful, godlike favorite son Jeb. I'd somehow missed the film's previous 700 references to H. W. being disappointed in W. and favoring Jeb, so I appreciated Stone once again making the film's themes extra clear. In the second fantasy sequence, W. is patrolling center field for the Texas Rangers—a team he once co-owned—and lets a home-run ball get away from him. You know, like he let greatness get away from him during his presidency, and shit.

Stone took a big risk making a biopic about the sitting president. That's the kind of ambition I like to praise and damn with My Year Of Flops. Alas, the film everyone was going to be talking about became the film the culture more or less ignored. Let's just hope Oliver Stone's *Palin* never gets green-lit.

Failure, Fiasco, Or Secret Success? *Fiasco*

Richard Dreyfuss On *W.*

The '70s ushered in a new era of unconventional leading men with offbeat looks and quirky personae. Richard Dreyfuss rode that wave to fame and glory as the Academy Award–winning star of hits like *American Graffiti, Jaws, The Goodbye Girl, Down & Out In Beverly Hills,* and *Stakeout.*

Richard Dreyfuss: Playing Dick Cheney was great. It was like a great meal. Unfortunately, it was done by a guy who took the politics out of the story, so it'll have no legs. He had an opportunity to keep a very important character in the film, and that character was you and me, the ones who really were, for a while, afraid of their own president. But by deciding to keep the story in the White House, it looked like business as usual, so the character couldn't appear. And there's no reason to see the film after you get past the performances or whatever. Josh [Brolin] is great, [Elizabeth Banks] is great, I'm really good.

And Oliver [Stone] is a putz who screamed that I was the worst actor he'd ever worked with, and I'd ruined his film, he had to cut around me. And I said, "Oliver, you've made one strategic error." He said, "What was that?" I said, "The junket has yet to come." And then I ripped him apart at the junket. They said, "What did you think of the film?" And I went . . . [Grimaces.] I answered the question. And as I'm doing now, I'm continuing to do that, because he was a bully, he was graceless at the top of his lungs, and he blew a great opportunity, artistically, commercially, whatever you want to call it. And I have a just-big-enough ego. I don't do favors for people who treat me like a pig. So as far as I'm concerned, you can lead this story off by saying, "Richard Dreyfuss still thinks Oliver is an asshole."

Nathan Rabin: Were you able to empathize with Cheney over the course of playing him?

RD: Empathize? No. I think that he was true to himself, you know? He really did believe that the executive branch was superior to the legislative and the courts. He really did believe that the executive had the right to tell Congress to go fuck itself.

NR: It was an imperial presidency.

RD: Yeah. And he believed in the PATRIOT Act. And there was never a conspiracy with the Bush people. They never planned anything. They just waited for our outrage, which never appeared, so they took the next step. We're the villains, because we have lost our outrage.

Book-Exclusive Patented, Pain-Free Case File: *The Great Moment*

In Preston Sturges' 1941 masterpiece *Sullivan's Travels*, the pampered, wildly successful comedy director behind such fanciful frivolities as *Ants In Your Pants Of 1939*, *Hey Hey In The Hayloft*, and *So Long Sarong* tires of pumping out mindless escapism and sets out to make *O Brother, Where Art Thou?*, a timely, socially relevant drama about the human condition. To prepare, he escapes the comforting womb of Hollywood and experiences poverty firsthand as an undercover hobo. He ends up on a chain gang for his troubles but learns he can do far more good for the ever-suffering masses as a maker of mirth than as a dour chronicler of the human condition.

In 1942, Preston Sturges, the pampered, wildly successful comedy director, set out to make a timely, socially relevant drama about the human condition and the cruelty of fate called *The Great Moment*. He was punished for his ambition with just about every indignity short of a stint on a chain gang.

When he made *The Great Moment*, Sturges was in the midst of one of the greatest streaks in American film, a five-year stretch that encompassed such unassailable apogees of cinematic comedy as *The Great McGinty, Christmas In July, The Lady Eve, Sullivan's Travels, The Palm Beach Story, The Miracle Of Morgan's Creek,* and *Hail The Conquering Hero*. Yet Sturges' success mattered little to his bosses over at Paramount. The debonair filmmaker watched in horror as *The Great Moment* was reedited against his will, his prologue discarded, the running time trimmed to 81 minutes, and the film's title changed twice (from *Triumph Over Pain* to *Great Without Glory* to *The Great Moment*). Then it lingered on a shelf for years. Upon its eventual 1944 release, moviegoers ignored it and critics dismissed it.

It was the beginning of the end for one of our greatest writer-directors. After *The Great Moment* spelled the death of his formerly fruitful relationship with Paramount, Sturges endured a disastrous stint co-running a nonstarting film studio with Howard Hughes. He suffered from mounting debt and projects that never got off the ground. Between the release of *The Great McGinty* and *The Great Moment*, Preston Sturges went from being seen as the miracle man with the magic touch to a difficult filmmaker whose best days were behind him.

Sturges' lively exploration of the birth of painless dentistry was fucked in myriad ways, most of them related to timing. The studio flinched at releasing a film called *Triumph Over Pain* during World

War II. Pain was everywhere. Audiences went to movies to escape pain, not to be reminded of it. To audiences smarting from the recent Depression and a bloody world war, the pain aspect of the film's original title negated the triumph part.

As documented in James Curtis' *Between Flops: A Biography Of Preston Sturges*, the filmmaker originally began the film with a prologue that begins, "One of the most charming characteristics of Homo sapiens, the wise guy on your right, is the consistency with which he has stoned, crucified, burned at the stake, and otherwise rid himself of those who consecrated their lives to his further comfort and well-being so that all his strength and cunning might be preserved for the erection of ever larger monuments, memorial shafts, triumphal arches, pyramids, and obelisks to the eternal glory of generals on horseback, tyrants, usurpers, dictators, politicians, and other heroes who led him, usually from the rear, to dismemberment and death."

There you have it, folks: Strap yourself in tight, eat some popcorn, put your arm around your best gal, and enjoy a film about a great man who finds himself "ridiculed, burned in effigy, ruined, and eventually driven to despair and death by the beneficiaries of his revelation." Decades later, the original prologue still feels bracingly dark, with its bleak vision of a world where fools who send men to horrible deaths are sanctified, while people who ease pain are crucified. At the beginning of World War II, it must have seemed borderline treasonous, especially its reference to "generals on horseback" leading from the rear. It's no surprise that the prologue was amputated from the final film.

Yet World War II was also, strangely, the perfect time to release a film about the development of anesthesia. Sturges posits that William Thomas Green Morton's refinement of sulfuric ether as an anesthetic marked the birth of modern medicine, the moment when pain stopped being a necessary evil and became controllable. Sturges gives us a secret history of Western medicine as a half-blind grasping toward progress from a motley assortment of semi-disreputable figures. Wouldn't Americans, especially GIs, want to learn more about the man who made it possible for them to doze dreamily during operations, oblivious to the pain of surgery? In this instance, the answer was definitely no. Ignorance was bliss.

The Great Moment deviates dramatically from the Great Man model of history by presenting its hero (Joel McCrea, also the star of *Sullivan's Travels*) not as a solitary genius but as a hardworking, ambitious, but not terribly bright failed medical student who revolutionizes anesthesia by building upon the work of colleague Dr. Horace Wells (Louis Jean Heydt), who popularized nitrous oxide as a painkiller, and pompous college professor Dr. Charles Jackson (Julius Tannen).

For the film's structure, Sturges returned to the achronological template of his screenplay for 1933's *The Power And The Glory*, a critically acclaimed drama about the rise and fall of an industrialist (Spencer Tracy); it was a key influence on *Citizen Kane*. In Sturges' original script, William's story is told in flashback by his wife, Elizabeth (Betty Field), and his assistant, Eben Frost (William Demarest). They trace a reverse American success story where triumph and innovation are followed by rejection, poverty, despair, and anonymity.

In case the darkness and futility of the subject's story aren't evident enough, Sturges planned to have the written prologue appear in front of its protagonist's long-forgotten gravestone. Instead, *Moment* opens with William being fêted by adoring onlookers as he presides over a parade in his honor. Sturges' jaundiced take on the fate of great men makes it on-screen in a less incendiary form via a prologue, arguing, "Of all things in nature, great men alone reverse the laws of perspective and grow smaller as one approaches them. Dwarfed by the magnitude of this revelation, reviled, hated by his fellow men, forgotten before he was remembered, Morton seems very small indeed, until the incandescent moment he ruined himself for a servant girl and gained immortality."

This bracing cold shower of a prologue is followed by an even more despairing sequence where Eben purchases one of his boss' medals from a pawnshop. It's dedicated "To The Benefactor Of Mankind

With The Gratitude Of Humanity." Eben brings the medal to Elizabeth, who recounts how no one showed up at William's funeral except herself and his children. The fight is lost before it's even begun. We've buried a sad, broken, defeated man before we've had a chance to get to know him.

The film then flashes back to William receiving news that Congress is considering a bill to award him $100,000 as a tardy reward for his service to humanity. For reasons too convoluted and complicated to go into, our hero never receives the money and is pilloried by the media as a scheming opportunist. Poverty, disgrace, and death await.

The film's first 10 minutes contain death, a lonely funeral, crucifixion by the press, a fortune that morphs into public humiliation, a great man's spirit being broken, and complicated legal and legislative wrangling. It's tragedy before triumph, the funeral before the birth of a great idea. Banking cynically on the popularity of Sturges' previous films, Paramount tried to sell *Moment* as "hilarious as a whiff of laughing gas." One can only imagine how audiences expecting another wacky Preston Sturges romp must have responded to this opening gauntlet of hopelessness and despair.

Before ether, William's interactions with customers resemble a Mexican wrestling match more than a medical procedure. It's all screaming and scary-looking torture devices and patients slinking away from the waiting room in abject terror. The bloodcurdling screams of patients haunt William's nightmares and jangle his nerves. There has to be a better way.

Our hero begins to stumble toward a panacea for pain when he accosts an angry and inebriated Dr. Jackson at a bar. Jackson flaunts his contempt for what he remembers as a "rather dull student" and says, "One of the cankers of our profession is the number of youths without funds or proper background who try to worm their way into it for the rich rewards they imagine it holds." Yet it's Jackson who accidentally gives William the idea that will make his career when he discusses the pain-deadening qualities of sulfuric ether.

In a genre rife with hagiographies, Sturges' biopic impishly begins its hero's journey to greatness with him badgering a misanthropic former teacher until that teacher is willing to do anything to end their unstructured conversation, even if it means giving a lowly dentist invaluable professional advice.

The world's first and only dental-ether tragicomedy, *The Great Moment* gets endless comic mileage out of ether and nitrous oxide's mind-warping effects on patients. Demarest, a longtime fixture of Sturges' repertory company, is a hoot as William's first and most enthusiastic patient, a professional human guinea pig who submits to ingesting ether out of a desire to clean up on William's double-your-money-back guarantee but continues taking it because he really, really likes getting high. The film balances physical comedy and wrenching drama in the terrifying/amusing moment when a horrified Elizabeth stumbles upon her husband, who has gotten high on his own ether supply. He's lying at his desk with a look of narcotized contentment, marveling approvingly at the metal rod he's jammed into his hand. If *Road House* has taught us anything, it's that pain doesn't hurt, especially when accompanied by William's magic elixir.

William's creation proves successful in a medical trial, but the Hippocratic Oath forbids doctors from using patent medicines with unknown ingredients, so William must decide between martyring himself for humanity's sake and revealing his secrets, or holding on to his patents and his shot at unimaginable riches.

By beginning at the story's tragic conclusion and working diligently toward the middle, *The Great Moment* ends with William's defining moment, his decision to sacrifice his own success so that others might be spared pain. *Moment* opens on a sustained note of funereal gloom but rouses itself to become a funny, vibrant, deeply sad look at the way the system fails dreamers and idealists. Paramount took the film away from Sturges, but his playful spirit pervades the production.

Paramount sat on *The Great Moment* for two years before dumping it into theaters with a trailer breathlessly promising a far-fetched yet improbably true yarn from "Hollywood's madcap Preston Sturges, who created that laugh riot *Miracle At Morgan's Creek.*"

With its emphasis on raucous slapstick and overheated prose, the trailer is designed to mislead, yet it accidentally tells the truth. The only drama Hollywood's madcap Preston Sturges directed doubles as a pretty terrific, surprisingly moving Preston Sturges comedy.

 Failure, Fiasco, Or Secret Success? *Secret Success*

Testifying Book-Exclusive Case File: *Gospel Road: A Story Of Jesus*

There once lived an icon notorious for the violent nature of his art. He was a dark, troubled soul plagued by rapacious personal demons, a man whose battles with substance abuse were legendary. Yet this tortured soul clung to faith as a life preserver in a sea of darkness. A man of fierce contradictions and even fiercer convictions, this shadowy figure used the power, money, and clout he made peddling bloody entertainment to spread the Gospel.

Ignoring the most sacrosanct commandment in all of entertainment—Thou shalt not invest thine own money—he sank much of his personal fortune into a supremely risky venture. Ignoring conventional wisdom, he traveled abroad to co-write, produce, and finance a movie about Jesus. Jesus had saved this tormented soul from himself and his compulsions; now he wanted to share that redemption with the secular world.

We all know how this story ends, don't we? With the mystery man in question triumphing over the skeptics and doubters en route to delivering one of the most commercially successful independent films of all time. Then he was undone by the Jew-run law-enforcement establishment and a sugar-titted lady cop one drunken night. Ah, but this isn't a book about winners. It's a tribute to the losers. So the man in question isn't Mel Gibson, and the film isn't *The Passion Of*

The Christ. No, I'm talking about Johnny Cash's half-forgotten 1973 religious drama *Gospel Road: A Story Of Jesus.*

In the late '60s and early '70s, Cash was, in the hackneyed parlance of *Behind The Music,* riding high. *Live At Folsom Prison* (1968) resurrected his flagging career and rebranded him as a proud champion of the underdog. A year later, *At San Quentin* did even better, thanks to a bleakly funny Shel Silverstein–penned number called "A Boy Named Sue." Cash's beloved network variety show exposed a whole new audience to country music. With the help of wife June Carter, Cash was finally winning his lifelong battle against pills and alcohol. After a lifetime filled with death, disaster, and self-destruction, Cash had reason to feel blessed and thankful.

Cash wanted to give back to a world from which he had taken so very much. According to a radio spot included on the *Gospel Road* DVD, the film originated with June Carter dreaming of her husband reading from a book while standing proudly on a mountaintop. Years later, Carter's dream came to fruition: As the framing device for *Gospel Road,* Cash's touchingly clumsy homage to the other JC, Cash reads from a Bible on a mountain in Israel.

Gospel Road opens with a sun rising hypnotically over the Holy Land before Cash, decked out in his customary black, turns directly to the camera and begins talking about the prescient words of the prophet Isaiah. The lines on Cash's impeccably craggy face tell a million stories of sin and salvation, of lost, whiskey-soaked nights of degradation, and triumphant mornings when the Lord's healing grace washed his soul clean.

Cash's performance reeks of high-school speech class. He recites Isaiah's words stiffly and theatrically, pausing to peer thoughtfully off-camera, as if contemplating God's unimaginable glory. Cash talks of would-be saviors long forgotten by history and of the one true savior.

He ends his opening narration by expounding, "Never a man spoke like this man [Jesus]. Never a man did the things on this earth this man did. And his words were as beautiful as his miracles. To many believers, their last desire is to be baptized in the Jordan River as Jesus was. They kneel at the holy places, places that are holy just because Jesus was there. They walked the way of the cross and shout 'Praise the Lord,' and they mean it. Now come along with me in the footsteps of Jesus, and I'll show you why they do." Cash raises his hands in a pantomime of religious rapture when he cries, "Praise the Lord!" Then he points conspiratorially at the audience. His performance is all the more powerful for its naked sincerity. He finally has an opportunity to play a fire-breathing preacher, with film as his unlikely medium and the audience as his unseen flock.

This opening gives the film a scruffy intimacy. We then cut to a shaky helicopter shot that just barely captures Cash flashing the peace sign. Gibson's Jesus was a warrior-God. *The Passion Of The Christ* lingered so fetishistically and lovingly over the physical agony of Jesus' death that it treated his life and teachings as an afterthought. Cash's savior, in sharp contrast, really is the Prince of Peace. What an incredibly sweet, quixotic way to begin a film about Jesus. *Gospel Road*'s pre-credit sequence once again finds Cash playing the great uniter sending out coded messages of solidarity to hippies, Jesus freaks, and mainstream Christians alike.

Cash narrates the film and provides the bulk of its soundtrack. His starkly beautiful voice dominates the film as he documents the life and times of Jesus, who is played as a boy by a shaggy-haired, pale, blond, blue-eyed little scamp (Robert Elfstrom Jr.) who'd look more at home waiting in line for tickets to a Jan And Dean concert than perambulating around Nazareth.

Consciously or otherwise, Cash and director Robert Elfstrom (who also plays a long-haired, sandal-wearing Nazarene carpenter with some crazy ideas about peace and love) turned Jesus' story into a religious head film. Elfstrom goes nuts with helicopter shots and prismatic effects; doing freaky shit with light and flares seems as important to him as laying down the Gospel. Cash's wall-to-wall narration and song score only add to the film's oddly psychedelic flavor. *Gospel Road* subscribes to the notion, popular throughout '70s cinema, that there's nothing more fascinating than watching a hippie dude wander around with an evocative song as his soundtrack. But this time, the hippie dude in question is Jesus.

Just as he adopted the form of a coyote and led Homer Simpson on a spiritual journey, Cash leads us on a greatest-hits tour of Jesus' life and times. We follow the Good Shepherd as he's baptized by John the Baptist, picks up his entourage of 12 followers who treat him like he's the first coming or something, is anointed the Son of God, and, to use arcane religious terminology, loses his shit and freaks the fuck out upon discovering moneylenders in the temple. We learn the origin of all of Jesus' beloved catchphrases, from "Let he who is without sin cast the first stone" to "Judge not, lest ye be judged" to "Ask and ye shall receive."

Gospel Road offers the gospel according to Johnny Cash. When Cash tells the camera, "Jesus addressed men as men and not as members of any particular class or culture. The differences which divide men, such as wealth, position, education, and so forth, he knew were strictly on the surface," he seems to be espousing his own radically egalitarian mind-set as much as Jesus'.

Though it follows Jesus' life in a linear fashion, *Gospel Road* frequently gives over to abstraction, as when Cash pontificates on Jesus' teachings during an endless helicopter shot of water glistening in the sun. *Road* is all about pretty images and pretty words; it doesn't particularly matter how the two fit together. In the film's boldest move, it places the crucified Jesus and his cross in the middle of a modern city, collapsing the impossible gulf between the past and the present in the process, and underlining the timelessness and contemporary resonance of Jesus' story and message.

"I bet Mary Magdalene walked this same beach I'm walking on. I wonder what Mary Magdalene really looked like. The Scriptures don't tell a lot about her, but what little is told has made her the subject of more speculation and controversy than any woman I've ever heard of. Jesus was to suffer much criticism for his association with people of questionable character." Cash narrates as he walks along the beach, still looking directly into the camera and emphasizing the words "questionable character" in a manner that underlines how directly it applies to him.

Within the context of the film, Cash didn't have to wonder what Mary Magdalene looks like, since June Carter plays her. The film never explains why exactly Mary Magdalene has a Southern drawl, or why a novice actor is the only thespian allowed to deliver her own lines, instead of having Cash narrate her story.

"You know, we can't forget the fact that Jesus was human," Cash reminds us in the film's key line. *Gospel Road* is ultimately as much about Cash as it is about Jesus. It is a film of trembling earnestness and unquestionable devotion. When Cash reflects on how he likes to imagine children frolicking with his Savior, the film becomes uncomfortably, even unbearably personal. Cash is revealing himself and bearing witness. The coolest motherfucker on the planet is willing to look defiantly uncool if it means saving souls. In this context, it almost seems unfair to criticize the film on aesthetic and artistic grounds, since *Gospel Road* is intended first and foremost as an evangelizing tool and a profound expression of personal faith.

Gospel Road makes its relatively brief running time feel like an eternity. It's more home movie than Hollywood, but that's much of its scruffy charm. It's really the story of Cash's faith; in its own hamfisted fashion, it embodies the yearning for deliverance and singular combination of strength and vulnerability that made Cash such an enduring icon.

Cash took the failure of *Gospel Road* hard. The public that had so warmly received him during his comeback didn't reject *Gospel Road* so much as ignore it, relegating Cash's peculiar passion project to sleepy Sunday school showings in church basements. *Road* marked the beginning of a dark period in Cash's life. He fell off the wagon, returned to pills and bad behavior, and entered a professional free fall that lasted until his *next* spectacular comeback, courtesy of Rick Rubin and the American Recordings label.

Yet I prefer Cash's amateur-hour take on Jesus to Gibson's far more technically accomplished version. You know, we can't forget the fact that Cash was human. That messy, naked, raw humanity and humility makes *Gospel* far more moving than it has any right to be.

Failure, Fiasco, Or Secret Success? *Fiasco*

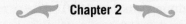

Chapter 2

Calamitous Comedies

Tenacious Teen Terrors Case File #54: *O.C. And Stiggs*
Originally Posted July 31, 2007

Back in the days when *The A.V. Club* shared an office with the *Onion* comedy writers on the fifth floor of an office building deep in the heart of Madison's popcorn district, I had the honor of knowing *The Onion*'s brilliant comedy writer Todd Hanson. I saw a lot of myself in Todd. He was, and is, a brooding, towering figure of infinite darkness, a sentient black cloud of a man responsible for pretty much every *Onion* article positing the universe as an unfathomably sadistic realm of bottomless cruelty.

Todd doesn't have interests; he has obsessions that consume him body and soul. In Madison, he was famous for his epic, intricately worded monologues about the art and ephemera that fascinated him. He was obsessed with Philip K. Dick and with Robert Altman, particularly the little-loved, wildly obscure Reagan-era *National Lampoon*–derived Altman teen sex comedy *O.C. And Stiggs*. At a Madison bar called Le Tigre, he favored us one night with an hour-long dissertation on what he considers one of the most misunderstood, underrated films of all time.

Altman was one of those glorious figures who couldn't have thrived or attained major mainstream popularity in any decade but the beautiful, crazy, endlessly generous and open-minded '70s. In the '70s, Altman was a cinematic colossus who churned out an endless series of masterpieces, some of which captured the zeitgeist en route to becoming huge, generation-defining hits, like 1970's *M*A*S*H*. After 1980's *Popeye*, however, Altman seemed intent on limiting his audience with each successive film. A giant of American cinema was marching defiantly from the mainstream to cult status to the fringes, and then to semi-obscurity. A naturalist intent on capturing the rhythms of everyday life became obsessed with fusing theater and cinema with efforts like *Come Back To The Five And Dime, Jimmy Dean, Jimmy Dean, Streamers, Beyond Therapy, Fool For Love,* and his 1984 masterpiece *Secret Honor*. Altman once belonged to the masses; by the time *O.C. And Stiggs* came along, he belonged exclusively to obsessives like Todd.

Altman famously bent countless genres and forms to his will: musicals, comic-strip adaptations, detective movies, Hollywood satire, the political miniseries, icy psychodrama, plays, and one-man shows. But according to conventional wisdom, it was the lowly teen sex comedy that ultimately defeated Altman in *O.C. And Stiggs*. The film was finished in 1984 but received such disastrous test scores that it was shelved for three years, then released to vitriolic reviews and nonexistent box office.

The pairing of Robert Altman and the teen-sex-comedy genre wasn't entirely the mismatch it might appear. A prankish, youthful irreverence courses through Altman's films, even his non-comedies. If '70s cinema was a lowbrow slobs-vs.-snobs comedy, Altman would be the John Belushi–esque Dionysus tossing Peter Bogdanovich in the pool, shattering his monocle, and soaking his silk ascot.

The interview with Robert Altman on the *O.C. And Stiggs* DVD provides a fascinating glimpse into the psychology of failure. Halfhearted defenses are offered. Actors are praised. Claims are made that critics and audiences misunderstood his project and its aims. There are weary concessions of friction and ultimately critical and commercial failure. In the most poignant part of the interview, Altman concedes that guests intermittently come over to the Altmansion and want to watch *O.C. And Stiggs*, sometimes to laugh with it and sometimes to laugh at it.

Altman argues that audiences and *National Lampoon* wanted Robert Altman's *Porky's* and were flummoxed when he delivered a satire of teen schlock instead. I think *O.C. And Stiggs* is a satire, but less of teen sex comedies than of the things that always enraged Altman: consumerism, hypocrisy, racism, and the general self-absorption of well-fed Caucasians. Altman occasionally comes off like the misanthropic cheap-shot artist his critics accused him of being—like all '80s teen sex comedies, this one seems to think homosexuality is inherently hilarious—but behind the snark lies principled contempt toward the complacency and sun-baked decadence of the Reagan '80s.

Adapted from recurring characters in *National Lampoon*, *O.C. And Stiggs* centers on a pair of bored, wildly codependent teens whose sole mission in life is to bedevil the Schwabs, a wealthy family led by Randall Schwab (Paul Dooley), an insurance kingpin whose hilariously stiff commercial concedes that his company simply won't tolerate such abominations as "drinking" or "the continent of Africa." The eponymous wisenheimers wage a campaign of psychological warfare against Randall for doing wrong by "Gramps" Ogilvie (Ray Walston), the crusty ex-cop granddad of either O.C. or Stiggs (damned if I can tell the difference). They call Africa on Randall's dime. They sabotage his daughter's wedding by getting his son, Randall Jr. (Jon Cryer), to go nuts with a machine gun.

Daniel Jenkins and Neill Barry play the eponymous mischief makers with the smirking superiority of people forever enjoying a private joke at the world's expense. Like the Van Wilders and Ferris Buellers to follow, they put invisible air quotes around everything they say and do. Yet in their own snotty way, they're out to comfort the afflicted and afflict the comfortable. They're simultaneously smug assholes and righteous avengers.

In the film's climax, the boys invite a wide cross-section of Arizona's housing-free population to party at the Schwab house. As things get increasingly out of control, the title characters call in Dennis Hopper's deranged veteran Sponson—a buddy of the boys and co-conspirator in their mischief brigade—to fly in with his helicopter and bring a little Vietnam to Casa De Schwab. As the veteran and his buddy fly over a pool-festooned suburban wasteland, they're at a loss for which gaudy nouveau-riche house to invade. "They all look the same!" Sponson marvels in horror as he surveys one Stepford home after another, in a sly commentary on suburban conformity that rings even truer today.

All the while, a television broadcasts the inane natterings of H. Ross Perot–like demagogue Hal Phillip Walker. Introduced in Altman's 1975 masterpiece *Nashville*, he riveted the nation in that film with questions like, "Have you stood on a high and windy hill and heard the acorns drop and roll?" and "Have you walked in the valley beside the brook, walked alone and remembered?" And perhaps most trenchantly, "Does Christmas smell like oranges to you?"

So when Hopper, playing a gonzo caricature of himself in full-on wild-eyed hippie-freak mode, invades the Schwabs, it's *Apocalypse Now* colliding with *Nashville* in a suburban Arizona bomb shelter in the mid-'80s. It's Robert Altman prankishly making one of his most reviled films into an unwitting, half-assed sequel to one of his most beloved triumphs. It's the grand glory of '70s cinematic ambition crashing helplessly into the soul-sick, mercenary '80s.

O.C. And Stiggs takes a while to get going, but by the time Sponson descends on the Schwab compound, the film has whipped up a fine, frenzied madness. In the giddy climax, the boys bring the war to the Schwabs. It's the return of the repressed, as the titular duo force Randall to confront the poverty and drunkenness of the black underclass (represented by Melvin Van Peebles' soulful wino and his homeless drinking buddies), the lingering scars of a disastrous war in Vietnam (Sponson), and, of course, the continent of Africa, via special guest star King Sunny Adé.

Altman's film resonated more strongly with me the second time around, in part because I was more familiar with its satirical targets. Having spent time in suburban Arizona, where new money goes to die a pampered spiritual death among jackrabbits, javelinas, and scorpions, I could better appreciate the cultural specificity of its satire.

O.C. And Stiggs boasts a terrific supporting cast, led by Martin Mull as Pat Colletti, a wealthy lush with a seemingly painted-on beard who luxuriates happily in his own booze-sodden decadence. I enjoyed the O.C. and Stiggsmobile, a deafeningly loud lemon on stilts and speed, and Bob Uecker's insane self-deprecating cameo as a loudmouth so intoxicated with the sound of his own voice that he never notices that no one is paying attention to anything he's saying (including himself, apparently).

I found a lot to dig about *O.C. And Stiggs,* but more than anything, I love Altman's style: the overlapping dialogue, the purposefully wandering cameras, the jittery zooms, and the long shots that suggest both sociological distance and the perspective of a bemused trickster god. Altman might not have succeeded in making a trenchant satire of teen sex comedies, but as is his nature, he twisted, contorted, and perverted his source material until it became the basis for something infinitely more wonderful and relevant: a Robert Altman movie. Then again, that's just the minority opinion of one frothing fanboy. Oh, and for the record, Christmas always *has* smelled like oranges to me.

Failure, Fiasco, Or Secret Success? *Secret Success*

Woody/Not Woody Case File #57: *Scenes From A Mall*
Originally Posted August 9, 2007

The late '60s Bond spoof *Casino Royale* and 1991's *Scenes From A Mall* both offer the strange spectacle of Woody Allen acting in non–Woody Allen movies. When he made *Casino Royale,* Allen was still a hot young comedian and cinematic neophyte. But by the time *Scenes From*

A Mall hit theaters, he was as much of a cultural institution as the Statue of Liberty, and nearly as immutable.

So it's understandably jarring to see Woody Allen, the quintessential New York snob, playing a ponytail-sporting Los Angeleno perfectly comfortable with the emptiness of his existence. That ponytail goes a long way toward negating the fundamental Woodyness of Allen's being, yet Woody remains Woody no matter how incongruous the setting. Paul Mazursky has Allen's Nick Fifer do things the real (and reel) Allen would never do. He buys Italian suits. He totes around a surfboard. He listens to music made after World War II. He says things like, "Christ, where's my fucking Saab?!" He seems comfortable in a mall. He goes hours without referencing Kierkegaard or Camus. Most shockingly, he has sex with a Jewish woman roughly his own age.

It's an existential conundrum: He's Woody, yet he isn't Woody. The ponytail and surfboard seem to exist in a different, infinitely more crass universe than Allen's Manhattan wonderland, yet the mannerisms, tics, and vocal inflections give him away. Even if Allen played Osama bin Laden, he'd probably still end up looking and acting suspiciously like *Annie Hall*'s Alvy Singer.

Bette Midler similarly tones down her trademark brassiness to play Nick's wife, Deborah, a successful headshrinker and book-writing person (that's fancy publishing-world speak for "author") celebrating the 16th anniversary of their marriage with a trip to the mall before joining friends for sushi. The day begins with the Fifers in a state of far-too-perfect domestic bliss. They marvel at how their marriage has managed to outlast all their friends' unions (this is Southern California, after all), send their kids away, and even try to engage in a little premall canoodling. The sight of an amorous, ponytailed Allen trying desperately to rip off Midler's gray spandex leggings in a fit of carnal passion will take years of therapy to purge from my memory.

At the mall, however, the couple's façade of matrimonial contentment begins to shatter when Nick confesses to a passionate affair with the 25-year-old wife of one of his clients. Deborah initially maintains

an air of poise and restraint, but before long, she's upsetting the narcotized calm of mall life with angry outbursts. She demands a divorce,
only to admit later to an affair of her own with a loving, caring, sexually skilled doctor played by Mazursky.

Between all the confessions, breakups, and impromptu reconcilia-
tions, the couple somehow finds the time to sneak into a screening of
Salaam Bombay! where Nick attempts to win his wife back by going
down on her in a theater. (Incidentally, if this Case File accomplishes
nothing else, I'd like it to at least introduce "seeing *Salaam Bombay!*" as
a euphemism for cunnilingus.) Judging by Deborah's orgasmic glow
exiting the theater, it's safe to say that Nick is the undisputed king of
seeing *Salaam Bombay!*

For the wealthy power couples of *Scenes From A Mall,* drinking in
the misery of street urchins from Bombay is just another consumer
choice in a pop world teeming with them. As the day progresses, the
tension and resentments bubbling under the surface of the Fifers'
marriage burst into plain view.

At its best, *Scenes* captures how the mundane details of a long-
shared history can pull a couple together while simultaneously tearing
them apart. Nick longs for the freedom and excitement of single life
yet is reluctant to leave the security and comfort of the nest. But it
ultimately doesn't seem to matter whether these self-absorbed suburban monsters break up or stick around to torment each other for
decades to come.

It's easy to see why *Scenes From A Mall* failed. Its characters run
the gamut from unlikeable to vaguely monstrous, and it's hard to
muster up sympathy for smug adulterers. *Scenes* also falls victim to
the Parental-Sex Rule: Unless you're a 17-year-old newly adopted by
Brad Pitt and Angelina Jolie, you don't want to imagine your parents
having sex, especially if they're Woody Allen and Bette Midler. We
want to imagine our parents as perfectly asexual, as devoid of genitalia
or sexual impulses as Barbie and Ken.

Late in the film, Nick, his surfboard, Deborah, and Fabio all
squeeze into an elevator together while a frustrated Deborah sexu-

ally violates Fabio with her eyes. In moments like this, *Scenes From A Mall* almost gets by on novelty value alone. And there are quiet, subtly powerful moments sprinkled throughout, as Midler's and Allen's faces reveal the extreme psychological and social cost of dissolving a marriage, however troubled.

Scenes never gains any traction as a comedy or drama, as an anti–Woody Allen movie or a Woody Allen movie of a different color. The couple's dark afternoon of the soul is more like an extended shrug. Yet the film retains the same strange morbid fascination as Allen's sad little ponytail, that telltale symptom of a man immersed in a midlife crisis. The *Scenes* DVD is depressingly spare, but I'd like to imagine that Mazursky shot at least one scene of Allen riding the surfboard he carries throughout the film as a visual gag. Woody Allen surfing: Now *that* would be funny.

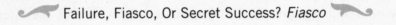 Failure, Fiasco, Or Secret Success? *Fiasco*

Book-Exclusive $20 Million Case File: *The Cable Guy*

As a child, it blew my mind that my father made something like $36,000 a year as a government bureaucrat. That worked out to almost a hundred dollars *a day*! To an 8-year-old, that represented an unimaginable bounty. I could barely comprehend what it would be like to have a hundred dollars for even a single day, let alone to make a hundred dollars *every day*, even on your days off. For that kind of money, my dad could buy six-packs of Mountain Dew *and* beer, a pizza, a cassette of the hottest new rock album, the latest *Playboy*, a Samantha Fox poster, and a stack of *Mad* magazines, then spend his entire day playing videogames before finishing off the night with a movie, popcorn, *and* soda, all without running out of money! This is how I imagined adults would live their lives if they weren't weighed down with children and families and stupid desk jobs.

So you can imagine how impressed I was to discover that my favorite movie stars and baseball players make a million dollars *or more* every year. It somehow seemed unfair that someone should be paid such inconceivable sums to play sports before adoring fans, or romance the world's most beautiful women.

Mind-boggling salaries for athletes and artists are so common-place these days that we've become jaded. But when it was announced that Jim Carrey would be making $20 million for his role in 1996's *The Cable Guy*, society responded the way my 8-year-old self did upon learning that my dad made a hundred dollars a day. *Twenty million dollars?*

It was one thing for Harrison Ford to make that much. In his films, he saved the world repeatedly. It would be churlish to begrudge him the spoils of his make-pretend heroism. But when *The Cable Guy* went into production, Carrey was only a few years removed from being the white guy on *In Living Color.* Worse, he was Canadian. It's bad enough that Canadians pass as Americans, have barbed penises to aid in their fiendish sexual proclivities, and plot covertly against their unsuspecting neighbors to the south. Now they looked like they were out to bankrupt our film industry with excessive salaries.

Ford at least pretended to do great things; Carrey was getting paid $20 million to behave like an ass. He was to receive the biggest up-front salary for any comic actor in history to do the kinds of things that earn fidgety, misbehaving 12-year-olds Ritalin prescriptions and one-way trips to military school.

Cable Guy began life as a Chris Farley vehicle about a hapless, awkward, but fundamentally sweet and nonviolent cable guy who accidentally played havoc with a customer's life. Director Ben Stiller liked the basic premise but not the screenplay, so he brought in Judd Apatow—a *Ben Stiller Show* writer and a veteran of smart television satires like *The Critic* and *The Larry Sanders Show*—to take the script in a much darker direction.

Given Stiller and Apatow's subsequent ascent to ubiquitous, prolific superstardom, it's ironic to think that hiring them as director and

41

script doctor/producer transformed a seemingly surefire blockbuster into a risky proposition. In Stiller and Apatow's hands, the screenplay morphed from a *Tommy Boy*–style buddy comedy to a more mainstream precursor to *Chuck & Buck*, a creepy, homoerotic black comedy about a disturbed loner and the sad sack he torments.

For the role of the straight man/Carrey's foil, the filmmakers chose Matthew Broderick, an actor who has spent the decades since his career-making turn in *Ferris Bueller's Day Off* exploring the infinite colors of the schlemiel rainbow. Actually, that's not fair, as the last few years have found Broderick playing everything from a putz (*The Stepford Wives*) to a yutz (*Marie & Bruce*) to a schmendrick (*Finding Amanda*) to a schmuck (*Then She Found Me*). The man has range.

Apatow reconceived the story as a dark riff on thrillers like *The Hand That Rocks The Cradle*, which boldly exposed the furtive menace posed by nannies, temps, cops, and myriad other professions that quietly house sociopaths intent on murdering you and your family. He also turned it into a meta-commentary on the way television warps the human psyche, a recurring motif in Stiller's films.

In *Reality Bites*, Stiller plays a man so twisted by working in television that he looks at Winona Ryder's homemade footage of her and her friends goofing around and sees a *Real World*–like reality show instead of an avant-garde masterpiece. In *Zoolander*, Stiller's sentient mannequin is more or less rendered mentally challenged by prolonged exposure to the fashion industry. In *Tropic Thunder*, Stiller plays a pompous actor who has been coddled and flattered by the culture of celebrity for so long that he's unable to delineate between movies and the real world. In *Permanent Midnight*, he plays novelist/screenwriter Jerry Stahl, a man driven to shooting junk by the indignity of having to put words in Alf's mouth. So it's no surprise that Stiller's dream project has long been Budd Schulberg's seminal showbiz morality play *What Makes Sammy Run?*, the archetypal tale of a man who makes it in show business by losing his soul.

So it's fitting that in *The Cable Guy*, Stiller once again plays a pathetic show-business figure, a disgraced former child star accused of killing his weak-willed identical twin. Stiller's dual role amounts to little more than a cameo, but he makes an indelible impression with a minimum of screen time. Playing a combination Menendez brothers, O. J. Simpson, and Todd Bridges, Stiller nails the furrowed-brow expression of intense concentration ubiquitous on the faces of celebrities on trial, a dour look that implicitly conveys, "If I just sit here quietly and look remorseful and serious, we can let these silly homicide charges slide, right, guys?"

The Cable Guy opens, naturally enough, with Broderick's Steven Kovacs flipping through the vast wasteland of the cable universe. We stumble through one garbled, staticy corner of the television hellscape to another: inane talk shows, *My Three Sons,* superhero shows, and tabloid coverage of the sibling murder trial. Stiller's unblinking camera renders the familiar creepy and unnerving. It's channel surfing as the preoccupation of the damned.

The Cable Guy (his actual name is never revealed) is four hours late, yet he appears enraged when he finally shows up. An unseen Carrey pounds relentlessly on Steven's door while repeating "Cable guy!" with mounting exasperation. The title character annoys us before his first on-screen appearance.

Steven unwisely takes the advice of his best friend (Jack Black, one of many future superstars in the supporting cast) and offers Carrey's Cable Guy $50 to hook him up with all the movie channels—even the dirty ones—for free. In doing so, he becomes complicit in his own undoing; that ill-considered nosh on the apple of knowledge leads to Steven's fall from grace.

Like Christian Bale in *American Psycho,* Carrey seems to be merely impersonating a human being. He's empty and vacant on the inside, so he throws himself into playing roles he's seen on TV: the affable cable guy with an overflowing roster of "preferred customers," the aggressive jock with the menacing tomahawk jam, the drinking buddy out to get his best pal laid, the love guru who hips Broderick to the aphrodisiac that is *Sleepless In Seattle,* and the karaoke rock star.

In the film's funniest sequence, the Cable Guy takes Steven to his favorite restaurant, a medieval theme eatery where he seems to know the beats of every line better than the dinner theater's cast. Janeane Garafalo, one of several *Ben Stiller Show* cast members in small roles, steals the scene as their "serving wench," a dispirited slacker whose commitment to historical authenticity doesn't extend to taking out her nose ring or washing off a thick coat of Goth makeup.

For Carrey's character, life is role-playing; since he doesn't have an authentic self, he inhabits roles he's seen other people play. Carrey the actor began his career as an impressionist. What are impressionists, ultimately, if not people who subvert their own identities to inhabit the voices, personalities, and affectations of famous people? *The Cable Guy* takes Carrey's persona into thrillingly dark places: He's playing his usual exemplar of comic aggression, but the repellent neediness and desperation at its core defies sentiment.

The Cable Guy's incursions into Steven's personal life become increasingly unhinged. When Steven's ex-girlfriend (Leslie Mann, later to become Apatow's real-life wife) goes on a date with a slick-talking smoothie (Owen Wilson), the Cable Guy, whose wardrobe seems stuck somewhere in the mid-'70s, viciously beats his pal's romantic rival in the men's bathroom. He pushes Steven past his breaking point, humiliating him in front of his parents and his ex during a game of "porno password" and getting him arrested. These events lead to a climactic conflict in a giant satellite dish, during which the Cable Guy delivers a painful speech in which all of his character's subtext spills embarrassingly to the surface, as he bemoans a childhood in which he learned the facts of life from *The Facts Of Life*.

The $20 million man resolves to "kill the [cathode-ray] babysitter" by destroying the satellite dish and his town's cable feed at the very moment when the verdict from Stiller's sibling homicide trial is being announced. Without the glass teat to suckle on, a couch potato played by Kyle Gass is moved to contemplate the unthinkable: reading a book.

According to a 1996 *Los Angeles Times* article on the film, Stiller shot a light and dark version of every scene to give himself more flexibility regarding the film's tone. *The Cable Guy* consequently has the distinction of being simultaneously too dark and too light. Columbia hired Stiller to give the film some of that *Ben Stiller Show* edge, but not *too* much; it had an investment to protect. *The Cable Guy* is extremely dark for a mainstream comedy, but not the pitch-black, uncompromising comedy it might have been had it been produced independently.

As a latchkey kid neglected by his alcoholic, promiscuous mother, Carrey's Cable Guy didn't see television as escape or entertainment; it was his whole world, a fantasy realm where children are always adorable, apple-cheeked, and well-treated, and murders get solved before the end credits roll. In this respect, the film recalls *Profit,* the exquisitely dark (and short-lived) mid-'90s Fox drama about a charming sociopath who grew up in a box with only the hypnotic glow of television for company. It also recalls my childhood.

Television was so much more than just a way to fill 12 to 16 hours out of every day during my wasted youth. I was addicted to television for the same reason the Cable Guy's younger self was: Its honeyed lies were infinitely preferable to my grim childhood realities as I was growing up in a group home. Like Carrey's pathetic dreamer, I even adopted a fake name gleaned from pop culture. Carrey dubs himself "Chip Douglas" after a character on *My Three Sons.* Upon moving into the group home, I inexplicably decided to call myself "Larry Miller" after the popular stand-up comic/character actor.

The Cable Guy hits awfully close to home. Maybe that's why I find it such a fascinating, resonant exploration of Stiller's career-long love-hate relationship with pop culture, even if, as a comic thriller, it's neither hilarious nor particularly suspenseful. Someone has to kill the cathode-ray babysitter, after all, and as a literal child of the industry (his parents are the comedy duo of Jerry Stiller and Anne Meara), Stiller was uniquely qualified for the job.

Failure, Fiasco, Or Secret Success? *Secret Success*

Fun With Animals Case File #61: *Freddy Got Fingered*
Originally Posted August 23, 2007

The notorious 2001 comedy *Freddy Got Fingered* has a reputation as both one of the worst films ever made and a movie so singularly bizarre that it's hard to believe it actually *got* made. Studios exist precisely to keep films this audacious from hitting theaters. I've never seen any of Tom Green's various shows, but I watched *Fingered* with open-mouthed admiration. It's the kind of movie you feel the need to watch again immediately just to make sure you didn't hallucinate it the first time around.

Fingered casts director and cowriter Green as Gord Brody, a 28-year-old aspiring animator who heads to Hollywood armed with little but a dream, a drawing of a bag of dripping baboon eyeballs attached to a balloon, and a complete lack of social skills. Gord bullies his way into the office of animation executive Mr. Davidson (Anthony Michael Hall) by pretending that the man's wife has died a hideous death, then dresses up as an English bobby and harangues him in a restaurant. Davidson looks at Gord's drawing and issues a stern judgment: "It doesn't make any sense. It's fucking stupid. What you need here is elevation. There has to be something happening here that's actually funny." It isn't hard to imagine studio executives saying the exact same thing to Green upon receiving the *Fingered* script. Thank God he didn't listen to reason. Or common sense. Or decency.

Did I mention the part where Gord pulls over to the side of the road, sees a giant horse cock, and grasps it lustily? It didn't really have anything to do with anything, but then neither does most of *Freddy Got Fingered*. It's a movie for the YouTube era; just about any 10-minute block functions as a perversely fascinating, surreal mini-movie with an anti-logic all its own. *Fingered* introduces a straightforward plot (dreamer moves to Hollywood to make it as an animator and toils at a cheese-sandwich factory until he gets his chance) solely so it can casually discard it. Gord's Hollywood adventures are largely over in about 15 minutes, at which point the film turns into a black-comic psychodrama about Gord's hate-hate relationship with his father, Jim (Rip Torn).

Nobody plays drunken, profane, rage-choked authority figures quite like Rip Torn. Torn attacks his role here like he's performing in an avant-garde art movie rather than a gross-out vehicle for a wacky MTV personality. And he's right to do so: Any resemblance between *Freddy Got Fingered* and a conventional studio comedy is purely coincidental.

Gord's rampaging id recalls such beloved man-children as Pee-wee Herman and *Wayne's World*'s Wayne Campbell. But where Pee-wee and Wayne represent guileless childhood innocence, Green represents childhood's dark side. To get back at his dad, Gord convinces a psychiatrist that Jim habitually molests Gord's straight-arrow younger brother (Eddie Kaye Thomas), who is subsequently placed in the Institute for Sexually Molested Children, even though he's clearly in his mid-20s.

Sprinkled throughout *Fingered* are gross-out setpieces executed with brazen fearlessness: Gord delivers a baby, then chews through the umbilical cord and swings the newborn around like a lasso. Gord takes Davidson's advice that he needs to "get inside" his animal characters by slicing open a dead moose and running around with it on top of him. In an especially queasy sequence, Gord's father drunkenly pulls down his pants and tauntingly dares his son to sodomize him. In my favorite scene, Gord delivers his big speech to his wheelchair-bound love interest, Betty (Marisa Coughlan), while "When A Man Loves A Woman" wails on the soundtrack and the deafening roar of a nearby helicopter threatens to drown him out. In moments like this, the film has more in common with early Jean-Luc Godard movies than gross-out Farrelly brothers knockoffs.

Did I mention all the gratuitous horse cocks? You'd have to hunt down bestiality porn to find so many throbbing horse cocks, or to see a grown man fondle the genitalia of large mammals so flagrantly. Watching *Fingered*, I wondered what the studio notes to Green must have been like: "Do you have to have so many giant animal cocks?

Doesn't the first giant animal cock get the point across? And wouldn't the lead character be more sympathetic if he didn't falsely accuse his father of incestuous child molestation? And the part where Betty is called a 'retard slut' . . . isn't that potentially off-putting to women in the coveted 18-to-35 demographic?"

In my line of work, it's rare and wondrous to witness the emergence of a dazzlingly original comic voice. I experienced that sensation watching *Freddy Got Fingered.* If you were to give a talented but deeply disturbed 12-year-old money to make a movie, I suspect it'd be a lot like this one. I've never seen anything like it. Green's directorial debut has balls of such unprecedented size and grandeur that they should be mounted and displayed at the Smithsonian.

I think it helps to see *Fingered* less as a conventional comedy than as a borderline Dadaist provocation, a $15 million prank at the studio's expense. It didn't invent the gross-out comedy, but it elevated it to unprecedented heights of depravity. Sure, it seems to have killed Green's film career, but oh, what a way to go.

❧ Failure, Fiasco, Or Secret Success? *Secret Success* ❧

Hippified Book-Exclusive Case File: *Skidoo*

The secret dream of the '60s counterculture was that the sexual and psychotropic revolutions rocking the free world would free squares and hippies alike. That quixotic hope resonates throughout the cinema of the late '60s and early '70s, a hippified belief that if the Man would just drop acid or indulge in a pot brownie or two, his consciousness would undergo a glorious transformation. He would morph instantly from Richard Nixon to Wavy Gravy. Millennia of guilt, shame, and repression (or as I call them, the Holy Trinity of the Jewish male psyche) would melt away, leaving only an ecstatic puddle of bliss. That myopic belief in the power of drugs to engender radical, dramatic spiritual growth is ever present in movies like *I Love You, Alice B. Toklas* and countless lesser works, like Otto Preminger's notorious, strangely fascinating 1968 debacle *Skidoo*.

The hippie dream promised a utopian paradise of open minds, plentiful mood alterers, copious nudity, a universal ban on the harshing of mellows, and government-imposed universal body painting. To middle-aged heterosexual men, it suggested something even more mind-blowing: guilt-free casual sex with nubile, obscenely flexible young women who'd been freed from guilt, self-consciousness, and inhibitions.

The counterculture boasted three potent cultural hydrogen bombs—pot, acid, and sexy hippie chicks of easy virtue—in its bid to seduce squares into grooviness. There was the deplorable practice of smoking marijuana, a consciousness-expander infinitely more powerful and mellow inducing than the Man's scotch, but burdened with none of the debilitating side effects—no hangovers, no addiction, no withdrawal, no DTs or hallucinations.

It's difficult to understand the '60s without dropping acid at least once. The first time I dropped acid—at a punk-rock show at my college co-op, appropriately enough—I suddenly understood, on an almost cellular level, the hippie fantasy of a revolution in consciousness that would free inhabitants of the prison of self from their dark, corrupt, fragmented realm, and usher in a brave new world where everyone was connected. During that initial rush, I felt a deep spiritual communion with gutter punks whose stench and sounds could be detected several area codes away. Then I came down and realized we were just a bunch of fucked-up kids taking drugs.

The last and perhaps most potent weapon in the counterculture's arsenal was the ripe sexuality of sexy hippie chicks, Manic Pixie Dream Girls whose spacey smiles and lithe young bodies promised to liberate brooding depressives from the grim realities of the workaday world. In *I Love You, Alice B. Toklas* and darker squares-meet-the-counterculture films like *Save The Tiger* and *Joe*, hippie Eves lead establishment Adams into a world of sex and toking. *Skidoo*, having already traumatized audiences with the image of Carol Channing in her underwear, thankfully gives protagonist Jackie Gleason a spiritual awakening instead of a sexual one. Nobody wanted to see Gleason's flabby Irish belly slapping angrily against some stoned little minx, including Gleason himself.

The more you know about the brilliant, mercurial, wildly controversial Otto Preminger—scion of one of Austria-Hungary's most prominent families and one of the most feared figures in American film—the more poignant *Skidoo* becomes. In a strange way, Preminger lived the movie; he dropped acid, collaborated with scruffy, long-haired countercultural types, and tried his damnedest to plug into the spirit of open-mindedness sweeping the country.

A successful director, producer, and part-time comic book villain—he played Mr. Freeze in the '60s TV *Batman*—Preminger wasn't about to throw it all away to live in a VW van and follow the Grateful Dead, but he clearly admired the hippie mind-set and the Black Panthers' brash rebelliousness. (Preminger's flirtation with Black Power is cruelly, though cleverly, chronicled in Tom Wolfe's classic article "Radical Chic: That Party at Lenny's.") But casting off the shackles of the establishment and embracing hippiedom isn't as easy as it seems.

It's no surprise that Preminger couldn't convincingly connect with the hippie mentality in spite of the best intentions. The film's cast reflected the violent conflict between Preminger's jones for capturing youth culture and his old-school aesthetic. To make the ultimate hippie acid film, Preminger apparently scoured the nursing homes of Hollywood to find the perfect cast for his suspiciously geriatric cinematic love-in. I suspect he posted flyers inscribed with the following words in retirement home rec rooms:

Otto "Moonbeam Sunshower" Preminger is looking for spunky senior citizens for supporting roles in ultimate hippie freakfest. Experience in campy superhero television shows and/or Judy Garland movies a plus; letters of reference from grandchildren welcome.

The posters yielded instant results: In addition to Jackie Gleason and a 77-year-old Groucho Marx, Preminger scored supporting roles for such young people's favorites as Arnold Stang, Mickey Rooney, George Raft, Peter Lawford, Slim Pickens, and Preminger's fellow *Batman* villains Cesar Romero, Frank Gorshin, and Burgess Meredith. And don't forget Carol Channing. Can't make a counterculture movie without Carol Channing.

In *Skidoo*, low-level hood gone straight "Tough Tony" Banks (Gleason) and his sidekick (Stang) spy on Tough Tony's flower-child daughter (Alexandra Hay) in a car with a hippie played by John Phillip Law, who looks like a cross between Tonto and Jesus, and communicates through Zen koans like, "If you can't dig nothing, then you can't dig anything, you dig?" Sitar noodling accompanies his stoned musings; apparently if you smoked pot in the '60s, an invisible sitar player followed you around providing mood music.

Our corpulent hero soon has more to worry about than his daughter's shaggy paramour when another mobster (Romero) tells him he's being called out of retirement to kill an imprisoned numbers man (Mickey Rooney) who plans to rat on enigmatic mob kingpin "God" (Marx). Tony is reluctant to kill (or "kiss," in the film's terminology) his best friend, but when his sidekick catches a bullet in the forehead, he realizes that he has no choice in the matter: It's an order, not a suggestion. While Tony glumly sets about executing his new assignment in Alcatraz, his daughter begins living the hippie nightmare: being stripped, then body-painted in a smelly van while spacey hippies sing old folk songs while toking and staring glumly at nothing in particular.

In prison, Tony meets his cellmates: a recidivist bookworm rapist (Michael Constantine) and Fred the Professor, a floppy-haired, walrus-mustache-sporting draft dodger played by Austin Pendleton, who steals the film with his loopy line readings and daft sweetness. He's the heart and soul, a gentle man in a cruel, impersonal, technology-crazed, fully automated world.

Speaking of fully automated and technology-crazed: Channing's

Flo Banks, decked out in canary yellow and feathers so she looks disconcertingly like a drag queen Big Bird, decides to seduce low-level mob flunky Angie (Frankie Avalon) into revealing the whereabouts of her AWOL husband. She attempts this in his tricked-out bachelor pad, a technological utopia/dystopia where everything is managed by remote control.

The film then unleashes a horror beyond words, beyond reason, beyond even madness: 46-year-old Carol Channing, stripped down to her bright yellow underwear, writhing suggestively on Angie's bed.

Skidoo suffers from a surplus rather than a dearth of ideas. It just needs a strong authorial voice to marshal all those weird notions and trippy conceits into a strong, cohesive whole. Take this example: While licking a piece of Fred's "special" stationery, Tony ends up accidentally ingesting LSD. The history of LSD freak-outs on film is long and painful. Taking LSD is a powerful, ineffable experience. It's hard to put into words, and even harder to render cinematically, so filmmakers resort to hokey surrealism, rinky-dink special effects, cheap camera tricks, over- and underexposed film, and other hackneyed attempts to capture the uncapturable.

Preminger was no exception. After Tony mistakenly drops acid, two characters shrink to munchkin size. He then begins seeing scarlet triangular orbs, disembodied eyeballs, guns, strange numbers written in bullet holes, and climactically, the floating disembodied head of God atop a screw. It's kitschy psychedelia-for-beginners as a bug-eyed Tony sweats his way to an epiphany: His daughter isn't really his daughter, and he's okay with that, having lost his ego at the behest of kindly spiritual guide Fred the Professor and LSD.

Skidoo is essentially about one man's liberation through mind-expanding psychedelics, yet pre- and post-LSD, Tony appears borderline suicidal. Gleason was going through a vicious depression when he shot *Skidoo,* and collaborating with a ruthless, glowering tyrant like Preminger—who tellingly had a lucrative sideline playing Nazis on stage and in film, most notably in *Stalag 17*—did little to improve his disposition.

In a film all about squares and freaks coming together in acid-and-weed-saturated bliss, Channing's character becomes the great uniter. Flo instantly *gets* the hippies. She doesn't need to drop acid to see the interconnectedness of all mankind. That's what makes her such a freak. Also strangely beautiful—but mainly a freak.

Skidoo ends the way it must: with Flo, inexplicably dressed as George Washington, singing the theme song and gyrating creepily like a marionette while leading a hippie armada of guitar-toting freaks onto Marx's floating fortress of uptightitude. With Tony's homemade hot-air balloon arriving on board the ship at the exact same moment. And with Tony and Flo celebrating their reunion by making sweet, sweet love (thankfully off-camera), thereby rendering everything perfect forever.

In the movie's groovy, generous world, even the bad guy gets away scot-free: The film ends with Fred the Professor and God in guru robes, sharing a joint and a wavelength as they sail off into their next epic trip.

Watching *Skidoo* for the third time—Christ, I really am a pop-culture masochist—I warmed to it not necessarily for what it is but rather for what it tries to be and what it could have been. In his biography *Otto Preminger: The Man Who Would Be King,* Foster Hirsch praises the film for its non-judgmental portrayal of the '60s counterculture. In Preminger's open, sweetly misguided film, hippies aren't just smarter, more spiritually attuned, and happier than everyone else, they're also more patriotic. The idea that hippies might just be better Americans than flag-waving cultural troglodytes like Tony is sneakily subversive and strangely winning. Preminger's celebration of a subculture he admired but didn't begin to understand serves as a singular time capsule of a time, place, and cultural divide that has only grown greater in the ensuing four decades.

Failure, Fiasco, Or Secret Success? *Fiasco*

Austin Pendleton On *Skidoo*

Austin Pendleton is one of those delightful character actors who elevate everything they appear in. The elfin Tony-nominated actor, playwright, and director has appeared in more than 40 films, including *Catch-22, What's Up, Doc?, The Front Page, The Muppet Movie,* and *My Cousin Vinny* in addition to his extensive work in the theater.

Austin Pendleton: The original screenplay the film was developed from was written by a guy I knew slightly in New York named Bill Cannon. He had written this movie called *Brewster McCloud.* He had seen me in a play and he had wanted me to play Brewster McCloud. It was in the early days of independent film. It was in the mid-'60s, I'd say. I read it and I loved it. I thought it was terrific and an incredible part. I couldn't believe it, because I had never been in a movie. So I said, "Great! I'll do this." But then he couldn't get it on. He couldn't get it produced at the time though it was ultimately made by Robert Altman.

So then he called me up, and he's like, "I've written a more commercial screenplay called *Skidoo,* and I've written a supporting part for you in that. So hopefully it'll be easier to get *Skidoo* made, and we'll attract some names for a couple of the lead roles, and you'll be really good in this supporting role, so then we can get *Brewster McCloud* made." And I said, "Well that's sweet of you." [Laughs.] *Skidoo* was like the *Brewster McCloud* screenplay: It was very '60s and very fragmented and the product of someone very, very talented. So then Bill called me one day and said, "I've sold *Skidoo!*" I said, "Great, dude. To who?" I thought it would be like early Brian De Palma.

Nathan Rabin: Or a Peter Fonda type.

AP: He said, "Otto Preminger." I said, "Have you lost your mind?" At that time and always since, I have been a fan of Otto Preminger's, but he's the last director I would think of for a thing like this. And he said, "Oh no, he's very excited about it." He'd shown Otto the *Brewster McCloud* script, and that would have been even more strange. He'd quoted Otto and did an imitation and said [Adopts Austrian accent:]

"I like *Brewster,* but I like better your *Skidoo.*" So then Bill told Otto, "Okay, but I want you to put this actor named Austin Pendleton in it." Otto tried to get me for a three-picture deal, and I told my agent, "I'm not going to do that." I don't know what I missed doing, but I said, "I'm not going to be tied down." I wish I had gotten a three-picture deal, as it happens, but anyway . . .

So I went out there and we began to shoot on the location, which was on the sound stage at Paramount, where all the prison scenes were shot. As I say, it was the first time I'd been in a part of any significance in a movie at all, and the technique of it, I just couldn't get hold of. I would miss my marks, I was incredibly self-conscious, and Otto kept being pleased with it. I didn't have a car, I was staying at a motel, at a place called the Players Motel, from which you could walk to Paramount. It was a hotel run for alcoholic actors, run by a couple of old actors who were themselves in AA. So the atmosphere around the pool was really depressing.

But I would get up early every morning and walk through the back alleys to Paramount. I would see over the buildings, see a big poster for American Airlines, see how many flights to New York, and all I kept thinking is, "I gotta get back to New York. I'm so unhappy here." And Otto was impatient. He got very particular about everything he wanted, and I thought everything he wanted was wrong. I was thinking the movie was going down the tubes, but I began thinking it was going even more down the tubes than I would have thought. It was like his competence seemed to be eluding him. I thought it would be like a smooth movie that was too old-fashioned. But it wasn't even that. Scenes were just going down the toilet. I kept calling my agent from the sound stage, saying quietly, "You've got to get me out of this." And she's saying, "Dear, it doesn't work that way. It's not like a play. It's just, 'No. You're in it.'" But I said it would destroy my whole movie career; I was never going to act again. And I was only 28. I was beside myself.

Then one day we were setting up a shot and Otto was getting increasingly impatient with me. But at the same time, I came in one day and he said [Adopts Austrian accent:] "I have good news for you: We're going to build you a new, much bigger part so you will be here quite a few more weeks!" And I thought, "Oh, shit! This is like a nightmare. And why can't he see how little this is working?" But still he was getting impatient with me. At first I thought, "Well, it's my first film, I can't hit my marks, can't do anything." And the first scene was one in which I was naked, by the way, and that freaked me out. It wasn't the way to begin. Then one day we were setting up a fairly simple shot: walking down the corridor outside the cells and coming to a stop, and then I go into a cell. And I didn't hit the marks. And Otto, out of desperation, cried out, "You are amateur!" And before I knew what was coming out of my mouth I said, "I know I am! What are we gonna do about it?" And he just turned on a dime and said, "No, no, I didn't say you're an amateur. I just mean you're inexperienced." From that point on, he started teaching me what remains about 80 percent of what I know about film acting.

NR: In *Skidoo,* your character represents the counterculture. Was that something you felt plugged into?

AP: I was very into all that.

NR: Why do you think the counterculture appealed to Otto Preminger at that stage of his life?

AP: Well I think . . . and he himself said this—he was a strangely open man. He said things like [Adopts Austrian accent:] "I regret that I had not been more like a hippie." And he also regretted never having had one homosexual experience. He told me that at one point.

NR: I'm guessing that wasn't a come-on.

AP: No, no. I didn't get the feeling. Never. If that was that, he didn't do that. He would never do that. He would with women, but I don't think he would ever come on to a guy. If I had said to him, "Well, Otto . . . ," then he might have gone along with it. It didn't occur to me. He was just talking about himself and his regrets. What the hippie movement meant to him was that if everybody were more open to all kinds of experiences, the world would be a better place. And that's what that movement was all about. You slept with everybody, you did every drug, and it did create—which he earnestly tried to re-create in that film, I don't think with much success—kind of a lovely vibe for a couple of years before everybody freaked out. And Otto was very moved by the idea of looking at life that way.

NR: The defense of *Skidoo* in Hirsch's Preminger biography is that it's a very non-judgmental take on the counterculture.

AP: That was the trademark of all his filmmaking. There's a real objectivity in the way he puts so much stuff into each shot. He doesn't try to favor one point of view over another. All his best films have that in them. But they all have it in terms of the kind of atmospheres and topics that he understood a little better. But he told me how touched he was by what the hippies were, how hippies saw things, how we saw the possibilities of life—that anything that didn't do somebody harm was worth exploring. He was genuinely moved by that.

Good-bye Blue Monday Case File #88: *Breakfast Of Champions*
Originally Posted November 27, 2007

Each generation picks its heroes. That's why Robert Altman's death inspired a tidal wave of grief. Altman spoke to my generation like few other filmmakers before or since. Altman had an eternally contemporary sensibility, hip, wry, smartass, and cynical, but with a sneaky streak of empathy and emotional depth. In that respect, he belongs as much to the present and future as the past. The same goes for Kurt Vonnegut.

Vonnegut is one of those rare writers capable of profoundly altering the way readers perceive the world. He possessed a genius for making the mundane and forgettable seem new, ridiculous, perverse, horrible, and cruel. He had an unparalleled gift for exposing the madness and folly of our materialistic world, and a deft ear for the mindless happy talk of commercials, taglines, ad copy, and all the ephemeral nonsense that whispers relentlessly in our collective ear, telling us that eternal happiness is just a few purchases away.

At the core of *Breakfast Of Champions* lies a principled revulsion toward the spiritual emptiness of consumer culture endemic to many of Altman's scathing social satires. So it's fitting that Altman wanted to adapt *Breakfast Of Champions* for the big screen in the mid-'70s with the great Peter Falk as businessperson Dwayne Hoover, the even greater Sterling Hayden as cantankerous science-fiction hack Kilgore Trout, and Ruth Gordon as the wealthy Eliot Rosewater.

Alas, when *Breakfast Of Champions* was made into a movie in the late '90s, Altman wasn't involved, though his good friend and long-time collaborator Alan Rudolph wrote and directed the adaptation. Altman produced many of Rudolph's films from this era, but *Breakfast* boasted an even more venerated producer with an even stronger reputation for valiantly fighting for Rudolph's artistic vision: Bruce Willis' brother.

Not coincidentally, Bruce Willis also stars as Dwayne Hoover, a fabulously well-to-do businessman rapidly coming apart at the seams. While the Midwestern backwater of Midland prepares for an arts festival, Hoover fights a losing battle to maintain his sanity. He is unwittingly on a collision course with Albert Finney's Kilgore Trout, a writer whose stories pad out the pages of dirty magazines and pornographic books. Nonetheless, he's been beckoned to appear at the Midland Arts Festival at the request of a wealthy benefactor. Meanwhile, back at Hoover's car dealership, jittery flunky Harry Le Sabre (Nick Nolte) worries endlessly that his boss will uncover his secret life as a transvestite, while childlike ex-convict Wayne Hoobler (Omar Epps) longs only to work for a man of Hoover's stature.

Breakfast deals with the conflict between the smiling, together face we show the outside world and the angry, burbling madness roiling just underneath the surface. It accordingly requires a lead actor touched with a spark of divine insanity, but Willis is too self-assured to inhabit the role convincingly. When he sticks a gun in his mouth and ponders the vast cosmic void, he's following the directions of the script, not responding to bad chemicals in his brain or the demented prerogatives of fate. History has taught us that no matter how many bad guys fire weapons in his direction, or how many Seagram's Golden Wine Coolers he's consumed, Willis will emerge smirking and triumphant. The alpha-male swagger that makes him one of our most bankable action stars also makes him a perverse choice to play a man lurching toward a personal and professional nadir from which he can never fully recover.

In a seedy hotel lounge, Hoover encounters Trout and asks for the meaning of life. Trout hands him a book that takes the form of a letter from the creator of the universe, explaining that everyone in the universe is an automated robot except for the recipient of the letter, who has the glory and the horror of being the only person on Earth capable of free will. This sends Hoover on a crazed spree of unprovoked violence.

As it heads into the home stretch, Vonnegut's novel becomes its author's story as much as his characters'. No longer content to watch from the sidelines, Vonnegut—that kindly, sadistic creator of his literary universe—becomes a character in his own novel, spying on the discord at the hotel lounge from behind mirrored glasses. Vonnegut makes his authorial presence felt in a thousand other little ways as well, from autobiographical asides (or faux-autobiographical asides) to his charmingly simple drawings to the jazz-like use of repetition and recurring themes and motifs.

Rudolph finds a way to integrate Vonnegut's drawings into the film, using them in the opening credits and sneaking them into the background like Easter eggs. The elegantly rumpled and ramshackle Finney proves an inspired choice to play Trout, Mark Isham's score does a much better job of balancing comedy and tragedy than the film, and Epps indelibly embodies his character's poignantly pathetic dreams.

But Rudolph gets just about everything else wrong. His screenplay takes pointless liberties with its source material, eliminating the author's presence and making Hoover's dead wife a spectral but apparently alive basket case stumbling about in a dreamy Thorazine haze. Most of all, Rudolph botches the book's tricky tone, a highwire combination of misanthropic satire, bleak philosophizing, and deep, aching sadness.

Adapting Vonnegut's *Breakfast* was always going to be a tricky proposition. It's a cartoon tragedy, a slapstick meditation on existence and the meaning of life. Without Vonnegut's indelible voice—an ironic, blackly comic howl of despair at an absent and perverse God—it devolves into a crazed cacophony of clattering cartoon caricatures, a headache-inducing parade of all-American grotesques. Vonnegut's corrosive philosophical satire stumbles nobly toward transcendence and grace, attaining a strange cumulative power in its heartbreaking final pages. Rudolph's adaptation retains only the stumbling.

Failure, Fiasco, Or Secret Success? *Failure*

Michael Jai White On *Breakfast Of Champions*

Michael Jai White is perhaps best known as the title character in the 1997 feature film adaptation of Todd McFarlane's cult comic *Spawn*. He had a memorable supporting role as a gangster whose flunky becomes the victim of the Joker's infamous "pencil trick" in *The Dark Knight* and played a superhero of sorts in the delightful blaxploitation parody/homage *Black Dynamite,* which he also cowrote.

Michael Jai White: I was confused, man. I didn't know what I was doing there. The day I got there, I knew I was going to do this scene with Buck Henry, but I hadn't met him yet. On the way to the set, I see Nick Nolte running down the street in a dress, and I'm like, "What is this movie about?" Even while I was on the set, I didn't quite understand what I was doing or what was going on. I did the scene with Buck Henry, and Bruce Willis was dancing on top of a car. It was so surreal. He danced on top of the car, which he wasn't supposed to do, destroying the hood of the car. They had to get another car. I didn't get a chance to read the script until I was there, and then I read the script, and I was like, "I still don't know what's going on." And I remember sitting in the theater not understanding. It felt like a bad dream. I didn't quite understand anything that happened.

Nathan Rabin: How did you end up in the movie if you hadn't read the script?

MJW: I don't remember how I got in the movie, to be honest. I got offered that job, and I remember my manager said, "You should do this. This is a Kurt Vonnegut novel with Bruce Willis in it. It could be big." My manager says, "This is a good thing." I always felt Albert Finney was one of the greatest actors who ever lived.

So I agreed to do it, but it was definitely a last-minute thing. I felt like maybe I was replacing somebody who fell out. And all I know is I was on my way to, I think, Idaho maybe? It was a blur. So I'm headed to Idaho all of the sudden, to shoot some scenes with Buck Henry. I'm thinking, "This is the guy who wrote *The Graduate*. He's the guy from *Saturday Night Live*." I was afraid to ask things. I was just in point-me mode. I didn't quite get anything. So it's just weird.

NR: Did you ever get around to reading *Breakfast Of Champions*?

MJW: Yeah, back then. I think I read it on set. I think I worked for only three or four days on that thing.

NR: But you were thoroughly confused, and still are 10 years later.

MJW: Right. If you were to ask me about it eight years ago, I could have given you a much clearer answer, but it's almost like that was erased from memory. Even now, as I re-create this, it's just a fog. It was like all of a sudden, two days later I'm off to Idaho to do something, and I don't quite know what.

Hickory Dickory Dock, George H. W. Bush–Era Playground Shock

Book-Exclusive Case Files: *Dice Rules* And *The Adventures Of Ford Fairlane*

When my first girlfriend dumped me, I made a spiritual journey to the Alley, a tacky quasi-Goth shopping complex in Chicago's Wrigleyville neighborhood, to pick up an item I hoped would transform me from a heartbroken shell of a man into a sentient ball of awesomeness: a black leather motorcycle jacket. It was the least practical item of clothing imaginable. Wearing it ensured that I was too warm in spring and fall, but too cold during the merciless Chicago winter. (The Alley, incidentally, was around the corner from what would become *The Onion*'s first Chicago office, a hovel where the entire *A.V. Club* staff squeezed into a tiny bullpen and the defining feature of the building was the overpowering stench of urine from an entry stairwell where bums would gather to relieve themselves after a long night of drinking rotgut.)

Oh, the magical powers of the leather jacket! It transformed an aggregation of skinny, ugly Queens dorks collectively known as the Ramones into the funnest rock band in the planet. It made a short, nebbishy Jewish journeyman actor named Henry Winkler into the personification of cool. More germane to this double Case File, a leather jacket transformed an undistinguished Jewish comic named Andrew Clay Silverstein—whose signature bit was a cute routine about Al Pacino, Sylvester Stallone, Robert De Niro, Eric Roberts, and John Travolta hanging out at the zoo together—into Andrew Dice Clay, the biggest, most controversial stand-up comic of the late '80s.

Considering what a joke he's become in the ensuing decades, it can be easy to forget just how massive Clay was at the time. He was a rock star of comedy who put out albums on Rick Rubin's American label, sold out Madison Square Garden for a solid week, and was primed for mainstream superstardom in the early '90s when he scored a superslick, Renny Harlin–directed big-budget action vehicle (1990's *The Adventures Of Ford Fairlane*) and his own theatrically released concert film, 1991's *Dice Rules*.

And he owed it all to a leather jacket and also the rank misogyny, xenophobia, and mindless hero worship of his fans. But mainly, the timeless cool of the leather jacket.

Dice Rules opens with a billow of smoke emanating from the neck of an empty sentient leather jacket that swivels around to reveal the words

"Dice Rules" in magical, glowing lipstick-red rubies. Clay sings a forgettable blues-rock number surrounded by adoring fans and a heavily mulleted backing band. Then the film segues into an almost 25-minute sketch positing a creation myth for the Diceman that borrows equally from early David Lee Roth videos, Jerry Lewis movies, *Welcome Back, Kotter,* and the revenge fantasies of disturbed 10-year-olds.

The Diceman was once like you and me: an übernerd with his hair slicked up into an Alfalfa cowlick. He had a domineering, verbally abusive, morbidly obese, shower-cap-sporting wife; an unfortunate predilection for wearing overalls over a lumberjack shirt; and a high, nasal whining voice that fell somewhere between Horshack and Eddie Deezen.

Everywhere he goes, the trepid hero of *Dice Rules* is abused. His mountain of a wife verbally castrates him. The clerk at the bank where he squirrels away his nest egg heaps scorn in his direction. Even his friends do nothing to hide their contempt. At a gas station, an impossibly young Eddie Griffin holds him responsible for the sins of white men everywhere.

Things look hopeless for this sad little schmuck until he stumbles upon a leather emporium where a gravel-voiced salesman (also played by Clay) shows him a jacket of destiny and utters words that will change his life forever: "Leather makes it happen. That's right. Anybody that was ever cool, that ever got the chicks, they wore the leather. James Dean. Leather jacket. Marlon Brando. Leather jacket. Arthur Fonzarelli. Leather jacket. Am I right or am I right? You can be one of those guys. You gotta want it, though."

With a single purchase, Clay makes a magical transformation from Jerry Lewis putz to Cinderfella. The concert film begins in earnest, with Andrew Dice Clay coming onstage at Madison Square Garden to perform before tens of thousands who otherwise would be occupied committing date rapes and/or beating up homosexuals. In that respect, Clay was performing a valuable public service by keeping these people off the streets for a few hours.

The applause is thunderous. The anticipation is palpable. These people don't *like* Clay: they *worship* him. Instead of crucifixes and rosary beads, they express their religious devotion with crude signs and homemade T-shirts adorned with Clay's catchphrases. The audience—which seems to score as much screen time as Clay himself—doubles as a museum of regrettable late-'80s fashion: stonewashed jeans, baseball hats with wacky messages, child-molester mustaches, big hair teased and permed to the heavens, enough hair spray to burn a continent-sized hole in the ozone layer.

After an eternity of Clay-fueled pandemonium, the Oracle speaks: "Korean delis. Indian newsstands. Greek diners. And ass-fucking parties every night of the week. That's New York. Howaya?"

The crowd erupts. In a preview of what's to come, there are constant reaction shots of Clay fans stomping their feet, clapping their hands, and holding ecstatically onto one another, lost in what is either orgasmic comic rapture or violent, possibly life-threatening seizures.

Clay begins slowly, with animal-themed bits on his dog eating his girlfriend out, his hatred of turtles, and the sneering attitudes of New York pigeons. In the grand tradition of elementary-school bullies, Clay picks only on people unable to defend themselves, but he warms up by snapping on creatures farther down the evolutionary chain. Before he can stick it to stuck-up amoebas, his rant veers into his misogynistic comfort zone.

Riffing on the 'tude of flying rats, Clay reflects, "You can be walking with your chick. All of a sudden, a bird shits on your nose. And your girlfriend will look at you like [Adopts Edith Bunker voice:] 'Honey, you have shit on your nose.' And you give her that attitude, like, 'What! Maybe I like it there. Now shut your fucking hole!'"

Going to a Clay concert in 1990 meant regressing proudly back to the fifth-grade lunchroom and quaking in awe at the cool kid who swears and wears a leather jacket and sneaks smokes from his drunk mom's purse and talks endlessly, profanely, enthusiastically, dismissively, and maliciously about all the skanks he's banging.

In Clay's caveman universe, guys just wanna get laid and women are all needy, desperate, parasitic shrews. People don't come to Diceman shows to laugh or be entertained. No, people come to Clay's shows to have their fear and hatred of women and minorities validated. They come to turn back the clock to a time before feminism and identity politics, and live, for an hour or so, in a world where women are interchangeable fucktoys and minorities are faceless verbal punching bags.

In rapid succession, Clay targets midgets, the Japanese, the twitchy, the handicapped, hunchbacks, and stutterers. "Ya ever listened to a stutterer? What the fuck are they trying to say? You're 30 years old. Talk like other people!" he admonishes. Yeah! And what's the deal with retarded people? Why can't they just read a fucking book, get a Ph.D., and land a lectureship at a small, prestigious liberal-arts college instead of always acting retarded?

After the interminable opening sketch, 45 minutes of vitriol, and a rapturously received recitation of Clay's signature dirty nursery rhymes, Clay just barely pads the film out to feature length by performing an Elvis song in the lip-curling, hips-swiveling style of the King; the aforementioned impressions of Sylvester Stallone, Robert De Niro, Eric Roberts, Al Pacino, and John Travolta at the zoo; and a perversely faithful performance of "Greased Lightning."

Like countless prepubescent girls, Clay has devoted endless hours to rewatching *Grease* and rehearsing its choreography. It's a weirdly innocent way to end 82 minutes of bad vibes and ugly sentiments, and a reminder that Clay once had a way to entertain people that didn't involve pandering to their worst instincts.

Dice Rules failed to reach beyond Clay's core audience, but that was a foregone conclusion in light of the much more high-profile failure of *The Adventures Of Ford Fairlane,* the film that was supposed to launch his career as a major movie star.

A move to the big screen was a natural for Clay. For what was the Diceman, if not a character he'd been perfecting for years? Yet in the years since *Dice Rules* and *The Adventures Of Ford Fairlane* bombed, the character seems to have taken over the actor. When he appeared on *Celebrity Apprentice* recently—a gig that defines late-career desperation—he acted as if he were still selling out Madison Square

Garden. There was a definite Norma Desmond vibe to it. In his mind, he was still big; it was the venues that had gotten small.

Clay's ego seems to have accepted only the rise, not the fall. When Clay talked to *The A.V. Club*'s David Wolinsky in 2008, he ended the interview by bragging about an imminent sex date with a "gorgeous redhead, over six feet tall, an hourglass figure, these big fucking tits, and an ass like a basketball." Is there anything sadder than a fiftysomething man boasting to an interviewer half his age about his girlfriend's basketball-sized ass? Three decades into his career, he hadn't evolved beyond bragging to the open-mouthed kids on the playground about how he totally touched this one girl's boob over the weekend and fingered the shit out of her.

The glory of *The Adventures Of Ford Fairlane* was that Clay fans no longer had to imagine him making out with all these hot chicks, then ordering them to scrub his toilet and wash his dishes; now they could watch the magic happen on a 20-foot screen in surround sound.

Clay's success with the ladies figures prominently in the voice-over narration that opens the film: "They call me Ford Fairlane, rock 'n' roll detective. I have the power to get into the hottest clubs, the hottest dressing rooms, and the hottest chicks. I admit it all sounds pretty nifty in theory. Then why am I here? Why do I wish the music industry and the rest of the globe would suck my Dick—Tracy?" Sure enough, Clay spends much of the early parts of the film dealing with a herd of Lycra-clad, oversexed skanks trampling all over one another for an opportunity to suck his Dick—Tracy, then clean up his sweet-ass beachfront lair. Ohhh!!!

The makers of *Ford Fairlane* faced a formidable challenge. How do you make Clay palatable to the mainstream without diluting his nasty edge? They begin by plopping him down in a milieu so sexist, sleazy, and heartless that Clay couldn't help but look like a white knight by comparison. The film takes place in the Los Angeles music scene of the late '80s, positing its wisecracking antihero as a potty-mouthed Sam Spade for the hair-metal era.

In a blatant act of pandering, screenwriters James Cappe, David

Arnott, and Daniel Waters give Clay sidekicks designed to appeal to every conceivable demographic. For the ladies, there's Jazz (Lauren Holly), a capable, steel-willed girl Friday. For the young people, there's a plucky orphan (Brandon Call) who idolizes the Diceman, and is known only as the Kid. Animal lovers get an anthropomorphic koala, and for the classic-rock crowd, Clay has an electric guitar once owned by Jimi Hendrix, something he can pick soulfully by a fire during his more pensive moments.

To give Clay credit, his rock 'n' roll dick is hateful only toward minorities not considered cool. So Fairlane praises Don Cleveland, a producer played by Morris Day, as "the only person in the business I could talk to without vomiting Day-Glo," and tells a rapper played by special guest star Tone Loc that while Clay may give him guff, he really does dig the new hippety-hop music—a sentiment he delivers with all the conviction of Elvis Presley assuring audiences that he loves the new music from bands like "the Beards" (aka the Byrds) in Presley's *'68 Comeback Special.*

Fairlane's misadventures begin when heavy-metal scuzzbag Bobby Black (Vince Neil) dies mysteriously and shock jock Johnny Crunch (Gilbert Gottfried) hires Fairlane to find his space-cadet groupie daughter Zuzu Petals (the charmingly out-of-it Maddie Corman). Fairlane's pursuit of the girl sends him ricocheting through a thick moral morass populated by exiles from the cast of *Hollywood Squares* during a music-theme week: Priscilla Presley as cold-blooded, rich femme fatale Colleen Sutton; Day as a hip producer reduced to working with an anemic-looking teen idol; sneering, mustachioed bad guy Julian Grendel (Wayne Newton); and wild-eyed, scenery-chewing Robert Englund as Newton's cackling, deranged henchman Smiley. Ed O'Neill steals the film as Lieutenant Amos, an antagonistic cop who never got over Fairlane blowing off his disco group during his days as a music publicist. Their bickering banter is stupid and juvenile, but intentionally so; call it meta-moronic.

Ford Fairlane is perhaps the best possible vehicle for Clay. Harlin and cinematographer Oliver Wood, who went on to shoot *Face/*

Off and the Matt Damon *Bourne* movies, give the film an electric, neon sleaziness awash in lurid reds and cool blues. Joel Silver was so impressed by Harlin's work here that he hired him to direct *Die Hard 2: Die Harder* based on its dailies alone. If Harlin could make Clay look like an icon of swaggering masculine cool, then just imagine what he could do with stars who didn't personify doucheiness.

Ford Fairlane is a live-action comic book sticky with the glitter and grime of the Sunset Strip and the sad glam-rock bastard child that was hair metal. It's a film of big hair and tight, tiny costumes; gleeful, unabashed vulgarity; and a charismatic hero with a certain cornball charm. It wasn't hurting for production values, either. It's a product of the Joel Silver adolescent-wish-fulfillment factory, so you better believe that shiny shit blows up but good, and that hired-gun scriptwriter Daniel Waters, well on his way to squandering the abundant promise of his script for *Heathers*, gives some of the dialogue a profane, pulpy panache.

Ford Fairlane has one big flaw: It isn't particularly fun or funny. My inner adolescent wanted to surrender to its puerile charms, but the adult in me wouldn't let him. Turn off the sound, and *Fairlane* is a candy-colored feast for the eyes, but the film is too inextricably rooted in the machismo, misanthropy, and misogyny of Clay's stage persona to qualify as even the guiltiest of pleasures.

Clay had every opportunity to cross over from cult hero to mainstream superstar—a high-rated HBO special, comedy albums, sold-out tours, a concert film, and a big-budget, Joel Silver–produced vehicle—but *Dice Rules* and *The Adventures Of Ford Fairlane* are rare instances where people lost money underestimating the taste and intelligence of the American public. Un-fucking-believable. Ohhhhhh!!!!!

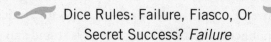

Dice Rules: Failure, Fiasco, Or Secret Success? *Failure*

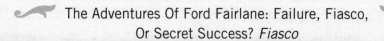

The Adventures Of Ford Fairlane: Failure, Fiasco, Or Secret Success? *Fiasco*

Trigger-Happy Teutonic Book-Exclusive Case File: *Postal*

On a chilly day in January 2005 in Chicago, three Chicago-based film critics for *The A.V. Club*—myself, editor Keith Phipps, and film editor Scott Tobias—descended on the screening room to catch an early-morning preview of the videogame adaptation *Alone In The Dark*. There was no real reason for all three of us to be at the screening. There was little chance we'd find ourselves passionately agitating for *Alone In The Dark* come awards time. A culture-wide debate on its aesthetic merits seemed unlikely.

Yet there we were all the same, inexplicably geeked about what was about to transpire. We somehow sensed that *Alone In The Dark* would be no run-of-the-mill crapfest. Our bad-movie Spidey senses were tingling uncontrollably with the promise that we were about to experience a film so spectacularly inept that it would instantly join *Santa Claus Conquers The Martians* and *Plan 9 From Outer Space* in the pantheon of anti-greats. A preposterous creature named Uwe Boll was sending out a trash-culture version of the Bat Signal, secretly alerting bad-movie aficionados that *Dark* was something special.

Our collective hunch was instantly validated by an opening-credit crawl that incoherently laid out endless exposition about terrifying beasties, lost Native American tribes, and other convoluted gobbledygook that explains and explains without actually explaining anything. This opening-exposition orgy obfuscates rather than edifies. The guffaws began early. They never stopped.

Boll got everything so wrong that it somehow felt right. It was perfect in its imperfections, like Boll's delusional belief that putting Tara Reid's hair in a schoolmarmish bun and covering her bloodshot, dilated eyes with glasses made her look like a Brown professor. Or the exquisitely redundant casting of Christian Slater and Stephen Dorff—the gold- and silver-medal winners in the Next Jack Nicholson Olympics—as the film's male leads. *Alone In The Dark* affirmed the ascendancy of a great bad filmmaker.

After stumbling giddily out of *Dark*, we were left to contemplate the enigma of Uwe Boll. The reality was far more spectacular than anything we could have imagined. If *Mystery Science Theater 3000* fans and message-board geeks could have created the ultimate bad film-maker, they couldn't have come up with a more perfect figure than Boll.

The Boll that emerges in the *Alone In The Dark* DVD commentary is a strangely hypnotic cross between Dr. Strangelove, a bizarro-world Werner Herzog, and a conspiracy theorist convinced that the American film industry exists solely to keep Uwe Boll down.

Boll's audio commentaries serve as Rupert Pupkin–like stand-up routines where, in a Teutonic bark, Boll rails against films that trumped his at the box office; accuses studios, actors, and theaters of institutional cowardice; makes casually racist comments; castigates Reid for not "losing her bra" for his film; and jokes about Owen Wilson's much-publicized suicide attempt.

In 2006, Boll didn't merely lash out petulantly at his online detractors like a 10-year-old in the midst of a temper tantrum; he literally challenged a handful of his most ferocious critics to box him. Is there a better way to settle artistic differences than with fisticuffs?

Given how terrible Boll's films are, how the hell does he keep getting the money to make more movies? The answer is perfectly in keeping with his demented carnival-barker persona. According to a 2008 profile in the *New York Times*, Boll's films have been funded through a loophole in the German tax system that allows investors to claim their investments as a write-off. And his films do much better at home than in theaters; according to the *Times,* theatrical grosses constitute only about 15 percent of their overall revenue.

Dr. Uwe Boll—he has a doctorate in literature, bizarrely yet perfectly enough—really is *The Producers'* Max Bialystock. Boll's 2008 *Postal* was his answer to *Springtime For Hitler,* only instead of a gay romp with Adolf and Eva, Boll promised madcap shenanigans with Osama bin Laden, 9/11, mass murderers, and a rogues' gallery of scoundrels, ne'er-do-wells, and glorified con artists that includes Dave Foley's penis, Verne Troyer, and Boll himself.

Postal was an adaptation of two notorious, vilified videogames (*Postal* and its sequel), but it was also an extension of Boll's shtick as an angry outsider railing impotently at the Hollywood establishment, the compromises of the film industry, and propriety. True to form, Boll announced a big 1,600-theater rollout for *Postal* that magically morphed into a four-screen release when I was assigned to review it. Well, sort of assigned to review it.

"You know, you don't have to do this. I know it's out of the way and playing at an inconvenient hour. We can always cover it next week, or on DVD. I'm giving you an out," my editor Keith offered, mercy in his eyes. But the die had been cast long ago. You know the role friends, family, love, community, religion, and public service play in your life? That's the role bad movies play in mine. I was born into this. Writing about ridiculous movies isn't just a job; it's a sacred calling. So the prospect of traveling an hour and a half to see *Postal* at a funky, only occasionally active repertory theater called the Portage was irresistible.

When I arrived at the Portage for the five o'clock screening of *Postal,* the man selling tickets seemed bewildered. "How, uh, did you find out about this screening? I mean, it's not even listed in [Chicago alt-weekly] *The Reader.*"

"I'm actually reviewing this for *A.V. Club,*" I blurted defensively. "Incidentally, how did this come to play here? Did Boll rent out the theater or something?" "Damned if I know," the ticket taker said.

I bought a grape Fanta and popcorn and entered the theater. The Portage is huge; it seats about 1,500. The absence of any other patrons made it seem even bigger. There were literally three times more people working the showing than attending it. Moviegoing, that consummate group activity, had suddenly become weirdly private. Screening Uwe Boll's *Postal* in a sacred cathedral of film was like a black-velvet Elvis painting occupying an entire wall of the Louvre: a terrible waste of a beautiful space.

When I got up to use the bathroom halfway through the film, the guy working concession quipped, "Do you want me to stop it for you?" When I left the theater, the projectionist came down and asked me what I thought of the film. I told him I'd expected something far worse, and he confessed, "The opening scene, you know, where the terrorists are arguing about the exact number of virgins they'll receive in paradise, it's almost, you know, kind of—" and then, measuring his words very carefully, "—mildly amusing." This mild amusement seemed to surprise him tremendously.

Postal begins by making sport of the single darkest moment in recent American history. It opens with a pair of terrorists in the cockpit of a plane headed into the World Trade Center, contemplating the exact nature of the reward awaiting them in paradise. They agree that martyrdom is a small price to pay for an afterlife involving 99 or 100 virgins, but what about 50 virgins? Or 10 virgins? What if they had to split those 10 virgins? How long would that last them? They decide to call Osama bin Laden (played by Larry Thomas, *Seinfeld*'s Soup Nazi), who regrets to inform them that due to an excess of martyrs, he can't promise any more than 20 virgins. This is a deal breaker, but before the terrorists succeed in taking the plane on a detour to the Bahamas, a group of Americans storm the cockpit and accidentally steer the plane into the World Trade Center. Cue the opening credits.

This opening is the closest any Uwe Boll film will ever come to capturing the wry verbal humor of a classic Bob Newhart routine. Boll then recalibrates the film's comic tone from "surprisingly subtle" to "screamingly broad" as he introduces us to a parade of All-American freaks.

Postal takes place in ironically named Paradise, Arizona, a white-trash hellhole where Job-like antihero Dude (Zack Ward) is leading a life that is almost like suicide. Settled into a trailer park with his morbidly obese, trash-television-obsessed wife, Dude inhabits the tawdry world of *The Jerry Springer Show*. His wife cheats on him, his neighbors detest him, and he steps into dog shit upon leaving his sad abode.

Trying to retain your self-respect while acting in a Uwe Boll movie is like trying to keep your head underwater without getting wet. *Postal* marks a milestone battle in Verne Troyer's ongoing war on dignity. He's aided in his quest by a perversely game Dave Foley as con artist/cult leader Uncle Dave; within five minutes of being introduced, Foley has exposed his flaccid penis; fallen asleep in a pile of nubile, nearly naked followers; smoked pot; and taken a dump on-screen.

Boll would not demand that his actors forgo their dignity without leading by example. He appears in *Postal* as himself, the lederhosen-wearing owner of Little Germany, a theme park funded by Nazi gold. Little Germany has come into the possession of a collection of sought-after dolls of a popular sentient-scrotum figure named Krotchy, which figures prominently in the plot. Dude and Uncle Dave want to abscond with the Krotchy dolls as a way of paying off Dave's debt to the IRS. Osama bin Laden and his minions, meanwhile, plan to use them to spread avian flu.

Whenever I visit Europe, I'm amused at how well movies depicting the United States as a cesspool of violence, lust, and insanity do overseas. *Postal* starts with the European conception of God's own U.S.A. as an ultraviolent realm where everyone packs heat and gunfights break out every half hour, then takes it to comic extremes. During a single shoot-out, Boll is shot in the crotch, a missile destroys a coffee stand called Grind Zero, children are murdered indiscriminately, and Verne Troyer, playing himself, punches a young person in the penis before ending up locked inside his own suitcase with only a glow-in-the-dark dildo for company.

Postal tops itself with every successive outrage. Soon, Troyer is forcibly sodomized by a thousand monkeys, and Uncle Dave is unceremoniously offed after discovering he's gay en route to a climactic trailer-park shoot-out where Dude delivers a big speech to the assembled hate mongers: "It's time to empty our hands of guns so we can fill our hands with hugs."

It isn't enough for Boll to take down every American institution and kill half the populace of Paradise. He ends the film with Osama bin Laden and George W. Bush skipping hand in hand through a field before a nuclear apocalypse. In *Postal*, American society is rotting from the inside out. The film pushes Ward's everyman to the point where grabbing a gun and killing a whole bunch of motherfuckers is the only sane, reasonable thing to do.

I was pleasantly surprised by *Postal* the first time around, if only because my expectations could not have been lower. It's less a film than a 100-minute-long juvenile prank, but it boasts a vulgar, confrontational energy that makes it surprisingly engaging. Of course, audiences don't go to Uwe Boll movies to laugh with him; they come to laugh at him. Boll makes it easy by being such a juicy target. With *Postal,* Boll finally wanted people to laugh at his movie. Understandably, that confused the irony-damaged "fans" who don't like Boll's movies so much as they "like" his movies, 'cause they're so "good" and their creator is such a "genius."

Postal reminded me why I love Boll even more than I hate him. There are plenty of bad filmmakers out there, but with the exception of *The Room*'s Tommy Wiseau, no contemporary creator of bad movies has cultivated such a strong cult of personality. Like Ed Wood before him, Boll lives his "art," even if that art revolves around empty provocation and terrible videogame adaptations.

At the risk of losing face in front of my fellow critics and readers, I have to admit that I, like the projectionist, found *Postal* almost, you know, kind of mildly amusing.

Failure, Fiasco, Or Secret Success? *Fiasco*

Dave Foley on *Postal*

With his boyish good looks and laid-back charm, affable straight man Dave Foley emerged as the breakout star of beloved Canadian sketch comedy group Kids in the Hall on their eponymous television show. After the troupe broke up, Foley starred as a news director on the cult sitcom *NewsRadio,* provided the lead voice in the Pixar film *A Bug's Life,* and appeared in the films *Dick, MonkeyBone,* and *Sky High.*

Dave Foley: The original script I got reminded me of late-'60s/early-'70s satirical pieces like *Little Murders,* the Jules Feiffer play. I thought it was a nice, dark, weird script. By the time I got up to Vancouver to shoot it, they had added in all the 9/11 stuff. I kept trying to talk them out of it, saying, "You're just going to kill the movie with this." *Postal* was also, of course, my cock's film debut. There was a scene where I was lying in bed with a bunch of naked girls and I said, "When I watch movies where there's some middle-aged guy lying in bed with a bunch of naked girls and he's fully dressed, that just seems creepy. So if they're going to be naked, then I should be naked too." Otherwise, it just seems weird.

Nathan Rabin: Were you hesitant about working with a director as infamous as Uwe Boll?

DF: That's one of the reasons I agreed to do it. I kept reading all these unbelievably angry postings on blogs by these Internet nerdy guys, pounding away at their computers writing [Adopts nerdy voice:] "He is totally destroying the integrity of this game! He must stop destroying the integrity of these wonderful games with his shitty movies!" You just think, "Here's an idea. Why don't you just tighten up your bathrobes and shut up?" They just hated him *so much*. That was also around the time he challenged all of his Internet critics to a boxing match, and a lot of them accepted, not realizing that he was a prize-winning amateur boxer and that he wasn't kidding, he was really going to beat them up. So all these Internet nerds came up to box Uwe and were a little shocked when they got in the ring and he actually beat them up.

NR: What's it like being directed by Uwe Boll?

DF: He's actually a really, really sweet guy. He's a really nice guy. I liked him a lot. His crew loves him, they're very dedicated to him. But movies are almost secondary to him. His real art form is being Uwe. It's almost like a performance-art thing. I think his real art form is the combat with fans and critics, and the movies are just artifacts of this creation that's bigger than his movies. While we were working on the movie, he was constantly looking at cuts of his last movie and preparing his next movie. As he's directing, he can't wait for the movie he's doing to be done. He's not interested in the movie he's doing; he's more interested in the next one, and the one he did before it.

NR: It's almost a machine-type situation.

DF: He's much more interested in the controversy concerning the one he just finished and preparing the controversy for the next one. I'm sure when he was doing the movie after *Postal,* he was obsessed with *Postal.* He likes the conflict with the public. He likes pissing off the bloggers.

NR: *Postal,* more than any of his other films, feels like a product of the confrontational Uwe Boll persona.

DF: I think he really did want to address a lot of the bullshit post-9/11 mentality, the idea that everyone becomes a hero. Not everyone's a hero. Being a victim doesn't make you a hero. Being murdered doesn't make you a hero necessarily; it makes you a murder victim. But people were talking about the people who died in the Twin Towers being heroes, and the country was going crazy. He did want to make a statement about that.

NR: Do you think that hurt the film?

DF: I think that crashing a plane into the Twin Towers at the start of the film hurt it. I said, "Look, even though I think a lot of that scene is funny, a lot of the dialogue in that scene is funny, if you do that, you're never going to get on a screen in North America. So why do it?"

NR: But presumably that was part of the reason he made the film, to be provocative, to deliberately piss people off.

DF: Yeah. To me, as long as it's funny, that's fine, but don't shoot yourself in the foot entirely, though God knows I've certainly done that myself in my own career.

Kicking A Man While He's Down Case File #132: *The Love Guru*
Originally Posted June 19, 2008

While researching this My Year Of Flops entry, I came across a 2006 *New York Times* article that time has rendered hilariously ironic. The article, titled "Mike Myers: Intentional Man Of Mystery," depicts Myers as the Stanley Kubrick of lowbrow comedy, a master technician who'd rather disappear from the spotlight for years than compromise his meticulous comic vision. Like Gallo Wines, Myers will serve no pee, masturbation, or nutsack joke before its time. The article describes Myers' lengthy hiatus from appearing in front of movie cameras "as a bid to recharge his creative batteries as well as a reflection of his perfectionism and high standards."

Though Myers declined to be interviewed for the piece, it paints a flattering portrait of him as a consummate artist methodically planning his next masterpiece, while less-talented peers like Will Ferrell, Adam Sandler, Jack Black, Ben Stiller, and Jim Carrey flood theaters with product. The implication is that they aren't nearly as devoted to their craft as Myers.

Myers fans had reason to be optimistic, however, as the prickly superstar had already begun road-testing his latest genius creation in comedy clubs throughout Greenwich Village. The character was a smiling, beatific, bearded guru named Pitka, who would eventually become the focus of 2008's *The Love Guru*.

Though infinitely less flattering, a scathing *Entertainment Weekly* profile of Myers from 2008 reiterates the Myers-as-genius-perfectionist line. *EW*'s Josh Rottenberg writes that Myers' "humor is based on artful contrivance, every detail machine-tooled with painstaking precision," then quotes *Love Guru* producer Michael De Luca as arguing, "Just because it's comedy doesn't mean it's not as important to Mike as *There Will Be Blood* is to Paul Thomas Anderson."

A smart, talented, accomplished writer-actor like Myers spending years meticulously creating, rehearsing, and refining an obnoxious one-note cartoon like Guru Pitka is like a group of brilliant scientists working around the clock for a decade to build a malfunctioning fart machine. Yet Myers and his agent were so confident about the commercial prospects of his latest creation that they began discussing sequels with Paramount more than a year before filming began. Though less prolific than his peers, Myers was a central component of three of the most successful comedy franchises of the past 25 years: *Wayne's World, Austin Powers,* and *Shrek.* The stakes and expectations were extraordinarily high for 2008's *The Love Guru,* his first foray in front of the cameras in five long years. If *The Love Guru* was even half as successful as *Shrek* or *Austin Powers,* it would mean a fortune not just in ticket sales but also in merchandising.

The Love Guru was a potential bonanza from a superstar accustomed to knocking it out of the park with each at bat. Yet between the release of 2003's underperforming *The Cat In The Hat* and *The Love Guru,* the public turned on Myers. The goodwill he engendered through *Saturday Night Live, Wayne's World, Austin Powers,* and *Shrek* got squandered through a series of mercenary sequels.

Myers was stupid enough to pick a very public fight with Ron Howard and his Imagine Films Entertainment juggernaut by pulling out of a proposed *Sprockets* film because he was unhappy with the screenplay. Here's the Kafkaesque part: Myers made an enemy of one of the most powerful people in Hollywood because he was unhappy with a screenplay he co-wrote. A certain level of self-hatred should be expected from funny people, but that took it entirely too far. A bitter Myers bitchily had Seth Green's heavy in *Goldmember* look more and more like Ron Howard with each passing scene. Myers really should have beefed publicly with a less-revered icon than Howard—someone like Maya Angelou, or the little dog that played Benji.

As more and more details came out about Myers' decades-long reign of jackassery, he came to be seen less as a troubled comic genius than as an asshole content to recycle the same tired shtick in film after film. Meanwhile, the Dresden-bombing-style publicity for *The Love Guru* made the tactical error of trying to sell Myers as a sensitive artist trying to create joy and laughter while recovering from a traumatic divorce and the death of a parent at a time when Myers' reputation was at an all-time low.

The Love Guru at least opens with an inspired gag. The sonorous sounds of Morgan Freeman gently usher viewers into the action. Then the camera pans down to reveal that Myers' second-rate guru is speaking through the "Morgan Freeman" setting of an East India Voiceover Machine. It's all downhill from there. The disappointments begin with Stephen Colbert's appearance as a sportscaster waging an unsuccessful battle against his addictions to sex and peyote. It's a running gag that's brilliant in theory, but it dies on-screen.

Once the film's premise is established—foxy Toronto Maple Leafs owner Jessica Alba recruits Myers' neo-Eastern spiritualist to fix the broken marriage of a hockey star (Romany Malco), so his team can win the Stanley Cup—Myers indulges in an endless, joke-light rendition of "9 To 5" that establishes a tone of insufferable self-indulgence.

The Love Guru barely passes the 80-minute mark, yet it still finds time for Myers to perform three—count 'em, *three*—songs, including a perversely straight rendition of "More Than Words." It's hard to believe this shit took three years to write.

It would be hard to imagine a bigger, more obvious target for spoofery than bogus spiritual teachers, but Myers never aspires to satire. Deepak Chopra was an early, vocal supporter of the film when it came under fire from an outraged, publicity-seeking Hindu cleric who, upset over its depiction of his religion, called for a boycott. He needn't have bothered: *The Love Guru*'s ads and previews did a much better job of keeping audiences away than any boycott could. Unless it was led by Ron Howard. People love that guy.

It is easy to see why Chopra dug the film; it's essentially an extended cinematic blowjob. Chopra, who has a cameo as himself, is depicted as the real deal, an authentic man of wisdom committed to making the world a better place.

But Myers is less interested in puncturing fake mysticism than in being the world's oldest grade-school cutup. That's why his guru behaves throughout like a naughty 8-year-old in the midst of a Pixy Stix rush. Myers cracks endless smutty jokes, giggles at his own juvenile antics, laughs at himself even when he isn't cracking wise, and smiles his trademark idiot grin of beatific self-satisfaction.

There's something faintly tragic about *The Love Guru*. It's the work of a famously unhappy man intent on remaining a man-child on-

screen forever. Myers is a cinematic Peter Pan thumbing his nose at the compromises of adulthood. Sublimely silly Myers vehicles like *Wayne's World* and *Austin Powers* invite audiences to regress to childhood alongside their man-heroes. That's a simultaneously seductive and poignant offer. Wayne Campbell and Austin Powers never have to grow up because they're deliriously happy the way they are. But *The Love Guru* makes a terrible case for perpetual preadolescence. It offers all the stupidity and immaturity, with none of the joy or innocence.

I still hold out hope for Myers. He's made us laugh before. It's possible, if not probable, that he will make us laugh again. Hopefully he will learn from *The Love Guru*. So let's end this piece as it began, with the deliciously ironic final paragraph from the *New York Times* piece lamenting Myers' regrettable absence from the big screen, and the shimmering promise of a spectacular return to film:

"For another year, then, at least, audiences will have to make do with Mr. Myers's voice as the big green ogre in *Shrek The Third*, his physical absence made easier by the notion that they've been spared the blighted vintages that might well have been the Myers product of 2004, 2005 or 2006—and that he's continuing to work, however deliberately, on a splendid '08."

As us Chicago baseball fans like to say: there's always next year.

Failure, Fiasco, Or Secret Success? *Failure*

Chapter 3

Musical Misfires And
Misunderstood Masterpieces

Beatles Smile-Time Variety Hour Without The Beatles Case File #51:
Sgt. Pepper's Lonely Hearts Club Band
Originally Posted July 19, 2007

During my lengthy stint as a video-store clerk, I used to play 1978's *Sgt. Pepper's Lonely Hearts Club Band* on the store monitors with some regularity. Being a huge Beatles fan, I figured even bad Beatles covers were better than no Beatles at all. So I should have been more prepared for the film's almost inconceivable awfulness. But as often as I played the movie for our unsuspecting customers, I never watched the monitor while the clattering abomination was playing, which protected me from its eviscerating power. I felt like Lot fleeing Sodom and Gomorrah: As long as I didn't look back, I was safe. But had I glanced even casually at the monitor and seen, say, Billy Preston in a gold lamé suit hurling magical laser beams while flying around singing "Get Back," or sexy henchmen robots destroying "She's Leaving Home," my brain would have turned into a pillar of salt.

To take the biblical analogy even farther, producer-mastermind Robert Stigwood even got legendary Beatles producer George Martin and engineer Geoff Emerick to play Judases and betray their old masters by having them produce and engineer here. Martin spent the '60s elevating pop music with his production wizardry and the subsequent years periodically desecrating the Beatles' legacy. In addition to arranging, conducting, directing, and producing the music in the *Sgt. Pepper* movie, Martin produced the soundtrack for the Beatles-themed Cirque du Soleil show *Love,* and a 1998 Beatles tribute album featuring Jim Carrey mugging his way through "I Am The Walrus" and Robin Williams and Bobby McFerrin dueting on "Come Together."

Like *The Star Wars Holiday Special, Sgt. Pepper* puts a beloved cultural institution in a new context so mind-bogglingly inappropriate that it engenders intense cognitive dissonance. Logic seems to dictate that the *Star Wars* universe shouldn't include a Wookiecentric special featuring the comedy stylings of Harvey Korman, Diahann Carroll trying to work Chewbacca's father into an erotic frenzy with a sexually charged song-and-dance number, a Boba Fett cartoon, and a special performance by Jefferson Starship. Yet *The Star Wars Christmas Special* undeniably exists, though George Lucas would like to pretend otherwise. A big-budget 1978 musical that transforms songs from *Sgt. Pepper's Lonely Hearts Club Band* and *Abbey Road* into a pilot for a *Beatles Smile-Time Variety Hour Without The Beatles* is similarly preposterous and far-fetched, yet the cinematic *Sgt. Pepper's Lonely Hearts Club Band* exists as well.

Still, there was method to Stigwood's madness. Wasn't the beloved *Yellow Submarine* a Beatles movie minus the Beatles? Sure, the Fab Four provided some songs, but their creative input was minimal, they didn't voice their animated doppelgängers, and their attitude toward the project was lukewarm at best.

Adapted loosely from the 1974 Off-Broadway musical *Sgt. Pepper's Lonely Hearts Club Band On The Road,* the film casts Peter Frampton and the Bee Gees as humble minstrels who rocket to superstardom after signing with a shady record label, only to watch their fortunes change after their magical musical instruments are stolen by the villainous Mean Mr. Mustard (Frankie Howerd), a real-estate scoundrel who receives directives from the evil computer on his pimped-out bus.

As Billy Shears and the Henderson brothers, respectively, Frampton and the Bee Gees must then use their vacant stares, amateurish pantomime skills, nonexistent charisma, and middle-of-the-road versions of Beatles classics to retrieve the instruments and bring joy back to Heartland. In the fierce battle between Frampton and the Brothers Gibb to determine who can emit less star power, everybody loses.

Sgt. Pepper takes a dark turn when Billy's love interest, Strawberry Fields (Sandy Farina), dies in a skirmish with Aerosmith. A despondent Billy tries to kill himself by jumping out of a building, only to have Sgt. Pepper (played by Beatles session player Billy Preston) pop up as the most Magicalest Negro ever and get his deus ex machina on by hurling magical beams of light that bring Strawberry Fields back to life, keep Billy from plummeting to his death, and for some reason, transform supporting players into members of the Catholic clergy.

Just when it seems like the film cannot get worse, a random selection of guest stars re-create the cover of *Sgt. Pepper's Lonely Hearts Club Band* for a final insult to everything the Beatles created. The closing number is a maraschino cherry of awfulness atop a 10-scoop sundae of bad ideas, incompetently executed. Is there any better way to end a "tribute" to the Beatles than with guest appearances from Dame Edna, Carol Channing, Keith Carradine, Sha-Na-Na, Hank Williams Jr., and Leif Garrett?

The Beatles explored a sonic and emotional template unprecedented in the history of pop music. There's infinite variety and sophistication in the band's humor alone. Paul McCartney brought cornball dance-hall baggy-pants broadness but also goofball absurdism, and John Lennon supplied vitriolic black humor and stinging social satire. Though it hit studios well before the Beatles reached their creative peak or underwent one of the most profound artistic evolutions in history, 1964's *A Hard Day's Night* feels fresh, edgy, hilarious, and hip today.

But Stigwood's film reduces the Beatles' diverse, literate humor to history's dumbest variety-show skit. *Pepper* combines the worst of the old and new. It ransacks vaudeville and silent film for its hokey jokes, grossly exaggerated performances, and groaning stupidity, but adds cheesy disco flourishes and special effects that wouldn't look out of place in a Rudy Ray Moore movie.

Pepper attempts to destroy everything resonant about the Beatles' music, stripping "She's Leaving Home" of its melancholy grace, "Good Morning Good Morning" of its caustic wit, and "A Day In The Life" of its epic, bipolar grandeur. At his most twee, Paul McCartney wrote cloying ditties that bordered on novelty songs. *Sgt. Pepper* takes this rare shortcoming in the Beatles' canon and runs with it. Guest stars Steve Martin and Alice Cooper respectively reduce "Maxwell's Silver Hammer" and "Because" to kitsch.

The musical performances fall into two discrete categories: bland, reverent mediocrities and creaky novelty songs. (The sole exception is Aerosmith's down-and-dirty take on "Come Together." Aerosmith escapes the epic pointlessness of this whole endeavor by making the song its own—a nasty, warped, peyote-soaked blues howler delivered with sleazy conviction.) Just because something works in one context doesn't mean it will succeed in another. At the risk of being controversial, I found *Sgt. Pepper's Lonely Hearts Club* inferior to the album that inspired it.

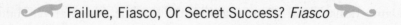 Failure, Fiasco, Or Secret Success? *Fiasco*

Madcap Musical Miserablism Case File #59: *Pennies From Heaven*
Originally Posted August 16, 2007

> *I have never spent two more miserable hours in my life. Every scene was cheap and vulgar. They didn't realize that the '30s were a*

very innocent age, and that it should have been set in the '80s—it
was just froth; it makes you cry, it's so distasteful.
                    —*Fred Astaire on 1981's* Pennies From Heaven

The '30s were indeed an innocent, blissful era of Jim Crow, lynching, and widespread institutional racism and sexism, a bygone era where Hitler got tongues a-wagging over in Germany and, as *The Onion's* book *Our Dumb Century* reminds us, all America had to fear was fear itself, a crippling, interminable Depression, and the specter of Hitler and Stalin splitting up Europe into two kingdoms.

Of course, the '30s were a time of innocence and escapism for Fred Astaire/Ginger Rogers musicals. Astaire made a fortune selling upscale fantasies to people beaten down by the Depression. He had a vested interest in making sure the harsh light of reality didn't invade the shimmering dreamworld of '30s musicals.

Pennies From Heaven has a better critical reputation than most of the films I've written about here, but it still found a way to make just about everyone unhappy, especially the people behind the acclaimed British miniseries that inspired it. In a strange way, the American *Pennies* both usurped and was usurped by its British counterpart. The accolades that greeted the limey *Pennies* ensured that the American version would forever be considered inferior, but the corporate muscle of MGM kept the English miniseries from being seen in the States for a full decade.

Rabid fans of cult writer Dennis Potter—who wrote both the British and American versions of *Pennies From Heaven*—were infuriated that MGM's remake took the original miniseries out of circulation until 1990 and that MGM didn't ask original stars Bob Hoskins and Cheryl Campbell to reprise their roles. MGM was horrified that the film grossed only a fraction of its $22 million budget. The film's three Oscar nominations must have provided little comfort. *Pennies* scored the Best Screenplay nomination that generally goes to challenging, innovative, and edgy films that the sleepy old dinosaurs who make up the Academy lack the testicular fortitude to festoon with nominations in higher-profile categories. True to form, *Pennies* lost to *On Golden Pond*.

Pennies bravely cast Steve Martin in his first dramatic role. Even more audaciously, it cast him as a largely unsympathetic character. We Americans treasure our delusions. The notion that you can doggedly pursue your dreams, follow your heart, believe in the transformative powers of music and love, and still end up in a hangman's noose for a crime you didn't commit seems downright unpatriotic. And we like our dreamers pure hearted and true, not sleazy, sordid, and ruled by sex and greed like Martin's sad little schemer.

In a revelatory lead performance, Martin plays Arthur, a sheet-music salesman trapped in a loveless marriage with sour-faced scold Joan (Jessica Harper). To escape a barren home life and a career sputtering headlong into Nowheresville, Arthur frequently slips into fantasies where he lip-synchs to Tin Pan Alley ditties and cavorts his way through production numbers worthy of MGM's legendary Freed Unit.

The plastic smiles and speed-fueled peppiness of dancers in old musicals have always struck me as strained and unnerving: They embody a painfully forced bonhomie that's downright creepy. *Pennies* brilliantly exploits that blatantly artificial pep in disquieting ways. There's similarly a haunting quality to the pop and crackle of ancient recordings where dead voices gather to espouse long-forgotten hopes and dreams. There's a reason creepy old records playing at unexpected intervals are a horror-film staple.

While making his rounds one day, Arthur becomes fixated on sad-eyed schoolteacher Eileen, played by Bernadette Peters, whose rag-doll vulnerability has never been more poignant.

Arthur's sexual fantasies are as tawdry and sad as the rest of his existence. He pressures a mortified Joan into putting lipstick on her nipples in a subplot as uncomfortably voyeuristic as anything in Todd Solondz's oeuvre. But his most cherished sexual fantasy involves paying an elevator operator $20 to look the other way while he and a game little minx have semi-public sex. *Pennies* has the temerity to suggest that under the coy double entendres, moony romanticism, and sly one-liners in old songs lies an animal hunger for sex. Martin plays this to the hilt.

Pennies begins with Arthur in a state of despair that only intensifies as the movie progresses. He achieves his dream of opening a record store, then watches it die. Eileen becomes pregnant, gets an abortion, and sinks into prostitution at the behest of Christopher Walken's tap-dancing pimp.

Walken's striptease tap dance to "Let's Misbehave" is rightfully acclaimed, but my favorite production number remains Vernel Bagneris' devastating solo dance to the title song. In the "Pennies From Heaven" number, Bagneris' accordion-playing murderer moves with otherworldly grace, his impossibly long limbs moving slowly and strangely, as if underwater. He begins the song amid the grim faces and permanent frowns of the dispirited rabble at a run-down diner before launching into a fantasy world where shimmering pennies rain down like gilded manna.

Pennies is fundamentally about the conflict between illusion and reality and the dual nature of escapism. Watching Astaire and Rogers glide around a ballroom for 90 minutes might help you forget your own troubles, but it also highlights the dispiriting chasm between the dreams Hollywood sells and the mundane lives of the moviegoers who buy them.

Arthur ends up getting framed for the accordion man's murder of a blind girl. As the noose tightens around his neck, the contrast between song-and-dance numbers and his unbearable life grows smaller and smaller until he begins talk-singing "Pennies From Heaven" through tears, accompanied by a ghostly unseen banjo as he awaits death. *Pennies* plays up the tragic divide between the fantasy worlds of Hollywood musicals and the sobering realities of life among the working poor. Late in the film, Martin blurs that line completely by first singing along with Astaire's celluloid image in a movie theater, then leaping boldly into the frame with Peters. I love musicals, but I also love

Heaven's merciless deconstruction of the genre. It gets under my skin and haunts my psyche anew with each viewing.

Pennies illustrates the truth of Noël Coward's famous line that it's "extraordinary how potent cheap music is," a quip that could double as Potter's epitaph. But don't take my word for it. Here's Martin's wholly unbiased take on the film's defenders and critics: "I must say that the people who get the movie, in general, have been wise and intelligent; the people who don't get it are ignorant scum."

❧ Failure, Fiasco, Or Secret Success? *Secret Success* ❧

Biblical Disco Freak-Out Case File #79: *The Apple*
Originally Posted October 25, 2007

Not too long ago, in a frozen tundra known as Wisconsin, my editor Keith created a feature called Films That Time Forgot as a way of channeling our shared bad-movie addiction to semi-productive ends. Selecting films for the feature necessitated a never-ending search for the sleaziest, weirdest, most obscure films I could find.

It was easy to see why time forgot most of these films: They were terrible and dated (sometimes amusingly so, sometimes not), and aspired to do little more than glean a few quick bucks out of the public's enduring appetite for violence, T & A, and/or gratuitous break-dancing sequences. But every once in a while, I'd uncover a secret gem that took up valuable real estate in my imagination.

There was, for example, *Death Drug,* a hilarious 1978 anti-PCP blaxploitation cheapie that begins with a seemingly stoned Philip Michael Thomas ambling around a pool hall and explaining that he has played many, many roles in his long and distinguished career. Why, he's played everything from a slick-dressing cop to . . . uh . . . He was in something else too, right? But of all the classic characters Thomas has played, one part remains close to his heart: the role of a

PCP-addled musician in *Death Drug*. Deep into his insane impro-
vised rant, Thomas assures the audience that there will be people in
their lives who'll offer them drugs that'll "get you so high, so high,
man, you'll need a parachute to come down," but that this film should
scare them straight.

Even without this VHS introduction, *Death Drug* would qualify as
the gold standard of camp, but what makes it such a singular boondoggle is that it clumsily inserts a music video from Thomas' Reagan-
era heyday into the middle of the action and expects audiences not
to notice that the lead character has suddenly aged dramatically and
is swanning his way through a music video even though the medium
barely existed when the film was supposed to take place.

The only Film That Time Forgot that can compete with *Death
Drug* for campy goodness is *The Apple*, a disco fantasia on biblical
themes from the director of *Over The Top* that was released in Germany in 1978 as *Star Rock* and stateside two years later under its new
title. According to show-business legend, audiences at *The Apple*'s
Hollywood première were so horrified by it that they angrily hurled
promotional copies of its soundtrack at the screen.

The Apple nakedly aspires to be the next *Rocky Horror Picture Show*,
with a little *1984*, *Hair*, and the book of Genesis thrown in. It's the
story of Adam and Eve reborn as an intergalactic Dionysian sex musical, only much stranger. The film takes place in the faraway future of
1994 and focuses on a hopelessly white-bread couple, Bibi (Cath-
erine Mary Stewart) and Alphie (George Gilmour), from Moose Jaw,
Canada. When the duo's nap-inducing brand of offensively inoffen-
sive folk-rock inexplicably wins over the crowd at a Worldvision Song
Festival, the hapless pair are wooed by a sinister music-world titan
named Mr. Boogalow (Vladek Sheybal), who is literally the devil.

Mr. Boogalow ushers the pair into a seductive nighttime realm
where sex is everywhere, temptation is omnipresent, and elaborately
choreographed Broadway-style production numbers are never more
than a few minutes away. Bibi quickly falls for a beefcake Boogalow
protégé (Allan Love), who woos her in a production number set in

91

hell, with the immortal couplet, "It's a natural, natural, natural desire / To meet an actual, actual, actual vampire!"

Having satiated her natural, natural, natural desires, Bibi can no longer go back to her vanilla life with Alphie. She becomes the newest star in Boogalow's constellation and delivers "Speed," a patriotic ode to America that doubles as a harrowing depiction of our nation as a desperate meth addict.

Alphie, meanwhile, sinks into a deep depression. Boogalow has somehow become powerful enough that everyone in the United States is forced to wear a triangular sticker promoting his record label (Boogalow International Music, or BIM) and observe the National BIM hour, a mandatory national-fitness program. Firefighters, leather-clad bikers, Coca-Cola bottlers, nuns, old people—all are forced to break into Broadway-style choreography during the National BIM hour.

Only *The Apple* has the audacity to dream up a future where a Simon Cowell–like Svengali is as powerful as Josef Stalin, and disco's bleary hedonism not only survived the '70s but grew in power until it conquered the world. Feeling adrift, Alphie eventually falls in with a group of sitar-stroking, bearded cartoon counterculture types wistfully described by their wizened leader (Joss Ackland) as "children of the '60s, commonly known as hippies." Alphie and Bibi are joyously reunited in time for a divine fellow in a sparkling white suit (also played by Ackland) to come down from heaven in a giant space car accompanied by videogame noises and offer to whisk his children to a fantastical space paradise where Mr. Boogalow has no power.

The peculiar genius of *The Apple* is that every time it appears the film cannot get any crazier, it ratchets up the weirdness to almost indescribable levels. It belongs to the subset of movies so all-consumingly druggy and surreal that they make audiences feel baked out of their minds even when they're sober. *The Apple* is both the perfect mind fuck to see while high and a movie that makes drugs seem redundant and unnecessary.

I think everyone in the world should see *The Apple*. It should be taught not just in film classes but in regular schools as well. It should replace the Bible and the Constitution as the cornerstone of our civilization. *The Apple* lifted my spirits, put a song in my heart, and completely validated my insatiable hunger to see an actual, actual, actual vampire by assuring me that such a seemingly sinful urge was simply a natural, natural, natural desire.

 Failure, Fiasco, Or Secret Success? *Secret Success*

Seven-Octave Butterfly-Shaped Case File #90: *Glitter*
Originally Posted December 4, 2007

In his last e-mail to me, my late friend and fellow critic Anderson Jones suggested that I write up 2001's *Glitter* for My Year Of Flops. Mariah Carey held a special place in his heart. I once asked Anderson if he'd ever been recognized in public during his stint on FX's *The New Movie Show With Chris Gore*. He said he'd been recognized once at a Mariah Carey concert. This seemed fitting. Carey's people were his people: They shared his deep commitment to superficiality, to the allure of big fluffy movies and sticky-sweet pop songs.

With this entry, I'm honoring a dead friend's memory by making glib jokes at the expense of one of his favorite artists. Call me a hero if you must (no, seriously: call me a hero, you must), but I'm just a guy doing my job. And being a hero. Mainly being a hero.

Glitter arrived at a crucial moment in what I like to call the "ho-ification" of Mariah Carey. Ho-ification occurs when an actress or singer stops being judged on her body of work and begins getting judged by the work she had done to her body. It's a ubiquitous pop-culture phenomenon in which an actress or singer decides that she wants to be recognized not just as an artist but also as a sweet, sweet piece of ass.

For Carey, the process began with the music video for "Honey," a tour de force of cheesecake iconography in which Carey indulged her 007 fantasies by playing Agent M and gallivanting about in the same bikini Ursula Andress wore in *Dr. No.* After "Honey," Carey was suddenly a woman with a message. That message was, "Hey, world; get a load of my tits! They're fucking great!" Her video concepts went from "having fun at the amusement park" ("Fantasy") to "jiggling about as a scantily clad racetrack ho-bag" ("Loverboy"), which perhaps not coincidentally was also the first single from the *Glitter* soundtrack.

Carey unleashed an avalanche of criticism when she handed out popsicles and indulged in an impromptu striptease during an infamous appearance on MTV's *Total Request Live,* well into what can be dubbed the crazification process. These public-relations disasters echo the scene in *Nashville* where Gwen Welles' painfully untalented looker dispiritedly takes off her clothes in a pathetic attempt to punish/win back a crowd by giving them exactly what she thinks they really want. Incidents like these speak to the fundamental hypocrisy at the heart of our culture's attitude toward sex and exhibitionism: We leer and ogle with impunity, then, once some vague, invisible line has been crossed, turn into disapproving prudes concerned only with protecting the innocence of children.

Glitter hit theaters at the worst possible time for Carey's previously blessed career. Her asexual early good-girl image was a distant memory, the ho-ification process had turned off as many fans as it created, and she was careening toward a nervous breakdown. The release of the film was postponed following Carey's hospitalization for "exhaustion." But the damage had already been done. A megastar who could previously do no wrong commercially suddenly could do no right.

Even her recording career began to suffer. The soundtrack to *Glitter* was nearly as big a bomb as the film it accompanied, in part because it faced much higher expectations. At the time of its release, it was unclear whether *Glitter* would mark the beginning of the end for Carey, or a bump in the road. She has subsequently rebounded on the strength of those terrible dog-whistle ballads they pipe into malls like stale air freshener, but *Glitter* had the potential to be a career killer.

In a performance that, to borrow an old Dorothy Parker line, runs the gamut of emotions from A to B, Carey stars in the semi-autobiographical drama as Billie Frank, a striver who grows up in an orphanage after being abandoned by her white father and drunken, self-destructive African-American mother. After getting discovered by a DJ/producer named Dice (Max Beesley, in the role that launched him to anonymity), Billie becomes a backup singer for Sylk, a talentless looker played by future *Top Chef* host Padma Lakshmi.

Dice eventually buys Billie's contract from Sylk's boyfriend, Timothy Walker (Terrence Howard), and instantly transforms her into a huge star. In its busy first hour, *Glitter* hops deliriously from one music-melodrama cliché to another, finding time to include my all-time favorite show-business movie trope: Billie and Dice are riding in a taxi when they hear Billie's song on the radio. She's made it! They like her! They really, really like her! Dice orders the cabbie to crank up the volume, while Billie orders, "Gimme a dime! Gimme a dime!" so she can call up her friends and order them to crank up the radio so they can hear her. Much jumping up and down, irrational exuberance, and girlish, high-pitched shrieking ensues.

But Dice isn't too keen on sharing Billie with the world. As her star rises, his descends. The busy rocket-ride-to-superstardom arc gives way to somber piano tinkling, and Carey's acting goes from strained smiles and perky head nods to frowny faces and forehead crinkling as she reflects on how sad it is that, like, her mom and dad totally abandoned her and stuff, and her boyfriend is going crazy.

In a delicious irony, Carey's character resents being forced to vamp her way through a music video whose concept seems to be Orgy at Plato's Retreat. *Glitter* consequently has it both ways. It gets to show off Carey's assets in countless skimpy yet strangely unflattering outfits, and it gets to insist that Carey is at heart a deep, soulful artist uncomfortable with cynical attempts to exploit her sexuality.

Timothy kills Dice right before Billie can go onstage at a sold-out show at Madison Square Garden and sing a big number about her late Svengali. As if that weren't enough to satisfy the 10-year-old girl in everyone, Billie then takes a limo to the country for a joyous reunion with her now clean-and-sober mom.

It's easy, and fun, to lampoon the film's lazy reliance on time-tested showbiz-movie conventions, but Carey really seems to believe in them, just as she really seems to feel the sentimental horseshit she screeches at deafening volumes in her ballads. There's a strange poignancy to the scene where Billie explains her fantasy that she'll someday become successful enough that her mother will feel a surge of pride and regret for having abandoned her. Everyone who grew up without a parent has felt that same maudlin sentiment, that desire to become big and successful and accomplished enough to make the slights of the past fade into nothingness. In moments like this, it's possible to see the woman behind the glistening façade, to get a sense of who Carey is as a person. There's a fragility in this scene lacking in the rest of her performance, a star turn that feels like an extension of her music-video vamping rather than an evolutionary leap forward.

"The glitter can't overpower the artist," a philosophical music-video director argues early in *Glitter* while engaging in a free-form stream-of-consciousness rant about the enigma that is Billie Frank. "Okay, we ask ourselves. Is she white? Is she black? We don't know. She's exotic. I wanna see more of her breasts." Here, the glitz overpowers Carey's wan presence. It's not even close. Also, I wanna see more of her breasts.

Failure, Fiasco, Or Secret Success? *Failure*

Seasons Of Cynicism Case File #98: *Rent*
Originally Posted January 1, 2008

A few years back, I was forced to watch *The Passion Of The Christ* to prepare for the final audition of my poorly rated, mildly disreputable basic-cable movie-review panel show *Movie Club With John Ridley*. I'd pointedly avoided seeing *The Passion Of The Christ* during its theatrical run. It was nothing personal: I just dislike Mel Gibson personally.

Since I missed out on seeing the film in a theater, I was reduced to watching it on a 12-inch screen in my hotel room after catching a six a.m. flight from Chicago to LAX on Southwest. I imagine that when Mel Gibson contemplated the ideal viewer for his self-financed labor of love, he didn't envision a leftist Jew watching the movie against his will on a tiny screen in a state of bone-deep exhaustion.

But even if I'd seen *The Passion Of The Christ* on an IMAX screen, I doubt I'd have liked it. I didn't go in expecting a revelatory experience. But I expected to respond to it on some level at least, to be moved or shocked or horrified, or experience convulsions of empathy toward the King of Kings as he endures the ass whipping of ass whippings.

I was, after all, the kind of neurotic Jewish kid who watched Christian televangelists on late-night television and bought into their fiery tirades about the horrors awaiting those who don't accept Jesus Christ. Yet watching *The Passion Of The Christ*, all I felt was slack-jawed disbelief. This was the movie everyone got so worked up about, this cheesy, ham-fisted grindhouse take on the crucifixion? This was the film that became a landmark in our culture's culture war, this blood-splattered, violence-fetishizing cornball Christian kitsch? *The Passion Of The Christ* was depressing, but for all the wrong reasons.

I experienced déjà vu watching the disastrous 2005 film adaptation of *Rent* the first time around just before its ill-fated theatrical run. I was once again gobsmacked that such a buzzed-about cultural phenomenon could be so transparently awful. This was the play that won the Pulitzer Prize, this Up With People take on the New York underground? This was the show that inspired such a fervent cult? This was the show that dragged Broadway kicking and screaming into the present?

It's hard to overestimate the role timing plays in transforming a theatrical smash into a cinematic flop. *Rent* creator Jonathan Larson died the day before the musical opened Off-Broadway. Criticizing Larson's brainchild in the aftermath of his death would be like strangling a cancer-stricken puppy on Christmas with a rolled-up American flag. *Rent* wasn't just a musical; it was an irresistible human-interest story, a pop-culture fable almost too good to be true.

The show people who brought Larson's Tony-winning pop triumph to the big screen patiently waited for the play's cultural moment to pass, then waited five more years, then a few more years after that, then finally pushed the project into development once it was little more than a quaint nostalgia piece.

Rent retained much of its original Broadway cast. While keeping the original cast is always a good idea in theory and often a good idea in practice, actors who convincingly played mid-twentysomethings in 1996 can't help but look a little long in the tooth come 2005. They look less post-collegiate than pre-menopausal. It's almost as if an entire decade had passed between the opening night of the Broadway smash and the première of the film fiasco.

That only adds to the surreal lack of verisimilitude plaguing *Rent*. They're fake twentysomethings playing fake bohemians in a wholly inauthentic take on la vie bohème (and *La Bohème*). When writing the play, Larson delved deep into his experiences and those of his boho buddies, but somewhere between the play and the big screen, any lingering traces of authenticity were systematically removed.

But seeing this a second time just after the New Year, I decided to go into *Rent* with a new attitude. No longer would I snicker and sneer. No, I would open my heart and mind to the magic, the music, the wonder of *Rent*. I was going to let the toe-tappingest movie ever made about AIDS, heroin, and poverty infect my soul with its stirring message of "No day but today."

It didn't work. Mere seconds after the film began, my cynicism returned. The opening song asks, in the most nauseatingly sincere manner imaginable, how one measures a year, then proposes a series of options. They are, in order:

- minutes (525,600 to be exact)
- daylights
- sunsets

- midnights
- cups of coffee
- inches
- miles
- laughter
- strife
- love

I measured the 135 minutes of *Rent* not in love, but in snickers, derisive snorts, and gales of unintentional laughter.

The film and play follow a series of scruffy bohemians as they try to change the world through their crappy art. There's Roger (Adam Pascal), a Jon Bon Jovi look-alike with big hair, AIDS, and a tormented past that keeps him from being able to accept the sexual advances of heroin-addicted, AIDS-stricken, yet really perky and fun stripper Mimi (Rosario Dawson).

Then there's Roger's roommate, Mark (Anthony Rapp), an aspiring D. A. Pennebaker making a revolutionary documentary where he films his friends and neighbors. Incidentally, there's a name for casual, ramshackle portraits of friends and neighbors shot on the fly: home movies. Last I checked, they're considered something to show bubbie and zayde when they visit, not art.

This dynamic duo and their crazily nonthreatening bohemian pals face a looming crisis in the form of handsome Benjamin (Taye Diggs), a former comrade who sold out and plans to evict his former pals from their Louvre-sized loft so he can build a "a state-of-the-art digital virtual interactive studio." The battle lines are drawn.

Benjamin offers the boys a Faustian bargain: He'll let them stay in their apartment if they can get a sassy performance artist played by Idina Menzel to cancel a protest where she wears tight pants, calls Benjamin a lapdog, and whines, "It's like I'm being tied to the hood of a yellow rental truck being packed in with fertilizer and fuel oil pushed over a cliff by a suicidal Mickey Mouse." Obviously, no wealthy real-estate dynasty can compete with the society-changing power of an underground performance artist's impish pop-culture allegory. So pigs bust the protest before she can disseminate more of her dangerous ideas.

Much singing and dancing ensue en route to the climactic death of a kindly, angelic character named Angel, who continues to hover benevolently over his friends like some sort of . . . what's the word I'm looking for here? You know, they made a TV show where these creatures touched people, and a movie where they were in the outfield, and a play where they were in America. I'm sure I'll think of it at some point after this book is published.

Mimi threatens to die until she's literally brought back to life through the power of Roger's terrible song. Ah, but what about the music, you say? Doesn't that redeem the whole sorry endeavor? No. No, it does not.

Larson's lyrics, maudlin powerless ballads, and MOR melodies are less Stephen Sondheim than outtakes from *The Apple*. It seems perverse to make a musical about Gen Xers, the most cynical and sarcastic generation known to man, that's wholly devoid of cynicism and sarcasm. *Rent* consequently feels like a Disneyland stage show about those nutty Gen Xers, with their bicuriosity and crazy drug addictions and shameless love of hoofing and crooning. In *Rent*, there's no problem that can't be overcome with singing, dancing, and/or moxie. The film doesn't just feel like a fairy-tale version of New York bohemia created for blue-haired tourists and clueless out-of-towners; it feels like it was created by them as well.

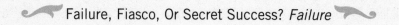 Failure, Fiasco, Or Secret Success? *Failure*

Let's Go Crazy Case File #102: *Under The Cherry Moon*
Originally Posted January 15, 2008

By 1985, an androgynous, three-foot-tall black man from Minnesota had reached the pinnacle of pop superstardom. Prince was a critic's darling and a popular favorite. He'd conquered the world of film a year earlier with *Purple Rain* and walked away with an Academy Award and a smash-hit, instant-classic soundtrack.

Yes, everything was coming up Milhouse for Prince. All those years of hard work were paying off. In times like these, Prince is habitually visited by an angry, persistent voice from somewhere deep within his purple-and-paisley soul. This agitated voice regularly issues a cry for professional suicide: "Things . . . going . . . too . . . well . . . fans . . . too . . . happy . . . career . . . proceeding . . . too . . . smoothly . . . must . . . sabotage . . . self . . . with . . . crazy . . . off-putting . . . stunt."

As usual, this insane inner voice urging self-destruction made valid points. But how could Prince best go about sabotaging his thriving career? Should he change his already ridiculous prance-about stage name to something so ludicrous it couldn't even be pronounced? Maybe something so bizarre it was subverbal, something that would make him a constant target in talk-show monologues and stand-up routines? Or should he scrawl "Slave" on his face and launch a long, public, widely mocked campaign to get out of his major-label contract by comparing it to unpaid servitude? How about an album of jazz-fusion instrumentals? What if he formed his own independent label and flooded the market with three-disc monstrosities and increasingly irrelevant solo albums? What if he passive-aggressively fulfilled Warner Bros.' desperate cry for a *Purple Rain* sequel with a flaky spiritual romance about an angel named Aura? Or he could very publicly become a Jehovah's Witness, that most respected and least ridiculed of all religious sects.

Oh, but there were *so* many different ways for Prince to fuck up his career! Over the course of his long, glorious, exquisitely checkered life, Prince would have an opportunity to try out all the aforementioned career wreckers. But in 1985, he happened upon an altogether more ingenious self-sabotage scheme. If those Hollywood phonies wanted another Prince movie so damned badly, he'd give them the craziest, least-commercial Prince movie imaginable, a black-and-white period romance heavy on dialogue and perversely light on musical performances. Maybe he wouldn't even sing at all! That'd show them.

I can imagine Prince's pitch. He'd look a studio suit firmly in the eye and say, "Look, I know this whole black-and-white thing sounds risky, but if it's any consolation, I'll be performing at most two or three songs. It'll be less about the music and more about dialogue and comedy. Oh, and the soundtrack will be vastly different from anything I've ever done, and my character will be an asshole. But that won't matter, because the woman I'm romancing—who'll be played by a white, British unknown, incidentally—will be a raging bitch. Also, I die at the end. And I plan to direct it myself after the original director is fired over 'creative differences.' And I'll film it almost entirely in France. In case you're worried that a hit soundtrack might accidentally fuel interest in the film, you should know I plan to give the soundtrack a different name from the movie. I'll call it *Parade*, and the film *Under The Cherry Moon*. Now may I please have $12 million for this can't-miss proposition?"

I suspect that after the ashen-faced executive picked his jaw up off the ground, he assumed that Prince was playing an elaborate practical joke and actually planned to make another *Purple Rain*–style conventional musical melodrama. You know, for the kids. Warner Bros.' doom was sealed.

Released in the summer of 1986, *Under The Cherry Moon* opens with glittery narration promising an escapist fairy tale about a bad boy redeemed by the love of a good woman. From the get-go, the film promises more than it can deliver. But for its first scene, at least, the prospect of a screwball Prince romance seems not only palatable but delectable.

As the film opens, freewheeling gigolo Christopher Tracy (Prince) is tickling the ivories while making goo-goo eyes at a potential meal ticket. He doesn't just make love to her with his eyes; he makes love to her, marries her, grows bored and disenchanted, cheats on her, proposes a trial separation, becomes lonely, and reluctantly reconciles with her exclusively via glances, winks, and lascivious stares. In this first scene,

Prince comes off like an impossibly glamorous silent screen star, a caramel-colored Valentino with big, wonderfully expressive eyes, oozing sex and glamour. It's a full-on seduction from a legendary lothario, pitched as much to the audience as his ostensible conquest. Michael Ballhaus' black-and-white photography is silky, decadent, and lush, an impossible dream of retro glamour.

Here, Prince's vision of a screwball comedy directed by Fellini comes gorgeously to life. Prince gives us not just a setting but an entire seductive fantasy world created by consummate old pros: regular Scorsese cinematographer Ballhaus and production designer Richard Sylbert, a two-time Oscar winner with credits such as *Chinatown*, *Dick Tracy*, and *The Graduate* to his name.

Then people start talking, and everything goes to shit. Christopher is a pianist whose affections can be rented by the hour but who pines for true love. He lives with effeminate sidekick/professional manservant Tricky (Jerome Benton), his half brother and endlessly game partner in crime, mischief, and androgyny. Perhaps the only heterosexual alive who can pull off wearing a puffy pirate shirt, Christopher keeps his customers satisfied with lascivious compliments like, "To not hear your voice each day is to die seven times by God's wrath / if I was anything other than human, I'd be the water in your bath." But when he happens upon society girl Mary Sharon (Kristin Scott Thomas, in her first role) on her 21st birthday, he's instantly smitten.

Thomas' character is written as an elitist snob who treats Christopher with aristocratic disdain and lets her sinister father control her. Yet she's introduced brazenly flashing high society, causing a wealthy dowager to faint in horror. After gleefully crowing, "How do you like my birthday suit? I designed it myself," Thomas settles down behind a drum set and leads the crowd in a funk-rock chant of "Let it rock. You just can't stop." Have I mentioned yet that the film takes place either in the '30s, the '40s, or some strange alternate universe that looks uncannily like the distant pre-rock past yet includes boomboxes, computers, cable, answering machines, and references to Liberace and Sam Cooke?

Initially repulsed by Christopher's leering advances, Mary repeatedly derides him as a "peasant." "It may seem strange to a hustler like you, but I go out with people my own age, special people. And they don't wear wedding rings, either," Thomas hisses self-righteously at Prince. He retorts, "Then they must be wearing diapers!" This, alas, is the film's conception of sophisticated screwball banter. There are elementary-school playgrounds with higher levels of intellectual discourse.

Withering insults like, "Maybe if you took off your chastity belt, you could breathe a little more better!" vex Mary to the point that she practices a series of equally devastating snaps to hurl Christopher's way the next she sees him, settling on, "You know, I could breathe a lot easier if the air weren't so polluted by your presence."

After treating this obnoxious playboy with withering contempt, Mary inexplicably falls in love with him and showers her exotic new lover and Tricky with gifts and money. But trouble lurks around the corner in the form of Mary's disapproving father. Will Mary end up with the mystery man who incites her wildest fantasies, or settle down with her stable, predictable, (unseen) boyfriend, Stuffy Q. Borington III? More important, will Christopher ever stop behaving like a petulant middle schooler and sing some fucking songs? Or will the audience simply be forced to choke down dialogue like the following:

Tsk, tsk, what a pity. Sometimes life can be so shitty. Here's a girl who's smart and pretty.

It must be easy to swim with a head as swelled as yours.

Mirror, mirror sevenfold, who's the finest dressed in gold?

If vintage screwball banter suggests a furious volley between two world-class tennis players, *Cherry Moon*'s version feels more like a lazy game of badminton between morbidly obese amateurs. In classic screwball comedies, the leads' rapid-fire surface bickering masks lust, attraction, and ultimately something nobler. Here, however, the leads' contempt for each other feels both deeply warranted and authentic; it's their growing attraction that rings false.

Prince and overqualified collaborators Ballhaus and Sylbert create a sinful, seductive world, then populate it with grating stick figures. Screwball comedies are all about pacing, speed, momentum, chemistry, wit, and the heedless, exhilarating forward rush of witty banter breathlessly executed. A woefully misbegotten would-be concoction, *Cherry Moon* is more like cotton candy with the weight and consistency of a brick.

Shortly after being shot by one of Mary's husband's goons, a deathbound Christopher (don't worry, in a too-little, too-late bid to give the audience what they want, Prince gets to sing in heaven alongside the Revolution, over the end credits) asks his true love, "We had fun, didn't we?" To tardily answer his question, no, we most assuredly did not.

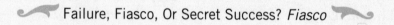 Failure, Fiasco, Or Secret Success? *Fiasco*

All-Singing, All-Dancing Book-Exclusive Case File: The Musical Version Of *I'll Do Anything*

> *I believe in screen tests. I believe in cutting people out if the dailies are bad. I believe in replacing people if the previews aren't there. Because I don't make movies for theaters that serve cappuccino in the lobby. I make popcorn movies. You want to know what I like? Come to my house, look at my lamps. That's what I like. But you're not going to find it in my movies.*
> —*Burke Adler (Albert Brooks) in* I'll Do Anything

I'll Do Anything puts the words that begin this Case File into Albert Brooks' mouth to establish his Joel Silver–like superproducer as the gauche embodiment of everything that's crass and mercenary about show business. As delivered with lip-smacking zeal at a machine-gun clip by Brooks' excitable schlock merchant, the monologue becomes a proud vulgarian's warped code of honor, a cultural barbarian's moolah-mad manifesto.

So it's ironic that James L. Brooks ended up living the mercenary creed of a character he created to epitomize everything that's monstrous (and secretly wonderful) about Hollywood.

Brooks filmed *I'll Do Anything* as a 140-minute musical with songs by Prince and choreography by Twyla Tharp. When the dailies were bad and the previews weren't encouraging, he castrated his musical by gutting the songs. Every last one of them. Yes, even the one where Rosie O'Donnell and Woody Harrelson rap. Brooks likes Tharp's choreography and Prince's light funk, but audiences wouldn't know it from watching the theatrical version of *I'll Do Anything*. They didn't even learn what kind of lamps its writer-director likes.

The musical *I'll Do Anything* has never been seen by the general public, but I was lucky enough to have a My Year Of Flops operative send me a bootleg DVD of the aborted version for use in this book. I watched the film as test audiences saw it, as a rough assemblage of scenes instead of a polished, finished movie.

In a desperate attempt to save his baby from being shown only in theaters serving cappuccino, James L. Brooks ended up killing it. A strange, overreaching musical was radically re-edited to become an intimate comedy-drama about the tricky intersection of art and commerce. A film that once sang its ambitions from the mountaintops became a meek, tuneless, albeit intriguingly personal and bravely sincere mediocrity.

It was to no avail. The Film Formerly Known As A Prince Musical flopped anyway. Audiences were understandably skeptical of an ex-musical with production numbers so terrible they were all excised before hitting theaters. *Anything* hobbled into theaters enshrouded in a thick cloud of failure and desperation. Brooks fatally lacked the courage of his convictions. He let disastrous test screenings destroy his labor of love.

The first of many, many ironies is that both cuts of *I'll Do Anything* are obsessed with test screenings, focus groups, and Hollywood's pathological need for approval. In the musical version, this theme is established in its very first scene, a brassy production number where a contingent of shaggy young singer-dancer-actor types share an orgasmic sense of post-show exhilaration following the première of a new play with Nick Nolte's Matt Hobbs as Jesus. Then a snake arrives in their show-biz Eden in the form of a tweedy critic panning the show on television.

Their dreams of living, in the immortal words of the opening song, "L to the A-R-G-E large!" are suddenly shattered, as nothing can compete with the godlike power of a geek with a pad and pen doling out a negative review on television.

A young, disconcertingly hunky Nolte (he didn't yet embody terms like "grizzled," "hard-living," "zombie-like," or "dead-looking"), wearing what appears to be a Tarzan wig, tries to cheer up a fellow actor by unconvincingly arguing, "Listen, no matter what this review says, the play was a great experience for me. I mean, it is about process, right?"

At the opening-night party, Hobbs hooks up with Beth, a hideous shrew played with the world's worst Southern accent by Tracey Ullman. Beth flatters Hobbs' creative ego by gushing, "Your feelings about your work are one of the things I love most about you."

We then cut to a shrieking baby and Beth screeching at her overwhelmed husband, "Don't pretend to be asleep just because you got the baby the last four times. What's the matter, is the artist tired?" At least she didn't speak ill of process. Never denigrate the process. This is one marriage that cannot and should not be saved, a doomed union with the words "Do Not Resuscitate" tattooed on its forehead. We then skip ahead six years. Beth and her daughter are long gone, and Hobbs' career is floundering.

That all changes when Hobbs blows an audition but picks up an unlikely pal/temporary employer in superproducer Burke and a love interest in Cathy Breslow (Joely Richardson), Hollywood's last idealist and one of Adler's employees. After the unsuccessful audition, Hobbs spies Adler lurching down the sidewalk and sobbing softly to himself while filled with the soul-shaking despair most folks reserve for the death of a child. It takes only his driver being 20 minutes late to reduce Adler's Master of the Universe to a state of childlike helplessness. "Look at me. You'd think I was a writer," he moans to Hobbs before hiring him as a chauffeur.

Brooks plays a man so at ease with his own superficiality that I almost didn't want him to evolve. His Silver surrogate loves the Hollywood machine. He's the kind of wheeler-dealer who lights up like a Christmas tree when Julie Kavner's character offers to show him where the tracking is done for upcoming movies. For Brooks' big shot, that is the real heart of Hollywood, a wonderland of pure commerce. Brooks invites sympathy for this showbiz devil; the emotional transparency and simplicity of his character is beguiling.

Brooks is so good that he throws off the balance of the film, as *I'll Do Anything* isn't really about Adler. It's about what happens when Hobbs' ex-wife reenters his life just long enough to inform him that she's going to jail for a long time and that their six-year-old daughter Jeanne (Whittni Wright) will now be his sole responsibility.

Jeanne is very much Beth's child. But *I'll Do Anything* posits Jeanne as such a blindingly cute moppet that she snaps up a major role in a sitcom pilot without even consciously pursuing an acting career. She simply accompanies her dad to an audition where the gods of television decide it would be a crime for her not to be grinning her way into America's collective heart every week as an adorably racist girl who learns life lessons at a multiracial orphanage.

I'll Do Anything's neurotic show-business types stop talking about their feelings just long enough to warble about their emotions in maudlin ballads and dance their feelings in splashy production numbers shot in long, involved takes that the director desperately hopes will hide his film's lack of visual style.

Good musicals make the inherently artificial act of people breaking spontaneously into song and dance seem natural. But there's a fatal disconnect between *I'll Do Anything*'s talky, touchy-feely chatfests and its strangely impersonal musical numbers. They seem to inhabit different universes. Even subpar Prince songs that sashay into the middle of the road with big plastic grins and jazz fingers a-flying can't give the film soul. The musical *I'll Do Anything* is the single whitest film ever made, with the possible exception of *Nights In Rodanthe* (which, ironically, was directed by a black man).

A musical that sends audiences home without a song in their hearts is in serious trouble. A musical that sends audiences home with only vague memories of being inundated with a mélange of interchangeable mid-period Prince quasi-funk is fucked. True, *I'll Do Anything* offers the odd spectacle of Nolte croaking a duet with Wright in a barroom rasp, but "Nolte Sings!" was an offer test audiences found easy to refuse. *I'll Do Anything* ended up being a victim of the very test-screening process it limply critiques. But the process—well, that had to be heartbreaking as well.

 Failure, Fiasco, Or Secret Success? *Fiasco*

It Ain't Over 'Til The Old Lady Sings Book-Exclusive Case File: *Mame*

Keenen Ivory Wayans is not known as a Confucius-like purveyor of profundities. But when *The A.V. Club* interviewed Anna Faris, she quoted him as saying something borderline wise: "There's no vanity in comedy."

Lucille Ball embodied that maxim on *I Love Lucy*. Ball began her career as a glamorous starlet, but in *I Love Lucy,* she was often a screeching, braying, flailing, desperate, lying, off-key mess. She was gloriously unencumbered by vanity. In her signature role, Ball played a big ball of misplaced ambition; she embraced looking awful and acting a fool. America loved her for it.

By the time 1974's *Mame* rolled around, Ball's philosophy had changed to, "Comedy is all vanity." Her involvement in the project began with the kind of pride that goeth before the fall. Ball became convinced that Rosalind Russell's portrayal of the title character on Broadway and in 1958's *Auntie Mame* owed a debt to her portrayal of Lucy Ricardo, and she was intent on collecting.

So Ball lobbied hard for the lead role in *Mame,* the film version of Jerry Herman's hit Broadway musical adaptation of *Auntie Mame.* Snagging that plum role proved her professional undoing. Why was Ball so surreally miscast? For starters, just about everyone other than Ball felt the role should have gone to Angela Lansbury, a musical-comedy vet who picked up a Tony Award for the part in 1966. Herman begged Warner Bros. to let the sexy, vivacious Lansbury reprise her role for the big screen. He failed.

Lansbury was a frisky 41 when she picked up the Tony for *Mame.* When Ball bulldozed her way into the lead, she was 61 and recovering from a broken leg. Casting Ball in the lead role dramatically altered the show's dynamic. With Lansbury on Broadway, *Mame* was about a dynamic middle-aged bohemian whose life changes course when she becomes the guardian of a towheaded moppet. With Ball in the lead, it became the story of a sexagenarian enjoying a few laughs before the sweet embrace of the grave. The proto-beatniks and freethinkers in 1958's *Auntie Mame* embrace Rosalind Russell's title character because she's the sexy, swinging life of the party. The eccentrics of *Mame* gravitate toward Ball because they miss their grandmas and suspect she's got a big silver bowl of butterscotch candies squirreled away somewhere.

Beyond the fact that she was at least 15 years too old for the role, there was the minor concern that Ball couldn't sing or dance. At all. In *I Love Lucy,* Ball's ghastly singing was a running joke; in *Mame,* it was a cause for alarm. She wasn't much better at hoofing, either. It's never an encouraging sign when a choreographer's main concern is his leading lady throwing out a hip.

Mame was supposed to open in late 1973, in time for Oscar consid-

eration, until executives took a look at the film and realized that even
in a world where 1967's *Dr. Dolittle* got nominated for nine Academy
Awards, *Mame*'s Oscar chances fell somewhere between nonexistent
and "are you fucking kidding me?"

The hyperbolic trailers for *Mame* try to transform the film's screaming faults into secret virtues, crowing that it's a "multimillion-dollar
production that took two years to capture on film," as if going over-
budget and overschedule were suddenly points of pride. The trailers
also alternately hail Ball as "the most unique and talented actress of
our time" and "the most versatile actress of all time," in a bone-dry
monotone. Then again, Ball is beloved for her portrayals of everything
from a kooky housewife to a slightly older kooky housewife.

Mame opens with Patrick (Kirby Furlong) being dispatched to live
with his eccentric Auntie Mame after his parents die. The kid arrives
at Mame's palace of decadence in the midst of a wild party. The soiree finds Mame sporting a hair helmet with sideburns and wearing a
lipstick-red pantsuit that looks like it was stitched together from one
of Santa Claus' discarded uniforms. Nevertheless, she's in her element,
presiding as a mother hen over a crazy coterie of artists and oddballs.

There's no point aiming for subtlety when you're playing a character this flamboyant, but it's hard to watch Ball vamp, quip, and pose,
pose, pose while outfitted in a sea of head wraps, sequins, and gowns,
and not see an aging transvestite. *Mame* caused Pauline Kael to wonder of Ball, "After 40 years in movies and TV, did she discover in
herself an unfulfilled ambition to be a flaming drag queen?"

The stock-market crash of 1929 wipes out Mame's fortune, but her
money troubles end when she's wooed by the colorfully named Beauregard Jackson Pickett Burnside, a wealthy, kind Southern granny
chaser with a crumb-catcher mustache and Foghorn Leghorn drawl.
Beauregard (played by Robert Preston) takes Mame and Patrick home
to meet his mama. He tells his mother, who resembles William H.
Taft in a dress, that she'll love Mame the second they meet, perhaps
because they're the same age.

After Mame finds happiness and security as the pampered wife of an American aristocrat, all that's left is for Patrick to grow up to be stuffy old Bruce Davison over the course of a single song. Having grown up the pet of a fearless feminist iconoclast, Patrick rebels by becoming a reactionary bore and getting engaged to an insufferable debutante (Doria Cook-Nelson). In *Auntie Mame*—which I watched solely as preparation for this Case File, and not, as I worried at the time, as a way of purging the last remaining vestiges of my heterosexuality—the sequences with the adult Patrick feel stiff and theatrical. Yet the film built up such goodwill that I didn't particularly mind.

But in the Lucille Ball *Mame,* there's a cognitive dissonance to the third act. How did a happy little boy who flourished in the incandescent warmth of his aunt's love grow up to be a small-minded jerk? Why are we supposed to care about a drip who wears the polka-dot tie, red carnation, and blue-and-yellow checkered suit of a sad clown?

Patrick's deplorable adult personality can be read as a reaction to his aunt's wildness. After a childhood spent playing second fiddle to a cyclone of progressive ideas, Patrick gravitates to the security and safety of living and loving among bigots. If life is a banquet, as Mame's motto contends, then Patrick has chosen to spend it consuming weak tea and watercress sandwiches. Mame's joie de vivre has infected and inspired everyone around her but the little man who matters most.

But mainly, these scenes exist so kooky old Auntie Mame can stick it to Patrick's snobby would-be in-laws (Don Porter and Audrey Christie) with badly dated sass. When Mame meets the in-laws-to-be, they propose buying their children the property next door so they can simultaneously keep their loved ones close and undesirables away. This causes Mame to dip into a nearby phone booth and transform into her alter ego, Superbohemian. Putting her theatrical flair to good use, she invites the snobs to her extravagant home, where she dramatically announces that she's purchased the estate next to theirs so she can start a home for single women.

The bluebloods are so shocked that their metaphorical monocles shatter in horror, and Patrick sees the error of his ways. The Davison-as-jerk scenes underline just how little we know about the supporting cast. They exist to give Mame people to play off and advance the plot. It's Auntie Mame's world; they just live in it.

The Jews-and-single-women-are-people-too message was somewhat anachronistic in 1958. By 1974, it was prehistoric. So much happened between '58 and '74: the JFK, RFK, and MLK assassinations, a sexual revolution, the French New Wave, Nehru suits, miniskirts, the fleeting popularity of the 1910 Fruitgum Company, tie-dye. *Mame* didn't change with the times; it was done in by them. It was part of a wave of slow-moving, pea-brained, exclamation-point-crazed musical dinosaurs (including *Dr. Dolittle, Star!, Hello, Dolly!, Paint Your Wagon*) that acted as if the '60s had never happened. These musicals appealed to a nostalgic yearning for a simpler age, but even squares found *Mame* easy to resist.

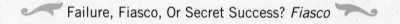 Failure, Fiasco, Or Secret Success? *Fiasco*

Chapter 4

It's A Bird! It's A Plane! It's A Flop!
Superheroes, Science Fiction, And Action

Lady And Gentleman, You Are Now Floating In The Floposphere Case File #46: *It's All About Love*
Originally Posted July 3, 2007

Watching Thomas Vinterberg's Dogme 95 breakout hit *The Celebration,* I experienced an intoxicating rush of discovery. I was excited about the film, but I was even more excited about Vinterberg films to come. If he could accomplish so much while adhering to the rigorous set of aesthetic strictures he helped create as one of the architects of the Dogme movement (a militantly naturalistic cinematic wave that made acolytes take a "vow of purity" and went from "bold new way of reinventing the language of cinema" to "bullshit PR stunt" in roughly 15 minutes), I could only imagine what he'd be capable of without the restrictions Dogme 95 imposed upon its filmmakers.

After *The Celebration,* Vinterberg was inundated with scripts and offers from money people eager to get into the Thomas Vinterberg business, but nothing struck his fancy. The real trick is to nab geniuses *before* they make their masterpiece, not after. Get in bed with Michael

Cimino after *Deer Hunter,* and you wake up the next morning with *Heaven's Gate,* a pounding headache, an empty wallet, and your office cleared out when you show up for work.

Vinterberg wilted under the pressure. He spent years working on a bizarre screenplay that seemed ripped painfully from the innermost recesses of his soul. It's a futuristic science-fiction love story that doubles as a moody meditation on love, loss, and a world spinning out of control.

Vinterberg's follow-up to *The Celebration,* 2003's *It's All About Love,* takes place in a near future troubled by grimly whimsical "cosmic disturbances." The world is freezing. It snows in July. Tap water turns to ice in seconds during cryptic freeze-storms. Ugandans begin magically levitating. People start dying en masse from lack of love, littering the streets with corpses whose hearts simply cease beating as much from a dearth of affection as lack of oxygen. Evil scientists repeatedly clone heroin-addled superstar figure skater Elena (Claire Danes, who's saddled with a shaky Polish accent that makes her sound vaguely vampiric).

It must have looked like an unholy mess on the page, but the producers probably figured that the man behind *The Celebration* could transform his script's fuzzy mélange of intriguing but half-baked ideas, lifeless characters, and cryptic social commentary into a satisfying, halfway-cohesive whole. They were wrong.

Vinterberg's *Celebration* cachet attracted a remarkable cast. Joaquin Phoenix and his soulful eyes of infinite sadness signed on to play John, a brooding, lovesick intellectual with a Ph.D. in Polish literature, which only sounds like the setup to a bad joke. Danes plays his estranged wife, a gloomy mega-celebrity with a bad heart, insomnia, and a history of drug abuse. Sean Penn plays Phoenix's brother Marciello, a sensitive soul given to loopy, pseudo-poetic, pseudo-philosophical monologues about the nature of the world and the importance of human connection. Marciello used to be afraid of flying; then he took medication that worked so well that now he can't do anything but fly. In another movie, that might qualify as a goofy throwaway joke, but Marciello literally spends his every scene expounding about the world from airplanes.

After an extended break, John returns to New York to sign divorce papers for Elena, only to be swept up in a web of intrigue and deception. Elena's family has commissioned at least three clones of her so that when Elena decides to leave the lucrative world of figure skating, they can replace her. But first, they must destroy Elena before she can screw up their plans. John helps Elena escape east, to an arctic hellhole where popular leisure-time activities include freezing and dying.

Vinterberg got it backward. When working with a tiny budget and Dogme guidelines, he crafted a movie as entertaining and funny as any Hollywood crowd-pleaser. Then, while working with big American stars, a budget of $10 million, and no restrictions, he made a film as weird and noncommercial as any gritty Dogme provocation.

As befits a film that closes with a monologue delivered by a man doomed to live out the rest of his life on an airplane—expounding about how, when it comes right down to it, it really is all about love—*Love* has a jet-lagged rootlessness and pervasive sense of dislocation. For all its faults, it captures that fragile post-9/11 mind-set of naked vulnerability and yawning doubt, before our souls again grew calloused and we developed an insatiable curiosity about the private life of Paris Hilton and the sweet 16 parties of the superrich. It poignantly evokes that strange historical epoch when it seemed somehow like the world would just stop, that the universe would punish us for the mess we'd made.

Though Vinterberg likely wrote the film before 9/11, it nevertheless conveys how the event single-handedly rewired our sense of the possible and the impossible, and upended our sense of reality. In a world where planes fly into buildings and zealots armed with box cutters can strike widespread terror in the heart of the richest, most powerful country in the world, why shouldn't Ugandans begin floating mysteriously? *Love* is filled with images that are simultaneously ridiculous, beautiful, and audacious, like a skating ballet with four Elenas gliding in unison that devolves into an ice-rink massacre as one Elena double after another loses her so-called life.

Like Wong Kar-Wai's strangely simpatico *2046*, *Love* finds a maverick abandoning logic in a quixotic quest for beauty and truth. With its doppelgängers, surrealism, abstract characters, and gorgeous, painterly long shots, *Love* feels like a waking dream, especially in a superior second half that delivers the science-fiction goods while plunging farther and farther into its own insanity.

So is *Love* ultimately a Fiasco or a Secret Success? It'd be a real stretch to call it a success, but it's exactly the kind of movie I wanted to highlight in My Year Of Flops, a film so stubbornly singular that it belongs to a sub-genre all its own—a mad, mad mix of science fiction, allegory, left-field social commentary, and romantic melodrama. If I weren't so damnably attached to my rating system, I'd give it a final score more in line with its free-floating craziness, like say, Three Floating Ugandans, Two and a Half Elena Clones, and Seven Loopy Marciello Monologues. Can I call it a Semisecret Fiascopiece? Heck, if Vinterberg can make a movie this defiantly weird, then I think I'm entitled.

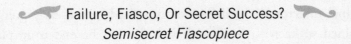

Failure, Fiasco, Or Secret Success?
Semisecret Fiascopiece

Mad Mutated Case File #64: *The Island Of Dr. Moreau*
Originally Posted September 4, 2007

In previous Case Files, I have proposed what I call the Great Gazoo Theory: that sometime in the mid-'70s, Marlon Brando began taking marching orders from the Great Gazoo, the tiny, effeminate green alien only Fred Flintstone could see. For example, Brando's behavior on the set of *The Score* is wholly understandable if you imagine the Great Gazoo hovering over his ear and whispering, "Hey, dum-dum, if you really want to show that Frank Oz fool what's what, call him Miss Piggy and refuse to talk to him."

The Great Gazoo Theory explains the totality of Brando's career from *Missouri Breaks* on. I expected it to sweep film scholarship. In my hubris, I predicted that it would be at least as influential as the auteur theory, if not more so, since it prominently involved a minor supporting character from the *Flintstones* universe.

The Great Gazoo worked overtime on the set of 1996's *The Island Of Dr. Moreau*. No sane human being could have made Marlon Brando take a role that required him to cover his face in white pancake makeup because he has "allergies to the sun" (a line that, due to Brando's slurred diction, sounds uncannily like, "I have an alligator for a son," which actually makes sense within the context of the film), use an ice bucket for a hat, speak in the effete diction of a *Masterpiece Theatre* host, travel everywhere with a tiny sidekick who looks like a fetus that just barely survived an abortion, and spend his last few moments alive tickling the ivories while trying to explain the differences between Schoenberg and Gershwin to terrifying sub-human beasties.

A certain derangement was hard-wired into the film's DNA. Original director Richard Stanley was fired in the early going yet remained so keen to work with Brando that he ended up playing one of the film's mutated man-animal hybrids. In *Moreau*, Brando symbolically passes down the straitjacket of supreme craziness to Val Kilmer, whose alternately droll and deranged performance suggests how Jim Morrison might have turned out if he'd turned to mad science instead of music.

David Thewlis sweatily inhabits the thankless lead role of Edward Douglas, an incredulous everyman rescued by the eccentric Montgomery (Kilmer) while adrift at sea, then taken to a mysterious island where Nobel Prize winner Dr. Moreau (who presumably cleaned up in the Crimes Against Nature category) is attempting to build a utopia and perfect nature by transforming animals into hideous half-human mutants and drugging and shocking them into submission. How could anything go wrong?

Dr. Moreau and Montgomery preserve an artificial calm, keeping the creatures in line with electric shocks when they misbehave and doping them with morphine, methamphetamines, "shrooms and some other shit" to "mellow them out" and "keep them coming back for more." Dr. Moreau, resplendent in flowing robes, behaves like a foppish doting dad, delivering bite-sized nuggets of civilization to his alternately worshipful and resentful minions in the form of Bible verses and piano recitals where he performs alongside his very own mini-me.

Brando doesn't enter the film until half an hour in and (spoiler alert!) he bites it a little over half an hour later. At that point, the steadily escalating insanity of Kilmer's performance reaches an apex: He dons white pancake makeup and white robes to launch into an unspeakably cruel Brando caricature that competes with—and at times even upstages—Brando's equally cruel caricature of himself. Kilmer doesn't play the role so much as lampoon it. There are subversive air quotes around every line. Kilmer does his damnedest to outcrazy Brando, and he succeeds with surprising frequency.

Though it's a tonal and thematic mess, *Dr. Moreau* is rife with indelible moments. Most of them belong to Kilmer, from the scene where he tenderly strokes a rabbit, holds it up to Thewlis so he can kiss it, then casually, briskly breaks its neck, to a death scene that hurls itself into the annals of camp history: swathed in white fabric, with white goo on his face, a drug-addled Montgomery impersonates a lisping, effete Dr. Moreau and reads aloud from Arthur Conan Doyle before he's killed by a trigger-happy mutant dog-boy. It is, perhaps, not the most dignified death.

The film coalesces into a blunt allegory about how the failures of society arise out of the flawed essence of human nature. Human nature, with its insatiable lust for power and propensity for violence, proves the semi-human islanders' undoing as much as their animal instincts. As Montgomery might argue, aren't we the real animals?

But by the time the manimals start firing automatic weapons at each other, any pretensions to social commentary have been lost in a

sea of empty spectacle. An indifferently filmed shoot-out is an indifferently filmed shoot-out, whether the gun lovers involved are Steven Seagal or puny man-animals.

Just before slurring one of the all-time great terrible last lines ("I want to go to dog heaven"), Kilmer utters, with sublime understatement, a line that could double as the film's epitaph: "Well, things didn't work out."

 Failure, Fiasco, Or Secret Success? *Fiasco*

Spaced-Out Oddity Case File #91: *Southland Tales*
Originally Posted December 6, 2007

I began eying 2006's *Southland Tales* greedily the moment I learned of its existence. Writer-director Richard Kelly saw his fortunes rise with those of *Donnie Darko,* his 2001 cult debut. While still in his 20s, Kelly was hailed as the David Lynch of his generation. Disastrously, Kelly seems to have believed the hype. The five-year gap between *Donnie Darko* and its follow-up only raised expectations for *Southland Tales.* Would the film represent a grand evolutionary leap forward, or a huge step back? Would it be his career-making *Boogie Nights,* or a sophomore slump?

With *Southland Tales,* Kelly offers not just a movie but a mind-melting multimedia experience, a vast, sprawling, absurdist universe, complete with three graphic-novel prequels. The film probably makes more sense to people who've read those, though I imagine that complete comprehension is impossible, even to Kelly himself. If a man as learned as cast member Wallace Shawn couldn't understand it after three viewings, what chance do any of us have?

So if *Southland Tales* feels like a third sequel to something that didn't make sense in the first place, that's because it is. In between *Darko* and *Tales,* Kelly worked on screenplays that unfortunately didn't get produced (a nixed adaptation of *Holes*) and screenplays that unfortunately did get produced (*Domino*). On the basis of *Southland Tales*, however, it's safe to assume that Kelly spent much of the intervening years smoking pot, reading *The Progressive*, and steadily going insane. Politics and good intentions have ruined more filmmakers than drugs and money combined. A little knowledge can be a dangerous thing, especially in tandem with too much ambition and too little self-discipline.

Southland Tales opens with a nuclear blast in Texas in an alternate-universe 2005, and an endless orgy of voice-over narration from haunted veteran Private Pilot Abilene (Justin Timberlake). The United States responded to a nuclear attack on July 4, 2005, by taking a fierce rightward turn. World War III brought the pain to Iran, North Korea, and various other supporters of evildoers. Now, a sinister entity called US-IDENT spies on the American populace and polices the world webernet with an iron fist.

A revolutionary group known as the neo-Marxists, populated disproportionately by distaff *Saturday Night Live* alums (Amy Poehler, Nora Dunn, Cheri Oteri), has brainwashed Iraq War veteran Roland Taverner (Seann William Scott) as a way of faking a Rodney King–like videotape exposing police brutality, in hopes of instigating a revolt against the repressive new social order. Meanwhile, Boxer Santoros, an amnesiac action star with ties to the Republican party (Dwayne "the Rock" Johnson, a real-life action star with ties to the Republican party), has written "a screenplay that foretold the tale of our destruction," but it's being ignored (no doubt due to third-act problems and a perfunctory diamond-smuggling subplot). Sarah Michelle Gellar plays Johnson's girlfriend, Krysta Kapowski, a porn star, current-events-chat-show host, and one-woman media empire whose most recent release is a pop single called "Teen Horniness Is Not A Crime." Got all that? Good.

Also involved: Booger from *Revenge Of The Nerds*, monkeys traveling through a rift in the space-time continuum, that weird old woman from *Poltergeist*, enigmatic spit-curled billionaire Baron Von Westphalen (Wallace Shawn), and Walter Mung (Christopher Lambert), an arms dealer who operates out of an ice-cream truck. Oh, and Bai Ling doing some weird snake-hipped dance aboard a mega-zeppelin. And Kevin Smith with a wizardly beard and (intentionally?) unconvincing old-man makeup that makes him look like the bastard offspring of Gandalf the Grey, Santa Claus, and ZZ Top. And a magical new energy source and a crazy new hallucinogenic drug. Oh, and the whole thing might just be an elaborate religious allegory. Or a dream. Or not.

Southland Tales is many things: a prescient glimpse into a looming apocalypse, a dark science-fiction comedy, pop-culture-damaged surrealism, and a passionate plea for the decriminalization of teen horniness. It's a film of rare courage, a one-of-a-kind trip through the looking glass, and a meditation on uncertain times and the sins of the Bush administration. It's also a gargantuan mess—disjointed, leadenly paced, and filled with ideas introduced and abandoned in the same manic, overheated rush.

It's as if Kelly jotted down every loopy conceit and crackpot idea he could think of, combined them with his dream journal, then decided they were strong enough that he could simply film his dreams and notes without going through the trouble of channeling them into a lucid, complete narrative.

Southland Tales debuted at Cannes in 2006 in a nearly three-hour-long version to less-than-stellar reviews. Kelly trimmed the film to a still-endless 144 minutes, but that couldn't save his weird little *Eraserhead*-looking baby from a quick commercial death.

I found a lot to love about *Southland Tales*. I dug the shaggy, loopy brilliance of throwaway lines like, "Scientists are predicting the future will be much more futuristic than originally predicted." Deep into the film, Kelly indulges in a stand-alone music-video sequence where a scarred, sinister Timberlake, decked out in a bloody shirt, stares menacingly at the camera and lip-synchs to the Killers' "All The Things I've Done" while drinking a can of Budweiser, as dancers in sexy nurse costumes writhe lasciviously in the background. Why?

Why not? Does it make any more or less sense than anything else in the film?

Some of *Southland Tales'* stunt casting pays huge dividends, like Jon Lovitz's bizarre turn as silver-haired, raspy-voiced psycho cop Bart Bookman, and Johnson's agreeably deranged performance. Johnson oozes self-assurance on-screen; that's what makes him such a convincing action hero. But here, he's as scared as a lost little boy. In that respect, his bravely bizarre, unself-conscious performance recalls Mark Wahlberg in *I ♥ Huckabees*. They're both exemplars of macho certainty playing lonely, confused characters who have no idea what they're doing, where they're headed, or how they fit into the big picture. I especially liked the way Johnson tents his hands together and lets his fingers flutter nervously, even girlishly. Johnson could develop into a terrific character actor.

Kelly unleashes such an endless, dizzying torrent of ideas, pop-culture references, and incongruous juxtapositions that some are bound to register. A fuzzy social satire, surrealistic tour de force, half-assed political treatise, and vanity project all rolled into one, *Southland Tales* hits its targets only about 5 to 10 percent of the time, but when it does, it makes a Nagasaki-level impact. I can't say I enjoyed *Southland Tales*, but I can't stop thinking about isolated moments and images. The man atop a floating ice-cream truck filled with heavenly light, shooting a mega-zeppelin with a shoulder-mounted missile, for example, will stay with me long after better, more coherent films have faded from memory.

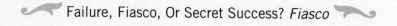

Failure, Fiasco, Or Secret Success? *Fiasco*

Wallace Shawn On *Southland Tales*

The son of legendary longtime *New Yorker* editor William Shawn, Wallace Shawn is an actor, playwright, screenwriter, and author known for the dark, incendiary nature of his plays. He has appeared in *Manhattan*, *My Dinner With Andre* (which he also wrote), *The Prin-*

cess Bride, and *Clueless* in addition to providing the voice of Rex the Dinosaur in the *Toy Story* trilogy.

Wallace Shawn: Well, I don't think anybody really had a literal understanding of the script, and I have to say, I was very influenced by the story of the English actor Ralph Richardson. Ralph Richardson had been offered *Waiting For Godot* by Beckett, and he read it, and he said, "Well, I don't understand a word of this, so I'm not going to be in it." And he later said that was the greatest regret of his life. And he always felt bad about it. He really wished that he'd been in it. Should've just said, "This is great, it's got something."

So I was kind of influenced by that, and I sort of thought—Richard Kelly had pictured me in the role of Baron Von Westphalen, so that was flattering and interesting. I saw his other film, *Donnie Darko,* and I thought, "Well, yeah. This is a very talented guy." He's younger than me, so it was a bit of a risk. I didn't understand it; I didn't understand what he was saying. Also, I have a very deep regard and respect for Karl Marx. I'm a left-wing person, and I've read Karl Marx, and I feel he was a great man. And the movie—I didn't know what to make of the fact that Richard Kelly kept talking about Karl Marx. Was he making fun of him, or did he respect him, or was it just that the name was funny to him?

Nathan Rabin: I think it may have been more of a Warholian kind of thing, where he was approaching him as an icon more than as a philosopher or political figure.

WS: I think you're on to it, sort of. He wasn't commenting on Marx's economic theories, it was something else. It was a bit Warholian. I had a lot of questions about whether I ought to get mixed up in it, but then ultimately meeting him, he's an unusually charming and appealing person. And he's very handsome, not at all the sort of weird, mad, creepy kind of person you would think had written that. I would have pictured that he would have looked, I don't know, more like me! I was surprised at the fact that he was not a bizarre little madman. He was someone who could go to any dinner party and delight old ladies as well as young girls. He was very un-weird in his presentation of himself.

NR: Did you ask him what he was going for, or if there was a sort of Rosetta stone to unlock what *Southland Tales* was all about?

WS: At first, I asked him a few questions, but I quickly could see that the answers were in the language of film. So you would simply add another layer of mystery. There was no way that he was going to translate this into something that you'd put in the *New York Times*. It didn't work that way for him. So I was astounded by the complete clarity and confidence with which each sequence of the film is made. The party on the spaceship, the blimp at the end, which is sort of a gathering of the elite of the United States. Everything is brilliantly done. Every single person that you see is magnificently cast, perfectly costumed. It's a totally confident vision. And when he has the porno actresses, they are all in a perfectly consistent world of their own. And when he goes on to the pier, though they go to a bar, all the people in the bar are still done with incredible confidence. So he knew exactly what he was doing in those ways. The meaning of the whole was definitely difficult to pin down, but that's not necessarily criticism. I did see it three times, and I liked it very much.

NR: Did you figure out more each time you saw it?

WS: Maybe a bit, but maybe if I'd seen it 10 times, I would have figured out more.

NR: Was this the long version, the one that played at Cannes?

WS: No, by the time I saw it, it was the shortened version.

NR: The long version would almost have to clarify things or provide clues or hints that the truncated version didn't.

WS: You'd think that, but I'm not sure. Because, as I say, in talking to him, you really move along into further questions. And then of course there are the graphic novels that are associated with the film, which raised further questions. It doesn't have a simple, clear plot or meaning that you're gonna one day get.

Big Green Brooding Case File #100: *Hulk*
Originally Posted January 8, 2008

2003's *Hulk* is perhaps the highest-grossing film I've written about, having brought in a gaudy $62 million in its opening week. But the film's box office nose-dived once poisonous word of mouth spread. *Hulk* represented a perverse case of bait and switch. The ads, poster, title, and fast-food tie-ins promised dumb fun about a big green monster who goes around smashing things. Instead, director Ang Lee and screenwriter James Schamus delivered an austere, cerebral exploration of the plight of an existential nowhere man. They screwed up a perfectly good smash-'em-up comic-book monster movie with their infernal "art" and "ideas."

Hulk is driven by two seemingly antithetical concepts. Lee set out to make a live-action issue of *The Incredible Hulk* that borrowed heavily from the visual vocabulary of comic books. So he divided the frame into panel-like segments via split screens, and employed cartoonish transitions. Second, he set out to elevate the plight of a humble scientist/giant green brute to the level of a Greek tragedy. To the eternal regret of Universal shareholders, he succeeded. He delivered a comic-book movie for folks whose idea of comic books involves Daniel Clowes, Chris Ware, and maybe Art Spiegelman. Its target audience is *New Yorker* subscribers rather than acne-ridden teenagers.

The film's opening echoes the elliptical storytelling of comic books. It begins in the '60s with the formative trauma of its protagonist's life: being ripped away from his birth family and placed with an adoptive family. The boy, irreparably scarred by his mother's death and his father's unexplained absence, grows up to be scientist Bruce Banner (Eric Bana). The deeply repressed scientist sulks until enraged, at which point he transforms into a green giant with an appetite for destruction. He's a good enough guy, but you wouldn't like him when he's angry.

Bruce soon gets a visit from his long-lost father (Nick Nolte), a maverick mad scientist with a look heavily indebted to late-period Unabomber. Bruce winds up waging a three-sided war against his crazy father, his own temper, and General Thaddeus "Thunderbolt" Ross, a gruff, authoritarian general played by longtime mustache enthusiast Sam Elliott.

In its first hour, *Hulk* boasts a hushed intensity that could easily pass for tedium. It's a bravely quiet film filled with solemn conversations conducted in near whispers. The Hulk doesn't appear in all his muscled-up glory until about 40 minutes in. Audiences who missed the opening credits could be forgiven for thinking they'd accidentally stumbled into an art movie.

Lee seems to go out of his way to avoid indulging in anything that might be considered fun. He appears hell-bent on denying a blockbuster audience the visceral kicks they angrily demand. Lee's Hulk smashes, but mostly he broods and aches. I appreciated the film's intelligent subversion of the comic-book movie. Yet me also like when Hulk smash stuff. Everyone does. That's why not even the film's failure could kill off the franchise.

Hulk can be chilly and inert in the early going, but it gains a strange cumulative power as it develops into both a sad family drama about the sins of the father and an elegant metaphor for the war on terror. The more the government tries to destroy Bruce's Hulkism without understanding it or its underlying causes, the stronger and more resilient it becomes.

Lee succeeded in defunifying one of pop culture's most beloved monsters, transforming a potentially camp spectacle into an experience more intellectual than visceral. And when it comes time for the Hulk to do battle with another monster in the hokey climax, Lee is as lost as a poetry professor at a demolition derby.

Hulk stands as a unique attempt to infect a blockbuster with the gravity and pathos of a small-scale drama. I suspect history will be far kinder to it than the present, especially when it's compared to the spate of comic-book adaptations that aspire to do nothing more than deliver the cheap thrills *Hulk* so assiduously avoids. Still, cheap thrills can be awfully fun, especially when accompanied by indiscriminate smashing.

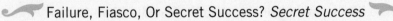 Failure, Fiasco, Or Secret Success? *Secret Success*

All-Time Action-Comedy Classic Book-Exclusive Case File:
Last Action Hero

There's a wonderful passage in Nancy Griffith and Kim Masters' book *Hit And Run*, a juicy account of Peter Guber and Jon Peters' disastrous stint running/ruining Columbia Pictures. At the company Christmas party, Guber delivered a bone-dry, punishingly corporate speech. Morale was low. A great malaise had swept over the studio. Partygoers struggled to stay awake.

Then, suddenly and with great bombast, a Hummer rumbled into the tent and zoomed up to the podium. A door swung open, and out sprang the world's biggest movie star, ready to save the day. Arnold Schwarzenegger pumped up the flagging spirits of industry girly-men with an animated pep talk about the unimaginable riches awaiting Sony and Columbia upon the release of its forthcoming blockbuster/all-time action-comedy classic, 1993's *Last Action Hero*.

If the soiree had been an '80s music video, the part of the wicked party starter who shows the squares how to have fun would have been filled by Van Halen, or possibly Twisted Sister, but Schwarzenegger inhabited the role beautifully. According to Griffith and Masters, having Schwarzenegger rock the Columbia Christmas party was less a nifty perk of getting into business with a giant movie star than the primary reason for green-lighting *Last Action Hero* in the first place. Reading *Hit And Run* and *Studio*, John Gregory Dunne's wonderful impressionistic account of Fox at the turbulent tail end of the '60s, it's easy to get the impression that movies get made largely to give studio executives something to brag about at cocktail parties.

And oh, did *Last Action Hero* give titans of the film industry something to talk about! Before the notorious flop became a source of tremendous shame, it was a source of enormous pride. Until it tanked, it looked like a surefire winner: a family-friendly, high-concept Arnold Schwarzenegger vehicle from the screenwriter of *Lethal Weapon* and the director of *Die Hard*.

The project began life as a spec screenplay by Zak Penn and Adam Leff, a pair of recent Wesleyan graduates with a million-dollar idea: What if a lonely boy raised on Hollywood blockbusters and genre crap could literally escape into the celluloid world of his favorite action hero? Alas, that premise proved to be a million-dollar idea only for the high-profile script doctors who rewrote the screenplay: first the screenwriting team of Shane Black and David Arnott, then the legendary William Goldman, who picked up his million for four weeks spent bulking up the relationship between the boy and the action hero who becomes his buddy, partner, and reluctant father figure.

The film was rushed into production to meet a June 18 release date that put it firmly in the wake of another summer movie that insiders thought might do okay, *Jurassic Park*. *Jurassic Park* and *Last Action Hero* were the battling behemoths of the summer of 1993.

Sony/Columbia went to ridiculous lengths to publicize its $120 million ($90 million for the film, $30 million for publicity) monster of a movie. This was back in the early '90s, when $120 million still qualified as a lot of money. Most spectacularly, Columbia paid half a million dollars to have Schwarzenegger's smirking mug painted onto the side of a space shuttle. The studio paid handsomely to have a glistening metallic enormo-cock penetrate outer space to create consumer awareness of *Last Action Hero*. It was simultaneously a brilliant, Barnumesque publicity stunt yielding millions of dollars' worth of publicity, and a mark of desperation.

As the film was raced to completion, bad buzz began to circulate. At a notorious early test screening, the results were so poor that the scorecards were shredded and Sony pretended the screening never happened. Black was called in for a last-minute rewrite for reshoots mere weeks before the film was scheduled to open, which happened to be a week after one of the biggest, most anticipated films of all time.

Still, Sony and Columbia put on a brave face. Executive Mark Canton called *Last Action Hero* "probably the greatest action movie of all time." Canton also called *Bonfire Of The Vanities* "the best movie I ever saw," which suggests he was either being disingenuous or had seen only several other movies. It is important to bear in mind, dear reader, that these are the men who determine which movies get made and how those movies are distributed and marketed. That explains an awful lot.

Columbia nevertheless held out hope that the primal power of Arnold Schwarzenegger toting around a big gun, tersely delivering wisecracks, and blowing holes through bad guys would overcome bad buzz, disastrous test scores, and Steven Spielberg's infernal dinosaur movie. I like to imagine Mark Canton holding court at a cocktail party and having the following conversation about the film's prospects:

Random partygoer: How were the previews for *Last Action Hero*?

Canton: Our glistening metallic enormo-cock will penetrate outer space to create consumer awareness of *Last Action Hero*.

Random partygoer: Did John McTiernan nail the tone? 'Cause looking at the script, it seems like it'd be tricky to get the balance of comedy and action right.

Canton: Our glistening metallic enormo-cock will penetrate outer space to create consumer awareness of *Last Action Hero*.

Random partygoer: Yes, but does the juxtaposition of violent spectacle and meta-textual, self-referential comedy work?

Canton: Our glistening metallic enormo-cock will penetrate outer space to create consumer awareness of *Last Action Hero*.

Random partygoer: Okay, this is clearly a dead end, talking business. How are the wife and kids?

Canton: Our glistening metallic enormo-cock will penetrate outer space to create consumer awareness of *Last Action Hero*.

You get the picture.

Last Action Hero opens with a scene from Jack Slater's (Schwarzenegger) latest pyrotechnic-filled exercise in ultraviolence, which pitches the conventions of the action movie to ostensibly comic levels. Heartless villain. Perpetually enraged black police captain who runs the emotional gamut from apoplectic to heart-attack-inducingly angry. Wisecracking, indestructible hero.

This points to the film's first big problem: Schwarzenegger movies already verge on self-parody. So a Schwarzenegger spoof seems redundant. The novelty of Schwarzenegger parodying his tough-guy image is undermined by the fact that Schwarzenegger spoofs his tough-guy image in pretty much every movie he makes. There's a self-deprecating edge to Schwarzenegger's performances, a knowing wink that lets the audiences know he's in on the joke.

Last Action Hero later segues from the reel world to the real world, as pint-sized movie lover Danny Madigan (Austin O'Brien) watches *Jack Slater III* in a glorious old movie palace that's about to close. Once upon a time, the theater was a sanctuary for movie lovers, but it's devolved into a doomed skid-row attraction whose only customers are Danny and a homeless man looking for a place to sleep.

Danny's life outside the theater goes from bad to worse when thieves break into the sad little apartment he shares with his mother, Irene (Mercedes Ruehl), but Danny gets the opportunity of a lifetime when kindly projectionist Nick (Robert Prosky) offers to show him a print of *Jack Slater IV* before it opens. Even more exhilaratingly, Nick gives Danny a magical ticket bestowed to him by Harry Houdini. Danny uses the ticket to journey from one side of the screen to the other.

A movie lover getting lost inside his favorite movie is a beautiful, resonant fantasy that previously fueled masterpieces like *Sherlock, Jr.* and *The Purple Rose Of Cairo*. The conceit of being a representative of Schwarzenegger's middle-school target demographic stuck inside a generic Schwarzenegger action movie feels more like cynical commercial calculation. McTiernan never seems comfortable with the film's satirical elements, so he delivers what he imagines audiences want: a straightforward Schwarzenegger vehicle that's maybe 15 percent more knowing, comic, and self-referential than its star's usual blood-splattered fare. In the parlance of *Hit And Run*, it's a "feathered fish" that doesn't quite belong in the action or comedy realm.

The film's best moments come from screenwriters too smart for their own good, scribbling playfully in the margins. In the film's sharpest gag, Danny uses the fact that Jack works alongside cartoon cat Whiskers (voiced by Danny DeVito) as proof that they're in a movie. Jack replies that of course his precinct employs a cartoon cat—he's one of their best detectives. The cartoon-cat subplot pays off unexpectedly when the cat returns to bail Jack out of a jam, but it also highlights the film's feathered-fish status. Why should audiences be emotionally invested in a fantasy world where cartoon cats work alongside wisecracking musclemen? The filmmakers should have either run with the notion that Jack's on-screen universe is a realm of pure fantasy where anything can happen, or abandoned the idea completely, instead of devoting about five minutes of screen time to comic-book fantasy and 115 minutes to its hero blowing shit up.

With *Kiss Kiss Bang Bang*, Shane Black's brilliant 2005 directorial debut, the hotshot screenwriter embodied Jean-Luc Godard's old maxim, "The best way to critique a movie is to make another movie." *Bang Bang* was everything *Last Action Hero* should have been: a movie-mad deconstruction of the buddy movie that radiated love for the English language.

Last Action Hero was seemingly destined to become one of the biggest hits of all time, until it became one of cinema's most notorious flops. The thorough botch of a seemingly foolproof blockbuster brings to mind a famous Hollywood aphorism from *Last Action Hero* script doctor William Goldman about the difficulty of predicting a film's failure or success: "Nobody knows anything."

Failure, Fiasco, Or Secret Success? *Failure*

Disgustingly Patriotic Case File #122: *The Rocketeer*
Originally Posted October 28, 2008

Anyone who tells you the appeal of moviegoing isn't at least partially voyeuristic is a goddamned liar and should be punched in the face repeatedly. We go to the movies to watch uncommonly beautiful people woo, romance, or reject other preternaturally fetching creatures in photogenic settings. As a young boy, I embraced movies as a socially acceptable way of looking at boobs. The fact that films were capable of art, truth, and beauty was a neat bonus.

It's been that way from the beginning. In a famous, perhaps apocryphal tale, early moviegoers were reportedly so terrified by the image of a train barreling toward them in the infamous early short "Oh My God, There Is A Real Train Barreling Toward You, You Are So Going To Die; Flee, Flee In Horror Unless You Want To End Up Flat As A Pancake, Your Internal Organs Splattered Against The Walls Of This Theater!" that they all began masturbating feverishly.

Later, movie studios realized that showing sexy women and men in erotically charged situations was nearly as arousing to filmgoers as the prospect of imminent death. The scandalously erotic possibilities of film terrified the Man, so he sent a joyless scold named Will Hays to keep movies from devolving, or rather evolving, into a sticky, sweaty mass of writhing bodies pummeling every orifice in an omnisexual fuckfest of historic dimensions. In keeping with our nation's history of hypocritical puritanism, the Hays Code dictated that kisses couldn't last longer than a millisecond, jaywalking must be punished with death, and single people shown hugging, cuddling, or hand-holding must immediately be run over by an out-of-control train.

But the Man couldn't control our daydreams, so filmgoers continued to fantasize in the dark. Moviegoing is simultaneously a communal and anonymous endeavor. Lusting after the same handful of beauties binds us together. Drooling over Marilyn Monroe united fathers and sons, beatniks and squares, Americans and people who wish they were American on account of America being so awesome. USA! USA! USA! (Sorry 'bout getting jingoistic there. A little-known provision of the PATRIOT Act dictates that the chant "USA! USA! USA!" must appear at least twice in all film columns lasting more than 120 entries.)

The language we use to talk about these figures of mass lust says much about the safe voyeurism of moviegoing. The term "America's sweetheart," for example, conveys our shared appreciation for women so glorious that a cultural consensus has been reached that they embody everything that is good and American about womanhood. Who doesn't love Audrey Hepburn, in spite of her being, you know, not American? Only a goddamned Nazi, that's who. And Nazis have no business pining for our Audrey.

Sex symbols, in sharp contrast, need only ignite the universal libido. America's sweethearts are always metaphorical virgins; sex symbols are voracious whores seducing us from afar.

An amusing subsection of the sex-symbol genus is what is quaintly known as the thinking man's sex symbol. That concept flatters cinephiles' innate sense of superiority. It implies that even their libidos are discerning. Let the ignorant rabble have their saline-inflated Pamela Andersons and Jessica Simpsons. These sophisticated souls prefer the rarefied likes of Maggie Gyllenhaal or Tina Fey.

Critics consequently walk a fine line between acknowledging the innate voyeurism of moviegoing and coming across as trenchcoat-sporting superpervs. Pauline Kael playfully acknowledged the voyeurism of cinephilia by giving her books suggestive titles: *I Lost It At The Movies, Taking It All In, Kiss Kiss Bang Bang, Going Steady, Deeper Into Movies, When The Lights Go Down, Afterglow,* and the infamous *Handjob By The Popcorn Stand.* Other critics let their prose drool for them. Reading *Nicole Kidman,* David Thomson's heavy-breathing "appreciation" of the Australian ice queen, I didn't know whether Kidman should send Thomson a thank-you letter or take out a restraining order against him. Similarly, Jeanine Basinger spends so much time panting over Tyrone Power in *The Star Machine* that I feared that she'd dig up Power's skeleton, dress him up in fancy clothes, and gush, "My goodness, Tyrone, you're even more divine looking as a rotting bag of bones! Why, if I were 20 years younger and you hadn't died 50 years ago, I don't know *what* might have happened!"

What does any of this have to do with this My Year Of Flops Case File on 1991's *The Rocketeer*? Well, I have always wanted to write the world's longest, most lascivious, and needlessly digressive introduction to an essay about a PG-rated family film. Mission accomplished, just like our glorious commander in chief said when he single-handedly won the Iraq War. USA! USA! USA!

More to the point, *The Rocketeer* features the most divine creature in the history of film: a 20-year-old Jennifer Connelly. Connelly plays a character whom the late comic-book artist Dave Stevens originally modeled after Bettie Page, whose strange, sordid career was predicated on being an impossible object of desire, a beautiful blank upon whom perverts could project their twisted fantasies. In Stevens' comics, the love interest is even named Betty, though the film changed the character's name (to Jenny Blake) and profession (from nude model to actress). Page lived to be seen, worshipped, adored. Connelly plays an idealized version of Page, the one Bettie Page wanted to be: an actress and a good girl, not the kind of virgin-whore who retains an air of innocence even while getting paddled by a mistress in bondage gear.

In *Career Opportunities* and *The Hot Spot*, Connelly radiated the steam heat of a classic sex symbol. In *The Rocketeer*, she's the quintessential America's sweetheart. Since *Requiem For A Dream*, she's become a frighteningly skinny waif who suffers disproportionately for our sins in an endless series of downers, earning her ambiguous status as a thinking man's sex symbol. She's mastered the art of being all things to all people.

Connelly isn't the only breathtaking aspect of *The Rocketeer*. It's a film of staggering glamour and beauty, an all-American tribute to the dangerous, exciting world of pulpy serials. Disney undoubtedly thought it had the next blockbuster franchise on its hands. It was not to be. A film series got snuffed in its infancy, leaving behind a raft of unsold *Rocketeer* action figures, cookie jars, lunch boxes, models, pins, cards, and videogames. Bill Campbell and Connelly both signed on for sequels that were never made. Even the biggest TV-ad push in Disney history at the time couldn't drive audiences to the film. In spite of okay reviews and okay box office, the film was a brutal disappointment to Disney.

Today, *The Rocketeer* stands as both a fascinating precursor to the film adaptation of *Iron Man*—though *Iron Man* made its comics debut decades before Stevens introduced the Rocketeer in a *Starslayer* comic in 1982—and as an antidote to the current spate of revisionist superhero efforts. We've been inundated with so many cinematic superheroes in need of therapy and mood stabilizers as of late that it's refreshing to see a superhero whose biggest psychological weakness involves neglecting his bestest gal in favor of flying.

As played by pretty boy Billy Campbell, Cliff, aka The Rocketeer, is a man devoid of existential angst and neurosis. All he wants to do is fly. He's unabashedly a comic-book hero. We are dealing with archetypes here, characters lustily embodied by the dependable likes of Alan Arkin (as Peevy, the crusty father figure) and Paul Sorvino (as sausage-fingered mobster Eddie Valentine).

The Rocketeer is defiantly old-fashioned. Like his mentors Steven Spielberg and George Lucas, director Joe Johnston injects the pulp ephemera of yesteryear with newfangled technological sophistication. Period films tend to age gracefully; *The Rocketeer*, like the Indiana Jones series, feels like it could have been made in 1940 or yesterday: It's timeless.

The filmmakers give *The Rocketeer* an epic scope and comic book sensibility. It's a movie movie: Many of the film's central characters are actors and filmmakers, including Connelly's radiant starlet; heavy Timothy Dalton as Neville Sinclair, a mustache-twirling bad guy modeled on Errol Flynn; and dashing Terry O'Quinn as filmmaker/ aviator Howard Hughes.

The Rocketeer's plot concerns a glistening, alluringly mammary-like rocket pack developed by Howard Hughes; it falls into the hands of mobsters, then gets discovered by hotshot flyboy Cliff and mentor Peevy. Cliff is immediately fascinated. What red-blooded American boy wouldn't want a jet pack of his very own? *The Rocketeer* taps into four fantasies shared by every strapping heterosexual American lad: flying, being a superhero, battling Nazis, and having sex with Bettie Page.

Cliff uses the jet pack to become costumed adventurer the Rocketeer. By superhero standards, the Rocketeer is a little lacking: He doesn't shoot fireballs or have X-ray vision or superpowers or titanium skin. He's just a handsome guy with a rocket pack. But rocket packs are so inherently awesome that they render other superpowers unnecessary.

The Rocketeer takes place in an alternate-universe 1938 Hollywood where Bettie Page is an innocent extra, Errol Flynn is a Nazi secret agent, Howard Hughes is a dashing Good Samaritan who happily sacrifices lucrative government contracts for the sake of the public good, and a rocket pack has the potential to shift the balance of power between the good guys and Nazi bogeyman. In that respect, it's like James Ellroy by way of Richard Donner's *Superman*. In reality, Hughes was less Mr. Smith than Mr. Burns. But in *The Rocketeer*'s flag-waving comic-book world, even mobsters and war profiteers are patriotic above all else.

The Rocketeer soars as pure spectacle. Every element feels perfectly in place. The dialogue is slangy and fun. The setpieces are constant and astonishing, including a swashbuckling epic where Jenny and Neville meet, the many flying sequences, a spectacular climax aboard an exploding Nazi zeppelin. The supporting parts are uniformly executed with panache. Bit players like a hulking mob flunky who looks like Boris Karloff after taking a few too many frying pans to the face illustrate the truth of Konstantin Stanislavski's famous line about there being no small parts, just shitty roles played by horrible fucking actors who waste everyone's time with their terrible performances. All this, plus the most gorgeous woman in history (other than my girlfriend) at the height of her nubile beauty. As a great man once said, "USA! USA! USA!"

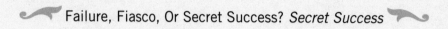 Failure, Fiasco, Or Secret Success? *Secret Success*

Chapter 5

Unsexy Sexy Films

Reality Bites Case File #56: *The Real Cancun*
Originally Posted August 7, 2007

On April 25, 2003, the pagan gods of cinema faced down a threat greater than piracy, the Internet, and the Wayans combined: reality television, the insidious cultural poison that transformed the medium of Edward R. Murrow and Rod Serling into a forum to explore the complicated psyches and love lives of Corey Feldman, Vince Neil, and various *Playboy* playmates and *Survivor* losers.

Cultural barbarians were clamoring at the gate, eager to corrupt a venerable institution that gave the world Ingmar Bergman, Jean-Luc Godard, and *Citizen Kane*—and, to be fair, two competing films about the lambada that famously pitted Golan against Globus. Our culture stood at a perilous crossroads. In just a few short years, the reality plague had completely transformed television. Now it looked primed to do the same to film. The test balloon in question? *The Real Cancun*, a potentially revolutionary "reality movie" from Bunim-Murray Productions, the demon spawn behind the MTV sensation *The Real World*.

From a production standpoint, reality movies boasted myriad advantages over fictional films. They were cheap, could be filmed and edited in a fraction of the time of their fictional counterparts (*Cancun* was filmed in 10 days, then hit theaters five weeks later), and didn't require demanding, expensive stars or batteries of screenwriters and script doctors. Most important, they featured the most powerful force known to man: boobs. Who needs Dame Judi Dench when there's an endless supply of strumpets willing to doff their tops for a shot at the limelight?

The Real Cancun's title says it all: "This is exactly like *The Real World*, only at spring break and with way more partying and boobs! Woo-hoo! Party! Party! Chug! Chug! Chug!" There's also a stylistic vocabulary to reality shows that *Cancun* shares, characterized by flashy editing, relentless appeals to prurient interests, and a wall-to-wall soundtrack of songs you're already sick of hearing.

The quasi-cinematic abomination follows 16 young people who head down to Cancun with two goals in mind: seeing how much liquor they can consume before passing out in a pool of their own vomit, and fucking random skanks and dumbasses. The hedonists here tend to blur together into a hideous writhing mass of drunken flesh, but a few souls stand out. There's the gawky horndog who refuses to drink until some hot party girls pressure him into downing body shots. Then there's a pair of platonic friends perpetually on the brink of becoming something more, and a woman who quips that her favorite position with less generously endowed men is with someone else. Oh, snap! In the hormone-crazed world of *The Real Cancun*, a land of well-developed pectorals and underdeveloped intellects, this passes for wit.

The Real Cancun isn't entirely devoid of drama: One guy pours a cup of his own piss on a skank after a jellyfish stings her. As a rule, I steer clear of reality shows. They tend to engender visceral loathing for humanity deep within me, and I want to fight my impulse toward misanthropy, not cultivate it like a psychic bonsai tree.

The film's most impressive feat involves making public nudity, lesbian make-out parties, and non-stop drinking not only unfun, but soul crushing. *Cancun* offers a horrifying glimpse into the kiddie-pool-shallow minds of folks whose greatest ambition in life is to emulate the extras in Mystikal videos. But underneath the partying, drinking, and meaningless carousing lie vast oceans of sadness. It's an ugly hangover masquerading as a party.

In a rare display of taste, the American public wholeheartedly rejected *The Real Cancun* and its cynical assault on cinema. It turns out people still want movies to mean something, even if it's just two hours in air-conditioned comfort watching shiny shit blow up good. I never felt prouder to be an American than when I learned that *The Real Cancun* grossed just over $2 million on its opening weekend.

Thank you, Mr. And Mrs. America and all the ships at sea! You saved yourselves (and me) from an endless deluge of dispiriting reality movies. Now if you could only do something about your insatiable appetite for *Saw* sequels, my life would be just about perfect.

Failure, Fiasco, Or Secret Success? *Failure*

Book-Exclusive, Freely Adapted Case File: *The Scarlet Letter*

Nathaniel Hawthorne's *The Scarlet Letter* is one of those unimpeachable masterpieces that scare impressionable high school students off reading forever. It's the kind of symbolism-heavy, portentous tome that makes "reading for pleasure" seem like an oxymoron. After being forced to wade through Hawthorne's dense forest of prose and weighty ideas about sin and hypocrisy, is it any wonder that weak-minded young people retreat into the unchallenging arms of reality television and *Us Weekly*?

Like so many of the dour magnum opuses that fill high-school syllabi, *The Scarlet Letter* is a bummer. But what if it wasn't? What if Hollywood sank its fangs into this great literary killjoy and turned it into a bloody, sexy melodrama about true love conquering all—one that ended with plucky heroine Hester Prynne, dreamy man of God Reverend Arthur Dimmesdale, and their adorable tot riding off into the sunset after a narratively convenient Native American sneak attack killed off all those disapproving Puritan scolds? What if it became an anachronistically flower-powered celebration of pure-hearted lovers triumphing over societal repression?

That was the beautiful, idiotic dream of 1995's *The Scarlet Letter*, a film that sought to improve upon Hawthorne's book by including all the scalping, attempted rape, skinny-dipping, extensive female masturbation, and pervasive interracial homoeroticism missing from the original text. Demi Moore reasoned that it was kosher for the film to change the book so dramatically because so few people had read it. Hollywood transformed an austere narrative into a randy cinematic romance novel, a bosom-heaving tale of ribaldry.

The filmmakers suffered for their sins. The trenchcoat set took one look at the film's ominous title and experienced traumatic flashbacks of battling their way through one of the most demanding novels ever to trouble an American teen's television-warped mind. The smart set, meanwhile, recoiled at the idea of turning Hawthorne's classic tale of sin and shame into a sexed-up, dumbed-down vehicle for a superstar who seemed to view book reading as an endeavor as esoteric and unpopular as learning Esperanto. Critics predictably eviscerated *The Scarlet Letter*, and it grossed little more than a fifth of its hefty $50 million budget during its domestic theatrical release.

Roland Joffé's film broadcasts its lack of fidelity for its source material with an opening credit crowing that it's "freely adapted" from Hawthorne's novel. Joffé preemptively ducks the inevitable deluge of critical brickbats by advertising, if not flaunting, his faithlessness to Hawthorne. It seems apt that a novel about infidelity should inspire one of the least faithful literary adaptations in American film.

This *Scarlet Letter* is many things. It's a shameless bodice ripper, a potboiler, softcore porn, and a sleazy wallow in sex and violence. It isn't, however, Nathaniel Hawthorne's *Scarlet Letter*. The "freely adapted" credit gives the film considerable wiggle room, but the film-makers really should have been honest with audiences and given it a new title, like *The Lusty Pilgrim,* and a tagline like "The man with the clerical collar . . . has this wench all hot and bothered!" or "He was a man of the cloth; she wanted to rip his clothes off." Joffé's heavy-breathing, soft-headed erotic drama splits the difference between *The Scarlet Letter* and *Red Shoe Diaries.*

Douglas Day Stewart's screenplay makes the mistake of imposing contemporary sensitivities on the literature of the past. He's written Hester Prynne as a sex-positive proto-feminist, a 1990s kind of gal stuck in the upside-down, backward world of the 1660s. He stops just short of including a prorecycling message in a film that neither needs nor can withstand a clumsy infusion of liberal sermonizing.

In a performance that suggests the world's horniest Disney hero-ine, Moore lends her patented air of steely determination to the role of a plucky freethinker who arrives in tradition-bound Massachusetts Bay in 1667 with a mind rife with rebellion, a tongue full of sass, and loins aching for sexual liberation.

With her much-older husband Roger Chillingworth (Rob-ert Duvall) ostensibly back in England, Hester purchases an easily aroused mute mulatto slave girl (Lisa Jolifee-Andoh) to leer lustily at her having sex and masturbating. (And, to a much lesser extent, so the slave girl can help Hester work the land and run errands.) Hes-ter instantly runs afoul of the glowering, repressive town elders, who scold her with harsh directives like, "Madam, you would do well here to use less lace in your dressmaking." That, I believe, was the Puritan way of calling someone a ho.

Yes, the powers that be are keen to give Hester a forced sassectomy, even before she's tending her garden one day and follows a bird and then a deer into the forest, where she encounters the life-changing sight of hunky Reverend Arthur Dimmesdale (Gary Oldman) dis-robing for a skinny-dip. From the lusty gleam in Hester's eyes, it's evident that the Lord has endowed Dimmesdale with more than just a gift for oratory.

The Scarlet Letter juxtaposes the sensual, natural world of Native Americans and its star-crossed lovers with the painfully repressed realm of the Puritans. In the film's telling, even adorable woodland creatures want Hester and Dimmesdale to fuck, social protocol be damned.

Tapping into his Sid Vicious magnetism, Oldham embodies the reverend as rock star, the preacher as pop icon. He pouts. He sulks. He inspires. He aims to stir the minds and consciences of his female parishioners but ends up affecting them profoundly farther down their anatomy. When Hester gushes while gazing adoringly at Dimmesdale ("It's rare for a man so young to speak with such force of passion"), she sounds more like a groupie prostrating herself before her favorite musician than a new parishioner extolling her spiritual leader's eloquence.

The Scarlet Letter posits Dimmesdale as the original emo heartthrob. He struts, emotes, and broods during his sermon like a 17th-century Ben Gibbard. Dimmesdale cuts himself repeatedly by rubbing his open palms against jagged tree bark in the pounding rain, because he feels everything so deeply. He digs books; when Moore's hormone-addled bibliophile lends him a bushel of books, he reads them all in a matter of days, many of them twice. He has enlightened attitudes toward liberated women and Native Americans. At home that night, Hester replays in her mind's cinema the image of Oldham's naked flesh gliding through the water. Meanwhile, her slave girl sidles saucily up to a peephole and gazes longingly as the naked, aroused Hester poses and pouts.

Then one day, Hester receives wonderful news: Her husband is dead! She is now free to explore her burning hunger for the good reverend. They consummate their illicit passion while the slave girl once again affords herself a front-row seat and slips her fingers into her honeypot as she helps herself to a bath. I had no idea that slave/owner relationships in 1660s New England were defined largely by frenzied masturbation. *The Scarlet Letter* is edifying and arousing, in an unedifying, non-arousing kind of way.

Dimmesdale and Hester pay for their stolen moments of pleasure with intense, almost unbearable pain. Hester is imprisoned when she becomes pregnant and won't disclose the name of the father. Upon her release, she is forced to wear a scarlet "A" for adultery. Equally ominously, Chillingworth isn't dead at all. Introduced spinning around madly while wearing the disembodied corpse of a deer as part of an Algonquian ceremony, he sneaks into town incognito and torments his wife while trying to discern the identity of her child's father.

At this point, the film trades sex for ultraviolence. A villager tries to rape Hester. Chillingworth, dressed in Native American garb, mistakes the rapist for Dimmesdale and murders and scalps him while letting out a cartoonish war whoop. Chillingworth's attempt to blame the scalping on indigenous Americans backfires, conveniently enough, when Dimmesdale is about to be hanged publicly after confessing his indiscretion, and a Native American arrow lodges in the hangman's neck. In the chaos, Dimmesdale, Hester, and their love child escape, in the happy ending no sane person could have expected or wanted. Hester and Dimmesdale share a lusty open-mouthed kiss as their baby climactically throws the cursed scarlet letter on the ground. Joffé gives audiences a Hollywood ending at the expense of everything Hawthorne's novel represents.

Film adaptations of literary classics serve a sneaky dual purpose as cinematic cheat sheets for lazy teenagers. As a celluloid CliffsNotes for backward students, *The Scarlet Letter* is hilariously misleading. In the years since *Scarlet Letter* slunk shamefully out of theaters and onto video and DVD, high-school teachers have undoubtedly been inundated with oblivious book reports on Hawthorne that look something like this. (Needless to say, if freshmen think the film will help them pass English, they're sorely mistaken.)

Webster's Dictionary *defines "shame" as "the painful feeling arising from the consciousness of something dishonorable, improper, ridiculous, etc., done by oneself or another." Author-person Nathaniel Hawthorne's* The Scarlet Letter *is primarily a book about female masturbation and interracial homoeroticism but it's also about shame and how it's bad and stuff. It is about a sexy married woman named Hester Prynne who sees a hunky preacher skinny-dipping and masturbates thinking about him. While she is masturbating, her foxy slave looks at her through a peephole and begins touching herself even though that is an invasion of privacy and probably a violation of the Third or Fourth Amendment.*

Hester Prynne and the preacher guy do it while the slave gets into a tub and masturbates and later frees a cardinal that symbolizes freedom or repression. The book takes place in the 1700s or 1800s because everyone looks weird and has a mustache even if they're not gay or a cop. I think it takes place in America but I'm not sure. The town fathers find out that Hester Prynne has been doing it because she's pregnant and make her wear a scarlet A for adultery.

Hester Prynne goes to jail because she won't snitch on the reverend guy. Later, Hester Prynne's husband, who everyone thinks is dead but isn't, spins around with a dead animal on his head and scalps this rapist guy while pretending to be an Indian. Also, there is a happy ending.

In conclusion, The Scarlet Letter *is a good book because it uses symbolism and has a lot of sex and a dude getting scalped.*

Failure, Fiasco, Or Secret Success? *Failure*

Desperotica Case File #86: *Body Of Evidence*

Originally Posted November 20, 2007

Body Of Evidence combined something audiences have always responded to positively (Madonna's sexuality) with something audiences have historically never responded to positively (Madonna's movies). Though Madonna has become synonymous with flops, she's racked up a few hits: *Desperately Seeking Susan, A League Of Their Own,* and *Dick Tracy.* A good rule of thumb: If a film instantly becomes a pop-culture punch line, then it's a Madonna movie. If it succeeds, it's a film Madonna happened to appear in.

In Jose Canseco's autobiography, *Juiced*, the Hulk-like steroid proponent writes that Madonna pursued him relentlessly during his baseball heyday, but that he found her insufficiently attractive. This struck me as absurd. In what universe is Madonna underqualified to give Jose Canseco a handjob?

Yet there's nothing natural about Madonna's sex appeal. It's a matter of attitude and lighting, iconography and shrewd calculation, exhibitionism and a finely honed gift for provocation. It's telling that many of Madonna's most fruitful artistic collaborations are with photographers and music-video directors. Depending on the angle and the outfit, Madonna can look like Marilyn Monroe reborn or the boogeyman's grandma.

In 1993's *Body Of Evidence*, Madonna's costume designers shoot for Old Hollywood glamour, but dead-end at dowdy and unflattering. Naked, Madonna is so flawless and creepily synthetic that she looks like a sentient sex doll. While it may be unseemly to dwell on her appearance, *Body Of Evidence*'s plot turns on her sexual desirability. Even the title is a panting double entendre about her character.

It's never an encouraging sign when a film repeatedly has to broadcast its femme fatale's sexiness. It should be evident in the way she walks, in the sway of her hips, and in a flirtatious glance, not in stiffly recited dialogue. Yet early in *Evidence*, opposing lawyers Frank Dulaney (Willem Dafoe) and Robert Garrett (Joe Mantegna) both feel the need to assert Madonna's attractiveness before the jury.

"She's a beautiful woman," Garrett thunders. "But when the trial is over, you will see her no differently than a gun or a knife, or any other instrument used as a weapon. She is a killer, and the worst kind—a killer who disguised herself as a loving partner." Now, far be it from me to challenge the veracity of anything said by Joe Mantegna, but I would argue that the worst kind of killer is one who wears a necklace made out of puppy skulls and a rain poncho made out of the torsos of murdered kittens. That's, perhaps, worse than a killer disguising herself as a loving partner.

Madonna's Rebecca Carlson has been accused of killing a wealthy lover with a bum ticker and an appetite for light bondage. Her weapon: awesome erotic overstimulation. Yes, it's murder by sex, as Garrett tries to convince a jury that Rebecca fucked her elderly lover to death by deliberately inducing a fatal heart attack during kinky, drug-fueled canoodling.

Half moribund courtroom thriller, half erotic thriller, *Evidence* alternates between florid scenes of sex-saturated courtroom shenanigans and endless, graphic romps in which Rebecca introduces Frank to the joys of public handjobs in crowded elevators, rough sex atop broken glass on the hood of a car in a parking garage, candle wax, champagne, and masturbation/bondage.

Alas, by the time *Evidence* flopped in theaters, Madonna's nudity was a wildly degraded commodity, thanks largely to the 1992 coffee-table book *Sex*, an encyclopedic compendium of kinks and carnal cravings designed to satisfy fetishes of every stripe. By 1993, the public was more familiar with the sight of Madonna's genitalia than their own.

Evidence tries to one-up *Basic Instinct* through the sheer quantity of its sex scenes, but it backfires. I never thought I would think this, but deep into the film, I got bored looking at Madonna's naked breasts. As a weird little kid, I was convinced that Madonna was a shameful harlot who would pollute the minds of innocent young people like my sister with her sinful devil music and brazen sexuality. Then adolescence hit and I became disproportionately grateful for Madonna's harlotry and devil music. Yet by the time I rewatched *Body Of Evidence* for this Case File, even I was suffering from Madonna exhaustion.

Sexploitation movies like *Body Of Evidence* fail at the box office in part because, all things considered, people enjoy masturbating in the comfort and privacy of their own home. How successful would even the funniest comedy be if audiences were legally forbidden from laughing in public? Would you want to plunk down $10 to see the new Judd Apatow movie if there were a chance you'd be arrested for shamelessly pleasuring your funny bone in full view of the general public? That's not such a problem if a dirty movie has artistic aims or social relevance, but *Evidence* nurses no ambitions beyond providing masturbatory fodder.

Body Of Evidence oscillates artlessly between legal pulp and soft-core porn until a big shocking final twist reveals that Madonna's strangely robotic sexual con artist is, in fact, the evil, duplicitous villain she appeared to be all along. Cue her violent death by gunfire, and roll credits.

With *Evidence,* one of the world's most popular sex symbols bombed as a screen vixen. Then again, I'm not entirely convinced that Camille Paglia didn't will Madonna into existence sometime in the late '70s. It's as if Paglia was sitting around one day and thought, "Wow, if only there was one virgin-whore-bitch-goddess-sinner-saint-icon-God who could embody every pretentious idea I've ever had. Then I'd be set." Bam! Suddenly a full-grown Madonna materialized out of thin air and began masturbating with a big black crucifix while dressed as Elvis.

Maybe they can include this film in a Paglia-taught class on, I dunno; Madonna, androgyny, gender subversion, and sadomasochism in popular culture as a form of social protest as part of an elective credit devoted to colossal wastes of everyone's time.

 Failure, Fiasco, Or Secret Success? *Failure*

Sex-Fantasy Island Case File #97: *Exit To Eden*
Originally Posted December 27, 2007

Here at My Year Of Flops Incorporated, we've explored a broad spectrum of unsexy sex films that collectively put the "blechhh" into sex. With this entry I'll explore the mother of all unsexy sex films: 1994's *Exit To Eden,* a once-in-a-lifetime cross between HBO's *Real Sex* and *Love, American Style.* It's a transgressive erotic drama! No, it's a wacky diamond-smuggling comedy with Rosie O'Donnell and Dan Aykroyd! No, it's a transgressive erotic drama *and* it's a wacky diamond-smuggling comedy with Rosie O'Donnell and Dan Aykroyd!

It's a surreally misguided attempt to make the kinky world of bondage and sadomasochism palatable to mainstream audiences by dressing Dan Aykroyd like the Gimp from *Pulp Fiction* and putting Rosie O'Donnell in revealing dominatrix gear. In the overheated parlance of the panting summary on the back of its video box, the film offers the scintillating promise of O'Donnell "thigh-high in leather and studs with a personal slave-boy to fulfill her every whim." That, apparently, was supposed to be a major draw: the prospect of Rosie O'Donnell squeezed into tight leather. Is there a more surefire erection killer this side of graphic photo books about the final stages of syphilis? How can anyone become comfortably aroused with the prospect of a half-naked O'Donnell looming just around the corner?

Sex and comedy are a tough combination to pull off. When was the last time you watched a sex comedy and found yourself thinking, "Wow! I'm laughing uproariously *and* I have a raging erection!" It's been illustrated time and time again that sex and comedy go together only when sped up and accompanied by Boots Randolph's "Yakety Sax." But what happens when the sexy stuff isn't sexy and the funny stuff isn't funny?

Exit To Eden began life as a non-comic erotic romance novel pseudonymously written by Anne Rice. Yes, there are some books that fill even Anne Rice with shame. It's never an encouraging sign when even a woman who dresses like an extra in a Bauhaus video well into middle age doesn't want to be publicly associated with a project.

What cinematic sensualist was called upon to bring Rice's erotic vision to the big screen? Adrian Lyne? David Lynch? How about the nice old grandfather behind *Happy Days* and *The Other Sister*? *Exit To Eden* was shepherded onto the big screen by Garry Marshall, a filmmaker with a preternatural ability to transform everything he touches into a banal sitcom.

So a straight erotic drama was turned into a cop comedy/Vaseline-smeared touchy-feely New Age romance. *Exit To Eden*'s starring cast combines two people who have no business starring in a big Hollywood film (Paul Mercurio and Dana Delany) and two people who have no business parading about publicly in S & M gear (Aykroyd and O'Donnell).

It's an old story, really. Lisa Emerson (Delany) was a doormat until an older lover introduced her to Dr. Martin Halifax (Hector Elizondo), who uttered magical words that would change her life: "I am a top, a master. You are a bottom, a submissive. Yet we are not different. We are in unison, to please each other. Just tell me your wishes. Welcome to my world . . . It is a world in which you have all the choices. You are a victim in life. I will teach you to always be in total control. I will teach you never to be a victim ever again. Never."

Dr. Halifax is the Yoda of deviant sex. I expected him to continue: "Life victim you are. Teach you I will. Control total will you have." A wallflower no more, Lisa becomes the headmistress of a fantasy pleasure island where she rules over an army of slaves and submissives, including Elliot Slater (Paul Mercurio), a love-struck photographer who made the mistake of photographing a pair of diamond smugglers played by Stuart Wilson and David Bowie's wife.

When the diamond smugglers head to Lisa's Pleasure Island to track down the negatives, wisecracking cop Sheila Kingston (O'Donnell) and partner Fred Lavery (Aykroyd) follow in hot pursuit, hoping to get to Elliot before the bad guys can retrieve the photos with extreme prejudice.

Once the film makes it onto the island, it veers among three distinct tones: the giggly, embarrassed sex comedy about O'Donnell and Aykroyd; a New Age romance; and the thriller-by-numbers action of the diamond-smuggling plot, which feels arbitrary even by the lenient standards of gratuitous diamond-smuggling subplots.

To help pass the time, I pretended *Exit To Eden* was secretly a Kubrickian science-fiction drama about a mysterious island staffed and populated entirely by sex androids. That would explain a lot, from the robotic performances and affectless line readings of Delany and her minions to the dearth of plausible human emotion on display. Certainly flesh-and-blood human beings would never utter lines like the following:

Very good, pretty eyes. Now I'm going to let you feel what you so much wanted to see.

Elliot was intrigued by erotica, but reticent to try it until now.

In this era of fringe-group lunacy, shouldn't we also preserve freedom of choice for this most intimate of choices: sex?

The BDSM elements of *Exit To Eden* amount to little more than kinky window dressing for a vanilla romance between a woman reluctant to give up power for fear of getting hurt, and a man afraid of embracing his kinks out of fear of being branded a pervert. Just how staggeringly banal and wholesome is the film's fierce head dominatrix? When Elliot asks Lisa what she likes best in bed, she giggles, "What do I like to do best in bed? I like to giggle. Cuddle and giggle. After a long day of smacking people, it's nice to cuddle."

It's a measure of the film's almost comic inertness that I wound up thinking, "I hope they get back to that scintillating diamond-smuggling subplot. All this sex is boring me to tears." Over 120 glacially paced minutes of cinematic torture, the film somehow manages to make kinky sex seem dull and tacky.

Exit To Eden is a doddering old square's take on the outer limits of sexuality, a blandly sentimental romance decked out in leather, lace, and spikes. In case there're any lingering doubts about its romance-novel soul, O'Donnell's narration ends with the following moral: "So what did I learn from this case? No matter what your sexual preference, true love is still the ultimate fantasy."

Exit To Eden was a huge critical and commercial flop domestically, though it did much better in Japan under the title *Happy Sexy Go-Go Naked China Beach Lady Fun Movie*. *Exit To Eden* was supposed to

open minds and liberate repressed libidos. Instead, it's an unintentional infomercial for sexual repression.

Failure, Fiasco, Or Secret Success? *Failure*

Maniacal Death-Orgy Case File #107: *Tough Guys Don't Dance*
Originally Posted April 16, 2008

Norman Mailer was a hero to many. He never meant shit to me. Though I have a soft spot in my heart for anyone with Mailer's genius for self-promotion (as seen in his tome, *Advertisements For Myself*), I have a hard time getting past the tough-guy posturing. Given Mailer's reputation, it's a miracle that he made it well into his 80s without dying of testosterone poisoning or meeting an undignified end wrestling a mountain lion. If Ernest Hemingway is the god of the great literary church of machismo, the great alpha-male all other two-fisted, hard-drinking wordsmiths prostrate themselves before, then Mailer is at least a minor saint, especially now that he's bare-knuckle brawling angels up in heaven.

Mailer toiled diligently to create the impression that he wrote with a half-empty whiskey bottle in one hand, a sawed-off shotgun in the other, and a dead hooker at his feet. Acolytes could be forgiven for imagining that he had gasoline and bourbon running through his veins.

Writer-director Mailer's 1987 thriller was the product of a brief period when beloved Israeli schlock merchants Menahem Golan and Yoram Globus, the geniuses behind *The Apple* and *Over The Top*, tried to buy a little respectability by throwing money at famous (or at least notorious) figures and hoping against hope that great art (or at least healthy commerce) would ensue.

So in the span of just a few years, Golan and Globus produced Barbet Schroeder's Charles Bukowski adaptation *Barfly* and *Death Wish 4: The Crackdown*, Jean-Luc Godard's *King Lear* and *Braddock: Missing*

155

In Action III, Norman Mailer's *Tough Guys Don't Dance* and *Masters Of The Universe.* It's tempting to place Mailer, that distinguished man of letters, on the side of artists and deep thinkers, but *Tough Guys Don't Dance* isn't even smart, pretentious trash. It's pretty much just trash.

Some DVDs are worth renting just for their trailers. *Tough Guys Don't Dance* is such a film. In the theatrical trailer, "America's most controversial author" addresses the camera directly while clutching a fistful of comment cards from a test screening. "Bold, innovative, wonderful!" crows the first one. "Stinks!" jeers the second. The comments that follow swing drunkenly between rapturous praise and scathing condemnation. "A movie not to miss" is followed by "a giant death orgy with lots of maniacs." "One of the best, most original films I've ever seen" is chased by "One of the worst ever. My grandmother could do better."

I could go on, but I'll skip over the praise and center on the hate-ration. "Whoever wrote this has never read a good book," Mailer reads from one card, before hurling it aside in a manner that unmistakably conveys, *"Read* a good book? I've only written, like, every good book, ever!" Ever the showman, he saves the best for last, literally winking at the screen after rasping, "The devil made this picture." That is clearly the highest praise Mailer has ever received.

This ballsy "You're probably going to hate this filthy, disgusting, hateful movie, which is an affront to good people and basic decency" approach was probably the smartest way to sell *Tough Guys.* The trailer isn't selling quality so much as danger, image, attitude, sex, sleaze, and Mailer himself. Mailer's performance throughout is a marvel: He's deadpan, but a shameless ham. If the film that this trailer so indelibly promotes were half as entertaining as its auteur reading comment cards, it'd catapult instantly to the upper tier of Secret Successes.

So it pains me to report that as far as giant death orgies with lots of maniacs go, *Tough Guys Don't Dance* is unforgivably dull. Or at least that's what I would have told you after seeing it for the first time. At the risk of contradicting myself, I would like to take back everything I've just written. I was shocked and delighted to discover that upon repeat viewings, nearly all of *Tough Guys*' flaws become subversive strengths. I knew going in that *Tough Guys* was a polarizing film. I never imagined that my opinion of it would shift so radically the second time around, from visceral hate to warped appreciation.

My reaction represents in microcosm the public's split response to many cult movies and notorious failures: loathing and ridicule, followed by revisionist acclaim. Cult films often fail in their initial release as art and drama, only to succeed with future generations as comedy and camp.

But enough pussyfooting: Let's get to the booze, broads, bodies, and bullets. You know, the good stuff. In his greatest bad performance, a ghostly pale, perpetually hungover, sex-obsessed Ryan O'Neal (such a Method actor!) stars as Tim Madden, a bartender, writer, chauffeur, drug dealer, and full-time fuckup in the midst of a downward spiral. His days blur together in a dispiriting orgy of drinking, fucking, and blackouts, interrupted by the occasional discovery of decapitated heads and accidental tattoo acquisition. Oh, and he might be a murderer. Or he might be getting set up by a psychotic, weed-addled small-town police chief (Wings Hauser) with a closet full of skeletons and a disconcerting habit of waving around a giant machete while stoned and drunk.

Or the guilty party might be a foppish bisexual multimillionaire dandy with an irresistible jones for the low life and a grudge against Tim for stealing his party-girl wife, Patty (Debra Sandlund). Tim and Patty, incidentally, met when Tim and his then-girlfriend Madeline Regency (Isabella Rossellini) answered a personal ad for orgy partners placed in *Screw* magazine by Patty and her then-husband (magician Penn Jillette), a group-sex-loving, fantastically well-endowed preacher named Big Stoop. During my first viewing, I remember thinking, "You know, this movie isn't anywhere near as much fun as a film with an orgy involving Isabella Rossellini, Ryan O'Neal, and Penn Jillette as a group-sex-loving, fantastically well-endowed Southern preacher named Big Stoop should be." The second time around, however, I dug the surreal incongruity of it all, particularly the words, "He must have the longest cock in Christendom," coming out of Ingrid Bergman's daughter's impeccably sculpted mouth.

Mailer caught flak throughout the years for his perceived sexism, but this film nobly depicts womanhood in its infinite variety. The film's strong, empowered female characters range in personality and disposition from cum-crazed cock addicts to jizz-hungry fuck monkeys to sex-obsessed orgy enthusiasts.

In addition to slipping the debauched likes of Patty and his ex-girlfriend the old salami surprise, Tim makes sweet, sweet love with a former porn star–turned–society wife (Frances Fisher) while her emasculated husband watches in horror. What initially struck me as bad pulp and vulgarity minus any redeeming energy or vitality eventually came together as a Gothic, tongue-in-cheek parody of blood-splattered tough-guy melodrama.

I even came to love that Mailer's he-men and she-sluts use words like "screw," "bang," "broad," and "dame" without a hint of irony. *Tough Guys* traffics in the lively patois of the scuzzy barroom. It's locker-room banter with a literary bent and caveman swagger. Here are some particularly juicy snippets of hard-boiled banter, Norman Mailer-style:

> *Certain dames ought to wear a T-shirt that says "Hang around, I'll make a cocksucker out of you."*

> *My blood itself was turning mean.*

> *You Yankees got tongues like tallywackers!*

> *Mr. Regency and I make out five times a night. That's why I call him Mr. Five.*

> *Your knife. Is in. My dog.*

And this exchange, between Tim and Hauser's police chief, Alvin Luther Regency:

Alvin: Life gives a man two balls. Use 'em. It's a rare day I don't bang two women. As a matter of fact, I don't sleep too well unless I get that second hump in. Both sides of my nature are obliged to express themselves.

Tim: Tell me, what are your two sides?

Alvin: The enforcer and the maniac.

Tim: Who do we have the honor of addressing?

Alvin: You've never met the maniac.

Hauser delivers the "enforcer and the maniac" line with irresistible lunatic abandon. A veteran of countless shitty B-movies, Hauser looks and acts like the demon spawn of Gary Busey and Rutger Hauer. It's a performance pitched at just the right level of frothing hysteria.

I was even won over by O'Neal's wan lead performance. As a malicious cosmic joke, Mailer undercuts his lead actor at every turn. He made the protagonist a passive, weak-willed shell of a man who turns white with fright at the first sign of danger, then cast the great tough-guy character actor Lawrence Tierney as O'Neal's rough-hewn dad, so O'Neal would look even more effete by comparison.

The apex/nadir of O'Neal's performance comes when he reads a horrifying letter and cries out, "Oh, God! Oh, man!" over and over while the camera swirls dementedly around him. O'Neal reportedly begged Mailer to cut out the scene to make himself look like less of a jackass amateur, but Mailer refused, cuz nobody tells Norman fucking Mailer what to do. Then Mailer screwed all of O'Neal's ex-wives simultaneously, did elephant tranquilizers, and beat a grizzly bear to death with his bare fists. Or so I would imagine.

Tough Guys Don't Dance works best as a darkly comic, horror-tinged melodrama about the emptiness of excess and the soul-crushing costs of pursuing mindless pleasure. Like Godard's *Weekend*, it's about the pleasuring of the body as the death of the spirit, about the agonizing moment when sex, drugs, and wild excess stop feeling like heaven and begin to feel like hell. It's populated by some of the most repellent hedonists this side of *Rules Of Attraction*, and written and directed with tongue firmly in cheek.

When I look back at the first half of this essay, I want to punch the fey asshole who wrote it right in his smug fucking face. Then, after he gradually regains consciousness, we can down some Jack and go out looking for trouble. Oh, God! Oh, man! Oh, God! Oh, man! I think Mailer, that crafty old dog, may just be having his wicked way with my fragile psyche after all.

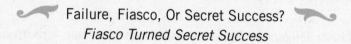

Failure, Fiasco, Or Secret Success?
Fiasco Turned Secret Success

Dominant-Paradigm-Subverting Case File #137: *Even Cowgirls Get The Blues*
Originally Posted May 13, 2009

When I told my editor Keith that I was thinking of writing about Gus Van Sant's 1993 comedy *Even Cowgirls Get The Blues* for My Year Of Flops, he mentioned that he'd read almost all Tom Robbins' books, then realized that he didn't particularly like them. When I asked why, he shrugged. "Eh, I was in college."

I never went through a Tom Robbins phase, but I have my own mini-pantheon of writers I will forever associate with college. For eternally status-conscious undergraduates, the books they read—or at least litter artfully around their living spaces, in hopes that peers (read: girls) will notice them and be impressed—play a big role in defining themselves. Heck, the fact that they read at all—instead of just watching fucking bullshit reality television like the sheep in [insert name of dorm/frat/sorority we don't care for]—plays a big role in how their self-images are forged.

So every year, a new group of freshmen establish their individuality, disdain for conformity, and rapacious intellectual curiosity—they're *seekers*—by reading all the books they're supposed to. They're looking for road maps for life, for mentors and life lessons from the sages their older brothers and sisters and parents and cool uncles followed before them, men and women with magical names like Allen Ginsberg and William S. Burroughs and Henry Miller and Malcolm X and James Baldwin and Tom Robbins. They're looking to them as keys that open doors to dangerous ideas and exciting new adult worlds.

Such college students are rebels steeped in tradition, or at least the tradition of rebellion. Accordingly, much of the literature they gravitate toward is synonymous with scenes, countercultures, movements, and attractive people who bathe less often than they should and drink and smoke pot and fuck indiscriminately. There's a grungy glamour to so much of our extracurricular freshmen reading, and it's rooted in the cult of personality of writers like Tom Robbins.

Much of what attracts us as young people in search of an identity boils down to sex. By "we," I of course mean "me." We're drawn like Kennedys to an open bar by the aura of sex, danger, kink, and transgression that clings to the oeuvres of artists like Burroughs, Ginsberg, and Robbins. I could tell you I was originally intrigued by *Even Cowgirls Get The Blues* because it is an adaptation of a cult novel by a major filmmaker, but the truth is, I really just wanted to see lesbians lesbianing it up in a sapphic Western wonderland.

I was a college freshman, appropriately enough, when I saw *Even Cowgirls Get The Blues* on videotape in 1994. It would be a year before I lived in a co-op myself, but I was looking for a cinematic contact high from the drugs, groovy vibes, and sexual free-for-all of the era it depicted. But mainly, I hoped to see hot chicks getting it on. My high ideals were both at odds with my baser instincts and perfectly in sync with them.

"The sur-*prise* of Sissy Hankshaw is that she did not grow up a neurotic *disaster*," Tom Robbins drawls in the narration that opens the film, as a pint-sized incarnation of a protagonist who will grow up to be Uma Thurman blows out her birthday candles while being fêted by a trio of Eisenhower-era suburban grotesques. The period detail is assaultive, the performances cartoonish, and the narration self-consciously wacky.

The heroine of *Even Cowgirls Get The Blues* was born with a genetic abnormality: freakishly large thumbs that will someday allow her to become the world's greatest hitchhiker. Her parents (played by counterculture icon Ken Kesey and Grace Zabriskie) want their daughter to live a normal life. But Sissy Hankshaw quickly becomes fixated on hitchhiking as a way of life, a ticket outta Squaresville and onto the holy open road.

After getting picked up by a sharp-dressed black man, Sissy opines on the virtues of American cheese ("It's the king of road food") and talks cosmically of embodying "the spirit and heart of hitchhiking. I have the rhythms of the universe inside me. I'm in a state of grace." She rattles on and on in language that clings to the page and stubbornly refuses to become cinematic: "You may say that my pleasure in Indianhood and my passion for car travel might be incongruous, if not mutually exclusive. But after all, the first car that ever stopped for me had been named after the great chief of the Ottawa."

In New York City, far from her spiritual home on the highways and byways of our great country, Sissy meets up with mentor the Countess, a feminine-hygiene magnate played by John Hurt. The Countess first tries to get Sissy to lose her virginity to a Mohawk Indian watercolorist played by Keanu Reeves, but when that proves a bust, the Countess tells her to travel to the Rubber Rose Ranch, a "beauty farm" named after a popular line of douches, so Sissy can make a triumphant return to modeling in a feminine-hygiene ad costarring some legendary whooping cranes.

At the Rubber Rose Ranch, a civil war has broken out between the overly coiffed, sweet-smelling forces of repression and a group of saucy sapphic sensualists who call themselves Cowgirls and rebel against the narrow-minded bourgeoisie by smoking pot, taking peyote, having mind-blowing orgasms, and not washing their vaginas. Seriously. In *Blues,* the scatological is political; the film is fixated on the ideological ramifications of body odor. The Countess' obsession with purging women of their vaginal odors is representative of society denying women their sexuality, independence, and autonomy. The Cowgirls, however, are fierce and untamed: wild, natural creatures free to explore their passions and impulses, forces of nature that can't be controlled, conquered, or co-opted.

I didn't remember much about *Even Cowgirls Get The Blues* from my first viewing, beyond its tragic dearth of hot lesbian action, but I do remember being mightily impressed by Rain Phoenix as Bonanza Jellybean, Sissy's love interest and the leader of the Cowgirls. Looking back, I wonder exactly what kind of crack I was smoking in 1994, because Phoenix is fucking terrible here. Hilary Duff terrible. Malin Akerman in *Watchmen* terrible.

A brilliant, seasoned actor like John Hurt can barely wrap his lips around this stilted, overwritten dialogue, so you can imagine how awful the following lines sound when delivered in a Keanu Reeves–like monotone by a rank amateur like Phoenix:

> *Cowgirls exist as an image. A fairly common one. The idea of cowgirls, especially for little girls, prevails in our culture. Therefore, it seems to me that the existence of cowgirls should prevail.*

> *Every living thing is a chemical composition, and anything added to it changes that composition.*

> *This here discussion is destined to become academic.*

The elaborate, almost sadistic wordiness of those phrases might have a pleasing, perverse rhythm in print, but on-screen, they groan and lumber, secretly beckoning audiences to check their watches and contemplate dinner plans. Robbins' loopy poetry and stoner lyricism died somewhere in the fraught journey between page and screen.

Whimsy has a way of becoming grotesque when rendered in the literal-minded vocabulary of film.

Ah, but back to the plot. At the Rubber Rose Ranch, Sissy falls in love with Jellybean, but Sissy's allegiances are divided between her new lover and her old mentor. Looking to get away from the craziness, she makes a spiritual journey to visit a mysterious figure known only as "the Chink," played by Pat Morita. Morita is either a profound mystic or a horny old mountain goat. Possibly both. There's a Chauncey Gardiner–like mock profundity to his home-made aphorisms. Or they're bullshit. Or they're simultaneously bogus *and* profound. Free your mind, square! Forget bullshit fake dichotomies!

In *Blues,* the spiritual is wrapped up in the physical, which is wrapped up in the scatological, and everything is a cosmic joke. The Chink treats the world like a perverse laugh. His belief system succinctly boils down to, "Ha ha, ho ho, hee hee." Morita's sham mystic gets Sissy high, then has sex with her. That's life: You save yourself for Keanu Reeves and end up losing your virginity to Arnold from *Happy Days.*

Morita plays the character with an exquisitely light touch, as an amiable goof. If only the film had followed suit. Instead, *Blues* stumbles when it should skip. Morita's performance and k.d. lang's dreamy music both seem to belong in a different version of *Blues,* one that doesn't suck.

Blues goes from bad to worse when Sissy accidentally injures the Countess with her gargantuan thumb. In the groan-inducing words of Robbins' narration, "A sorrowful Sissy had her thumbs transport her to the one person she knew who could disarm her. Or should we say, de-*thumb* her." Thurman has her glorious thumbs reduced to normal size and loses her mojo in the process.

Meanwhile, back at the Rubber Rose Ranch, the Cowgirls have taken the whooping cranes—the beauty ranch's pride and joy—as hostages and are feeding them peyote to keep them from becoming pawns in the Countess' tawdry empire of shame and repression.

People sometimes complain about terrible adaptations ruining great books, to which the common and proper retort is that books will always exist as autonomous, untainted entities. *Blues* proves especially resilient; no matter how badly Van Sant tries to translate Robbins' text into cinematic form, it clings to its literary roots. It simply will not become a movie. In spite of Van Sant's considerable talent, *Even Cowgirls Get The Blues* feels throughout like the world's most elaborate, expensive staged reading.

I don't want to dissuade anyone from reading Tom Robbins. By all means, read Tom Robbins, young person, especially if you think it will help you get laid. Live. Love. Dream impractical dreams. Set out on a spiritual and intellectual journey of self-discovery with folks like Tom Robbins as your guides and gurus, even if you'll probably wind up with a mortgage, a drinking problem, a bad back, and a lifetime of regrets. (Man, I feel like I'm delivering the world's most depressing graduation speech here.) Don't let me kill your youthful idealism and curiosity. Life will do that for you soon enough.

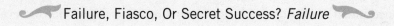

Failure, Fiasco, Or Secret Success? *Failure*

How Do You Solve A Problem Like *Lolita*? Book-Exclusive Case File: *Lolita*

Rereading *Lolita* for this Case File was like getting a chummy letter from an old friend. That might seem like an odd sentiment, considering that *Lolita* takes place largely in the psyche of a pedophile, alcoholic, and murderer. But revisiting *Lolita,* I discovered anew how much I like Humbert Humbert.

What's not to like, beyond murder, statutory rape, snobbery, deceit, sham marriage, sinister calculation, kidnapping, lying, and pedophilia? What I responded to was not Humbert's deplorable morals but rather a voice that is erudite, brutal, self-lacerating, viciously funny, sad, perversely wise, and oftentimes just plain perverse. Above all, Humbert speaks to us in a voice that is so brazenly modern that the book might as well have been written tomorrow.

More than half a century later, *Lolita* doesn't feel like a period piece. Vladimir Nabokov is still the smartest guy in the room, a man who perfected a highly evolved form of snark decades before "snark" became a nauseating buzzword. The world Humbert describes with such delicious disgust is recognizably our own, a naughty pop realm of motels and billboards, highways and ubiquitous advertising where the emptiness of pop culture assaults us from every direction in the form of clamorous pop songs, B-movies, and glossy magazines adorned with this week's reigning pretty boy.

It's a mad world filtered through the myopic prism of a madman. Humbert Humbert is the ultimate unreliable narrator. While professing to reveal all, he tilts everything in his favor. *Lolita* inhabits a moral universe so corrupt that it all but absolves its simultaneously self-deprecating and self-serving narrator of his mortal sins. Humbert presents himself not as a wolf in a henhouse, but rather as a wolf surrounded at all sides by mega-werewolves and figures beyond even H. P. Lovecraft's imagination.

So you see, ladies and gentlemen of the novel's imaginary jury, Humbert is ultimately blameless. It was that devilish minx Dolores Haze who seduced him. He was powerless before her nubile charms. He was likewise blameless in the unfortunate death, deceit, and betrayal of her mother. Surely a woman that pretentious, deluded, and worst of all gauche deserved to die. Actually, being run over by an errant automobile in the prime of her handsome womanhood was too good for such a monster of banality.

Humbert isn't even the worst pedophile in *Lolita*. That dubious honor belongs to Claire Quilty, shape-shifter, intellectual, appreciator/defiler of truth and beauty, sexual adventurer, orgy enthusiast, and child pornographer. Compared to his sinister shadow self, Humbert is a pussycat. Humbert ultimately isn't even to blame for his sexual attraction to preadolescent girls. Or rather that's what Humbert would have you believe. There are two big problems with Humbert's account: He's mad as a hatter, and he's lying.

Having written a memoir, I can attest that narrators have entirely too much power. The people I write about in *The Big Rewind: A Memoir Brought To You By Pop Culture* don't get the back half of my book to tell their version of the events chronicled within. It isn't *Rashomon*. It isn't a democracy, or a message board where the ghosts of my past can confront me. The reader is at my mercy. It's my version of the tale they're buying.

In the same vein, we see the tragicomic world of Humbert Humbert solely through his eyes. He seduces us with his wit, intellect, eloquence, and cracked romanticism. He renders us complicit in his crimes. This charming devil's greatest trick is not convincing the world that he doesn't exist, but rather that he's really not that bad, that it's the world that's mad and cruel, not him. Humbert may be a victim, but he's also a victimizer. Only in his own mind is he equal parts predator and prey.

"How did they ever make a movie of *Lolita*?" famously teased the tagline for Stanley Kubrick's deeply flawed, deeply compelling 1962 adaptation of Nabokov's masterpiece. It refers, of course, to the thorny problem of trying to smuggle an adaptation of a book about a man's passionate affair with a 12-year-old temptress past the puritanical busybodies of the early 1960s.

But it also speaks to an even larger problem facing filmmakers hoping to do right by Nabokov: So much of the book's brilliance is fundamentally unfilmable. It's rooted less in film-friendly fodder-like dialogue and plot than in the exquisite nastiness of Humbert's narration, in the unspeakably cruel, viciously funny little character studies of the sad souls who populate his tawdry tale. Humbert is like the world's meanest, funniest sociologist, casting a cold, judgmental eye toward the American booboisie in their natural habitat. He takes in their bizarre customs, laughable pretensions, shameless perversions, and pathetic delusions with visceral disgust. He's equally ruthless with himself. We see the world through Humbert's eyes as a realm of unspeakable beauty and unrelenting horror. He gets under our skin. We become one with Humbert.

Kubrick's film captures the dark comedy and scathing satire of Nabokov's novel while draining it of sex. Part of this is attributable to the times; had Kubrick filmed a doggedly faithful, literal adaptation, his film would have been banned in every country, and he'd be sent away as a child pornographer and moral degenerate.

Kubrick felt *Lolita* dragged after Humbert and his Lolita consummate their strange, cursed union, so he essentially skips directly from the hell of Humbert being around Lo without being able to consummate their strange bond to the torment of being at the mercy of a petulant, bratty lover who can destroy his life with a few words to a teacher or a policeman. He doesn't allow our antihero even a few moments of carnal heaven in between. In a 1969 interview with Joseph Gelmis, Kubrick said he bitterly regretted not being able to do justice to the erotic elements of the novel; he also reflected that he'd never have made the movie if he'd known the kind of restrictions censors would impose on his work.

While Kubrick gives us an understandably sexless *Lolita,* there's also a lot about it he gets right, beginning with the casting. Few actors convey inner torment like James Mason. In the 1956 Nicholas Ray masterpiece *Bigger Than Life,* Mason plunges deep into a moral abyss as a man driven so megalomaniacal by cortisone and the all-American lust for success that he's willing, even eager, to murder his son to make a point. So playing a man who lives to fuck little girls is a cakewalk by comparison.

The supporting roles are cast with equal aplomb. Shelley Winters engages in brilliant self-parody as a tragically tacky housewife convinced she's an intellectual. In Nabokov's brilliant turn of phrase, she's a "handsome woman" who represents to Humbert the infinite horrors, physical (womanly hips, full breasts, and wrinkled, sagging skin) and psychological, of the adult woman.

The casting of Peter Sellers proved even more inspired. Beefing up the Claire Quilty role remains the only way either Kubrick's film or the

1997 adaptation improved on the source material. In the book, Quilty functions as a ghost, a phantom whose presence is felt throughout but whose actual appearances are sporadic. He's Humbert's shadow self, a double who trumps him in every sense. Humbert writes and teaches about art; Quilty creates it. Humbert must pay for Lo's body; she willingly gives Quilty her heart. Quilty even tops Humbert in perversions; where Humbert is content with a single nymphet, Quilty needs to film a whole gaggle of children fornicating in novel formations in order to get it up. He even manages to die a more pathetic death than Humbert.

In many ways, Sellers seems to be playing himself, a sexually tormented chameleon uncomfortable in his own skin and happy only when adopting various masks. Just as there seems to have been no "real" Peter Sellers, Quilty is such a creature of the theater that he seems to exist only while pretending to be somebody else. When Humbert tries to get him to confess and atone for his sins at the end of the book—acting as a sublimely hypocritical priest/executioner—the best Quilty can muster is a bad vaudeville routine and a slapstick chase around his haunted mansion.

Where Kubrick was cursed by being able to show too little, Adrien Lyne, in his well-intentioned but hopelessly misguided 1997 adaptation, is cursed by being able to show too much. Lyne lingers over the erotic aspects of the book to such an extent he misses everything else. But his film does have one huge advantage over Kubrick's version in Dominique Swain's transcendent Lo, the daughter of Melanie Griffith's poignantly pathetic Charlotte Haze. Where Sue Lyon played Lo as a bleached-blond 25-year-old sexpot in the body of an adolescent, Swain plays her as a woman trapped in the purgatory between girlhood and adulthood. She's the Lo of Nabokov's novel, a reddish, coltish eternal ingenue with impossibly long limbs and a precocious seductiveness borrowed from teenybopper magazines and the popcorn movies she devours voraciously.

She's simultaneously brazenly sexual and disconcertingly girlish, as when she dances to an inane ditty with unself-conscious abandon. Swain's fearless performance alone gives the film a transgressive sexual charge only hinted at in Kubrick's version. It also made the film a prohibitively tricky proposition for American studios and a minor cause célèbre for a handful of prominent intellectuals—and also Erica Jong.

A 1998 piece by Jong in the *New York Observer* maps out the case for Lyne's *Lolita* in the shrillest, most hyperbolic terms imaginable, positing the film's inability to find theatrical distribution as yet another sad case of a serious European artist (in this case, the man behind *Flashdance* and *Indecent Proposal*) trying to bring great art to the masses and being confronted at every turn by the monkey-like screeching of puritans convinced the film was a ringing endorsement of pedophilia. In Jong's fevered imagination, Francis Ford Coppola and Steven Spielberg should take to the streets to protest what she describes as the film's "de facto censorship" at the hands of cowardly studios.

Is there an element of truth in Jong's rant? Perhaps. In addition to being residents of the greatest country ever (USA! USA! USA!), we Americans tend to be a little on the puritanical/hypocritical side where sex is concerned, especially when it comes to the young people. It's entirely possible that Joe and Jane America would blanch at paying bloated ticket prices to see a sexy film about a pedophile in a theater where they could easily be spotted by their pastor, grandmother, third-grade teacher, and Bible group. It's also likely that studios took a look at what Jong describes as a "$58 million art movie" and thought, to borrow the title of an early George Jones single, "There's no money in this deal." American studios would release sex fights between toddlers if they thought it would fatten their coffers.

Lyne brandished his supposed fidelity to Nabokov's novel as a sword of righteousness in his battles with would-be censors and critics. Yet he managed to preserve much of the book's text while completely missing its spirit. This is evident from the very first image of Jeremy Irons' Humbert Humbert swerving drunkenly in a giant old boat of a car en route to his showdown with Frank Langella's Claire Quilty. Irons purrs narration from the book, caressing each word as he lingers fetishistically on his memories of Lo. Words that ooze irony in the novel are uttered with hushed, breathy romanticism. Apparently no one told Lyne that *Lolita* is a comedy.

We then segue from this endgame to the ostensible cause of the protagonist's erotic fixation on nymphets: his tragically unconsummated romance with a childhood sweetheart. Lyne films Humbert's romanticized memories of his doomed romance as a cross between a half-remembered dream and an artsy perfume ad. It comes across not as the skeleton key that unlocks the most tortured secrets of its protagonist's troubled psyche but as a pedophile's self-mythology. It feels like a lie designed to trick readers into seeing the protagonist as a true romantic irrevocably scarred by the death of his first true love, instead of as a dangerous sex criminal.

Over the course of Nabokov's *Lolita*, Humbert's unreliable narrator performs a delicate psychological striptease in which he reveals only what he wants the audience to know. Yet he still exposes himself as a misanthrope devoid of empathy and oblivious to anything but his sexual conquest of Lo. Watching Irons brood thoughtfully and gaze longingly throughout *Lolita*, I was struck with the notion that Lyne had made a *Lolita* Humbert Humbert would endorse, one that would vindicate him in the eyes of history. Lyne's *Lolita* unleashes Humbert's sexuality while castrating his wit and misanthropy.

To cite a single example, Kubrick stages as brutal black comedy the scene where Mason's Humbert reads a letter in which Charlotte professes her *amour fou* for her handsome lodger in the most histrionic manner imaginable and begs him to flee the house permanently while she's gone unless he wants to be with her forever as man and wife. Humbert reads Charlotte's maudlin sentiments—her wholesale misuse of basic French in a pathetic attempt to appear worldly is a particularly deft touch, *n'est-ce pas*—with withering sarcasm and undisguised contempt, laughing a dark, cruel laugh during especially earnest, overwrought parts. True, Nabokov never actually writes that Humbert laughed derisively as he read the letter. But how could he have responded any other way?

Nabokov and Kubrick's Humbert is a cracked actor who must adopt a series of socially acceptable poses—visiting educator, harmless lodger, loyal husband, single father—to keep the world from seeing his true self. In moments like these, that façade of normalcy and propriety cracks and we see Humbert as he truly is—a petty tyrant who snorts derisively while a dreadful but sincere woman nakedly pours out her heart.

Now compare this to how Lyne stages the scene. In Lyne's version, when Humbert reads the letter in Lo's bed while cradling one of her teddy bears, it's the voice of Griffith's lovestruck Charlotte Haze we hear. Irons' face reveals next to nothing: not contempt, not disdain, not revulsion at such a grotesque display of emotion, just a mischievous hint of delight when Charlotte asks him to become a father to her daughter. This is a subtler reading of the scene, but it's also less powerful. A scene of cathartic black comedy becomes one of muted drama.

Where Lyne skimps on black comedy, he goes overboard with sex. Lyne gives us a gauzy, soft-focus, softcore version of Nabokov; think of it as *Lolita After Dark*. Kubrick brought to *Lolita* his genius as an ironist. He molds the material in his image. Lyne does the same, transforming one of literature's funniest, darkest comedies into an endless procession of pretty pictures set to Ennio Morricone's swooning score.

By making the film a period piece and lingering over period trappings, Lyne robs the book of its urgency and modernity. It becomes something that happened to dead people long ago. In the process, it loses much of its transgressive charge. Lyne does, however, do justice to the title character. Since *Lolita* is seen through Humbert's eyes and he sees Lo as a sexual creature above all else, we almost lose sight of Lo's remarkable resolve.

There is a moment of enormous power in the Lyne version where

Lo lets out an animal moan of despair upon learning that her mother is dead, and we realize just how deeply she's been wounded. She's lost her father, her brother (a detail Humbert sees fit to mention only in passing, as if it were no more consequential than the passing of a house cat), and now her mother, leaving her at the mercy of a sexual predator. But her spirit remains unbroken, and she retains a spark of life and a streak of mischievous wit. Lo is the book's hero; her triumph is the resilience of the human spirit. She's strong enough to go through hell yet still be able to give herself—if not her heart—to her husband, a good, decent, simple man who is the opposite of both Humbert and Quilty.

Lyne's *Lolita* comes close to redeeming itself with a heartbreaking scene where Humbert visits the now married and pregnant Lo, looking dowdy, plain, and millions of miles removed from the frolicsome nymphet of Humbert's imagination. In this scene, the past takes on an almost physical presence as Humbert discovers that he really does love Lo, not just the glorious ghost that troubles his imagination. Lust has turned to love. But it's too late.

Like the *Simpsons* episode where Lisa rejects the romantic advances of Ralph Wiggum, if you freeze-frame either the Kubrick or Lyne *Lolita,* you can literally pinpoint the exact moment when Humbert's heart breaks and the tiny little shred of hope he's clung to zealously in the face of overwhelming blackness disintegrates. It's when Lo gets a dreamy, faraway look in her eyes and gushes that Claire Quilty was the only man she *really* ever loved, that everyone else—her husband, Humbert—was just a poor substitute. It's not that Lo was averse to giving her heart to a sexual deviant; it's that Humbert was the *wrong* sexual deviant. After that, all that's left for Humbert is murder, incarceration, and the sweet release of the grave, followed by an eternity of hellfire. But nothing Satan could hurl at Humby could wound him more profoundly than the ecstatic gleam in dear, tragic Lo's eyes when she beams about her beloved Claire.

Nabokov described *Lolita* as a product of his "love affair with the

English language." Lyne's *Lolita* ironically includes more of Nabokov's words than Kubrick's but misses their meaning and context. He's created a kinder, gentler Humbert Humbert. He's cleaned up Humbert's act while doing him the ultimate injustice: transforming a great literary monster into a lovelorn sap.

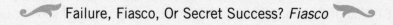 Failure, Fiasco, Or Secret Success? *Fiasco*

Chapter 6

My Year Of Flops Jr.: "You Know, For Kids!"

When Middle-Aged Puppet-Men Attack! Case File #78: *Pinocchio*
Originally Posted October 23, 2007

When *Life Is Beautiful* began to conquer the United States, it made writer, director, and star Roberto Benigni the most beloved Italian export since pizza. By the time Benigni's nightmare reign of whimsy had reached an end, he was the most reviled Italian this side of Mussolini. He had devolved into a fascist of the heart whose message seemed to be, "Love me and my adorable antics, or I crush you like a bug. Oh no, I use up all my English making love-threat-promise to the moon!"

Benigni's meteoric rise and precipitous fall serve as cautionary warnings about the dangers about overstaying your welcome. The impish man-child had been a familiar face to arthouse denizens for decades, thanks to his uniformly awesome collaborations with Jim Jarmusch, and a huge star in his native Italy and Europe for much longer. Yet in spite of an ill-fated, American-made attempt at reviving the *Pink Panther* series with Benigni in the lead role in the early '90s, the incorrigible Italian ham was largely an unknown quantity state-side until late in the decade.

Life Is Beautiful changed all that. On paper, a heartwarming family comedy–drama set in a concentration camp must have looked like a recipe for disaster. When Jerry Lewis mined similar territory in 1972's *The Day The Clown Cried*, the result was the most notorious unreleased movie in history. Yet when Benigni mugged his way through the bleakest corners of Nazi Germany, he became an international icon.

Beautiful opened to mostly strong reviews and unprecedented box office en route to becoming one of the top-grossing foreign films of all time. Our country's embrace of Benigni reached its apex when he won the Academy Award for Best Actor and *Beautiful* won Best Foreign Film. In an ecstatic frenzy, Benigni leaped on top of chairs rushing to the podium, where he expressed a desire to kidnap, then make love to everybody, and other assorted nonsense. The Oscar clip-reel moment simultaneously cemented Benigni's place in American pop culture and hastened his decline.

As a backlash quickly gained momentum, Benigni became less adorable by the second. Parodies of Benigni's antics started popping up everywhere, from *The Simpsons* to *Saturday Night Live*. People began asking troubling questions. Was Benigni a modern-day Charlie Chaplin or a less-hirsute Robin Williams? Was *Life Is Beautiful* a timeless testament to the power of imagination and hope, or a crass vanity project? Had we as a culture been suckered? Was the emperor of middlebrow whimsy at least a tad bit underdressed?

Benigni's decision to follow *Beautiful* with a 2002 adaptation of *Pinocchio* with himself in the lead role answered all those questions. What sane 50-year-old casts himself as a little boy? Then again, what sane human being thinks, "You know what would be the perfect setting for a heartwarming family movie? A concentration camp!"? One of those bad ideas made Benigni's stateside career. The other took it away.

The casting of a clearly middle-aged man as a prepubescent scamp would be enough to sink most movies. But the American release of *Pinocchio* amplified that miscalculation by replacing Benigni's instantly recognizable voice with that of journeyman American actor and voice-over specialist Breckin Meyer. In a bizarre bit of intergenerational ventriloquism, the voice of a 50-year-old Italian pretending to be a puppet boy was overdubbed by a twentysomething American.

Pinocchio tries to explain away its never-ending parade of jarring incongruities with twinkling narration that ushers viewers gently into a land where "animals can speak, a child can look like a grown-up, and very often grown-ups can act like children." The narrator neglects to mention that in this magical land of Fantastical Vanity Projects, the words people speak are often bitterly at odds with the movements of their lips.

Pinocchio opens with an impish log being made into a puppet blessed with the gift of life. Breckini's papa oozes pride as he puts the finishing touches on his wooden brainchild: sagging skin, wrinkles aplenty, and a rapidly receding hairline. It's adorable that in this version, the kindly puppet maker chooses to make a puppet roughly his own age: He's less a child surrogate than a potential canasta partner. Breckini comes alive and prances about wearing more makeup than a two-dollar Parisian whore and a smock that looks like it was made out of any Jewish grandmother's floral-print slipcovers.

In spite of stern warnings from his cricket sidekick/conscience, Breckini quickly develops a taste for trouble. Instead of going to school, he heads to a puppet theater, where he's nearly devoured by a sentimental giant, who ultimately takes pity on him and gives him five gold coins. The coins quickly find their way into the pockets of the Cat and the Fox, scoundrels who don black executioner hoods redolent of both Ku Klux Klan robes and the prisoner-abuse scandal at Abu Ghraib. Then they string Breckini up on a tree branch and leave him to die in front of an impossibly huge and luminous moon. The Blue Fairy (played by Nicoletta Braschi, Benigni's real-life wife, and voiced by Glenn Close) takes pity on the poor, misguided puppet and saves him from certain death.

This establishes a pattern from which the film seldom deviates: Breckini must choose between doing right and doing wrong. He invariably chooses wrong, suffers disproportionately, and faces imminent destruction, only to be bailed out at the last minute by the Blue Fairy, the film's trusty, oft-employed deus ex machina. Many of these grim elements are taken directly from Carlo Collodi's original novel, but that doesn't make them any less jarring.

If the image of Breckini dangling from a tree isn't enough to traumatize tykes, just a few minutes later, a group of rabbit pallbearers show up at his bedside with a coffin. The rabbit pallbearers are supremely peeved, and they slink away glumly when Breckini makes a miraculous recovery.

Breckini eventually ends up behind bars with fellow juvenile delinquent Leonardo (voiced by Topher Grace) who confides in hushed tones, "I've got something to show you." Leonardo then whips out a sweet candy phallus of a lollipop and regales Breckini with the story of how he purloined 29 lollipops from a candy store before a cop busted him. "I was just about to lick the first one," Leonardo shares conspiratorially, "and then I heard a policeman call out to me, 'Put that tongue back, robber. And hand back those 28 lollipops you have in your pocket.'"

Oozing envy, Breckini pleads, "Will you give me one little lick? Just one?" Leonardo willingly acquiesces. "You lick here, me there. You lick first," he demands. They then take turns double-teaming the lollipop with long, passionate, open-mouthed, obscenely sensual licks.

After being released from jail, Breckini encounters a gravestone suggesting that the Blue Fairy died from Pinocchio-related causes. Distraught, he pleads, "How do you become dead? I wanna be dead too!" Other than homoeroticism and miscalculation, Benigni's *Pinocchio* is distinguished by a perverse, consistent morbidity in the form of rabbit pallbearers, hangings, and the ever-present specter of death.

Breckini eventually follows Leonardo to Fun Foreverland, a paradise where suspiciously mature-looking "boys" frolic, play, wrestle, and prance about in a girl-free environment.

Still more pain and humiliation await Breckini. He's transformed into a donkey, made to work in a sleazy circus, subjected to the vocal stylings of Regis Philbin, and tossed into the ocean to await a watery grave. Yet the Blue Fairy bails Breckini out of every bind, then makes him into a real boy.

In the transcendent Disney version, *Pinocchio* emerges as a powerful coming-of-age allegory about forsaking the pleasures of adolescence and embracing adult responsibility. Yet Benigni's career is predicated on remaining a child forever. If he had listened to his sober inner adult, he'd never have attempted a project this insanely ambitious or ambitiously insane.

Rewatching *Pinocchio*, I admired its unsupportable belief that audiences would somehow be willing to overlook the incongruity of a 50-year-old Pinocchio and surrender their defenses at the altar of childhood innocence. *Pinocchio* is exactly the sort of weirdly compelling, utterly singular personal project I wanted to pay homage to with My Year Of Flops, even if I wouldn't recommend it to anyone but the morbidly curious.

Pinocchio was originally envisioned as a collaboration between Benigni and Federico Fellini, but I doubt even Fellini could have redeemed a project this fundamentally flawed, though he might have pushed the project's innate weirdness to dizzyingly surreal levels. I suspect that the Italian version is preferable to its American bastardization, and while I planned to watch both before writing this entry, I was sent two copies of the dubbed version. There are limits even to my pop-culture masochism. Unlike Benigni, I know when I'm licked.

 Failure, Fiasco, Or Secret Success? *Fiasco*

Roberto Benigni On *Pinocchio*

Excitable, rubber-faced cut-up Roberto Benigni is an Academy Award–winning writer, actor, comedian, and director. A huge star in his native Italy, Benigni made an indelible impression on American arthouse audiences with scene-stealing appearances in cult classic Jim Jarmusch films like *Down By Law, Coffee & Cigarettes,* and *Night On Earth* before triumphing internationally as the writer, director, and star of the 1997 Holocaust comedy-drama *Life Is Beautiful.*

Roberto Benigni: *Pinocchio* was a big success in Italy, but it didn't go very well around the world because it was a very particular project. Very Italian and very scary also because it was a bold move, having Pinocchio acted by a man of 50 years old. So it was a very, very special project. I put in this movie all my energy, all my oomph, I would say. It wasn't received very good around the world, but it's a project that I love very, very much.

And you know, there are some movies that are loved and some less. But I am really very proud to have presented one of the most wonderful characters for Italy and the world too, because Pinocchio is a universal subject. Now, Walt Disney did a very American version, which I like very much. But I tried to do this Italian version of *Pinocchio* with a lot of liberty, and a lot of visual imagination. But it was also very hard, very difficult to understand. And I understand the reception of the movie. It could be difficult for some of the audience.

Nathan Rabin: Were you worried that because you were 50, audiences wouldn't accept you in that role?

RB: Sometimes it happens, this is not a problem. In United States, they give me such a generous reception of *Life Is Beautiful,* my previous movie, that really I owe to United States a lot of love, because they were so generous at me with this movie.

NR: People also were a little confused, because in the American version your voice was dubbed. What was the thinking behind that?

RB: Sometimes the dubbing, you know, it's really a difficult thing to understand. In Italy, we are used to the dubbing because they dub every movie, you know. But not in United States. They think it's better to not dub the movie. It's a problem. We don't know how to present a movie, because subtitles also are difficult, especially for a movie like *Pinocchio,* which is addressed to boys, to children. So they cannot read the entire time. And I am an actor who talks very, very much during the movies, so it's a problem.

NR: Right, but why dub your voice? You have such a—

RB: I know, but I repeat I am really so happy about *Pinocchio* because I did what I felt. It's a very honest movie. And if it's not received very good—for example, in Italy and Japan they loved the movie a lot. So sometimes it happens. But this is, I repeat, very, very normal.

Fuck You, Jew Case File #96: *Santa Claus: The Movie*
Originally Posted December 25, 2007

There's nothing lonelier than being a Jew on Christmas. When someone says, "Merry Christmas," all I hear is, "Fuck you, Jew." When someone says, "Happy holidays," what he really means is, "Fuck you, Jew." When they say "Happy Chanakoonah," that's ultimately just another way of saying, "Fuck you, Jew." When someone at work says, "Hey, Nathan, can I borrow your *Juno* screener?" all I hear is, "Fuck you, Jew." Man, I really need to go back on my meds. Fucking seasonal depression.

Ah, but Christmas isn't really about religion, you say. It's that most wonderful time of the year when people forget their troubles and join together to worship the Great God of Commerce and his little buddy Jesus. We pay tribute to the Great God of Commerce with maxed-out credit cards, personal checks, and plain old cash. But then, in a culture-wide fit of passive-aggression, we turn our backs on Him by bombarding children with movies, television shows, and songs where materialism is climactically renounced and everyone learns the True Meaning of Christmas. If these renunciations of greed succeed, then they make everyone involved lots and lots of money, year in and year out.

1985's *Santa Claus: The Movie* represented a transparent attempt to spin a *Superman*-like franchise out of the world's most indulgent gift-giver. Actually, Santa Claus and Superman have more in common than films produced by Ilya Salkind and cowritten by David New-man. They both can fly. They're both magic. They both got to witness the sad decline of Kevin Spacey's film career up close—Santa in *Fred Claus*, Superman in *Superman Returns*. And they both fucked Margot Kidder back when that meant something.

Like *Superman, Santa Claus: The Movie* offers an elaborate cre-ation story for one of our culture's most beloved icons. Santa (David Huddleston) was just your average jelly-bellied gift-giving enthusiast until a group of immortal little people make Santa an offer he can't refuse: Deliver presents to all the gentile girls and boys on Christmas for the rest of eternity in exchange for immortality and the ability to fly. For a morbidly obese gentleman on the verge of a heart attack, that's an irresistible deal. Besides, it isn't as if he has much choice in the matter: He can either deliver toys until the end of time or he can wake up in bloody sheets next to Prancer's severed head. Elves don't fuck around.

The film's surprisingly not terrible first half cruises through all sorts of landmarks in Santa Claus' evolution. At one point, the jolly son of a bitch expresses a suspiciously socialist belief that "every child should get a present," but then he learns the error of his ways and implements his patented double-checked list delineating the naughty from the nice.

As long as it's fixated on the goings-on at the North Pole, the film remains on solid footing. The elves' workshop is so bright and cheery, it's easy to forget it's a sweatshop, and the special effects are slick and convincing, especially where flying is concerned. But the moment the outside world comes into play, the film's cornball charm disappears.

Santa needs an assistant, so he hooks up with an enterprising elf named Patch, played by Dudley Moore. Alas, Patch's modernization of Santa's factory results in shoddy workmanship, defective toys, wide-spread sobbing, and a furious backlash against Ol' Saint Nick. Chil-dren associated with him are terrorized. Bullies taunt a rich orphan (Carrie Kei Heim) by sneering, "How can you be so dumb, Cornelia? Everyone knows he gives out shoddy cheap toys. My daddy says he's an old fake." Another pint-sized hooligan twists the knife by braying, "My parents gave me a doll that says whole sentences on a cassette. You don't have any parents, so nyaaaahh!"

After the Christmas disaster, Patch resigns in disgrace and heads to New York, where he offers his services to sinister defective-toy merchant B.Z. (John Lithgow), a cigar-chomping archvillain desperately in need of good PR. I hope someday to be rich enough to smoke giant cigars while cackling maniacally.

Patch and B.Z. set out to beat Santa at his own game by giving out fantastical lollipops that allow people to fly. Literally. How can Santa compete? He can't, so he sinks into a holly, jolly suicidal depression. It's a good thing the elves hid all the knives, ropes, and sleeping pills from their morbidly obese boss until his ennui lifted. When an elf diplomatically shows Santa a new doll that wets itself, all Saint Nick can muster is a dispirited, "But does it fly?"

In spite of its title, *Santa Claus: The Movie* ignores Santa for long stretches of its dreary second half in order to focus on the low-wattage antics of a pair of moppets: a rich girl (Heim) who says things like, "Would you like some cookies? They're from Bloomingdale's!" and a Damon Runyon–esque scamp (Christian Fitzpatrick) who gazes longingly into the window of a McDonald's at a happy family enjoying the beloved fast-food chain's wide array of delicious products. The two form a bond that transcends class lines when the girl leaves a mouth-watering can of Coke and leftovers for her homeless Santa-loving pal.

B.Z.'s greed ultimately gets the best of him. When Fitzpatrick's scamp discovers Lithgow's evil scheme to sell dangerous, potentially deadly flying candy canes, he ends up bound and gagged until Santa shows up to save the day. And quite possibly save Christmas. And deliver a death blow to his unwanted competition. It's the free market at work!

As the film lurches to a close, the tone veers between the curdled dark comedy of Lithgow's scenery-chewing, highly theatrical performance and maudlin, sentimental speeches like, "People don't seem to care about giving a gift just so they can see the light of happiness in a friend's eyes. It just doesn't feel like Christmas anymore" and "If you give extra kisses, you get bigger hugs. That's what Santa's wife is always saying."

Then there are elf-themed puns: Patch insists that the magic lollipop's flying powers are "elf-explanatory," that he does not lack "elf-assurance," and that ultimately, "Heaven helps those who help their elf." Plot proves the death of *Santa Claus: The Movie*. Whenever the film strays from Santa's well-worn mythology, it flounders, and the cynicism at the film's core rises to the surface. As with so many Christmas movies, the anti-materialist sermonizing feels disingenuous, since *Santa Claus: The Movie* is a moneymaking venture first, second, third, fourth, and fifth, and a creative endeavor a distinct sixth.

Yet *Santa Claus: The Movie* ended up angering the Great God of Commerce by losing a mint for Tristar. There would be no sequels, no remakes, no Superman/Santa crossovers where Santa Claus is forced to kneel before Zod . . . just a bleak yuletide for everyone involved.

〜 Failure, Fiasco, Or Secret Success? *Failure* 〜

Totally Tween Case File #118: *Bratz: The Movie*
Originally Posted September 17, 2008

While on vacation, I briefly became addicted to A&E's *The Two Coreys*. In my favorite episode, Corey Feldman, concerned that his tragicomic bud Corey Haim has become a pill-popper, convinces Todd Bridges and Pauly Shore to confront Haim about his substance abuse. As Bridges and Shore contemplate the task at hand, they're overcome with a profound sense of life's ridiculousness. How did they get there? What crime did they commit in a past life to merit this karmic mind fuck? Even Pauly Shore, Todd Bridges, and Corey Feldman found the prospect of a semi-intervention featuring Pauly

Shore, Todd Bridges, and Corey Feldman to be surreal. You know your life has spun out of control when Pauly Shore is lecturing you about responsibility.

I know the feeling. There are times in everyone's life when the randomness of fate blindsides you. Don DeLillo, Kurt Vonnegut, and David Foster Wallace masterfully chronicled the often ugly, sometimes sublime preposterousness of our universe. They allow readers to take a step back and see the things we all take for granted in a new, disorientingly foreign light, to see the bizarre in the familiar and the familiar in the bizarre.

I experienced a similarly uncanny sense of life's absurdity when I sat down in a small, cold room on the 16th floor of a nondescript building in downtown Chicago with a platoon of pasty, shabbily dressed middle-aged men in 2007 to watch a series of flickering images and shiny, happy noise called *Bratz: The Movie,* a live-action movie designed to sell a popular line of skanky plastic dolls. Here's what the American Psychological Association had to say about these plastic pop tarts:

> *Bratz dolls come dressed in sexualized clothing such as miniskirts, fishnet stockings, and feather boas. Although these dolls may present no more sexualization of girls or women than is seen in MTV videos, it is worrisome when dolls designed specifically for 4- to 8-year-olds are associated with an objectified adult sexuality.*

Alas, those spoilsport eggheads in the APA were no match for the Bratz spokesman (you gotta wonder whom *he* killed in a previous life), who defended the dolls with the withering retort, "The Bratz brand, which has remained number one in the UK market for 23 consecutive months, focuses core values on friendship, hair play, and a 'passion for fashion.'"

Bruno Bettelheim argued that a proper appreciation of "hair play" is a vital component of every child's emotional development. And Abraham Maslow made "passion for fashion" a cornerstone of his hierarchy of needs. But *Bratz's* inspiring message of hair play, cultivating a passion for fashion, and friendship is largely wasted on the killjoys in the APA. Also, film critics.

The folks at the screening room were, perhaps, not the ideal audience for a movie about clothing-obsessed teenage girls. When the film began, I wondered why *Bratz* was being screened for critics at all. Did the *Bratz*keteers expect us to respond to their product with anything other than disdain? Couldn't *Bratz: The Movie* just as easily be titled *Not Screened For Critics: The Movie*?

Bratz's first sequence establishes a tone of psychotic peppiness, as the Bratz approach choosing outfits for the first day of high school with orgasmic glee. Ah, but *Bratz* isn't afraid to delve into deep issues. One of the girls has divorced parents. Another left her turquoise shirt at her friend's house.

Bratz veers into *Afterschool Special* territory when one of the girls literally runs into a boy who's cute but also deaf, and they have the following exchange:

Brat: What are you, blind?
Totally Hot Deaf Guy: No, but I'm deaf.
Brat: What?
Totally Hot Deaf Guy: I'm deaf.
Brat: You don't sound deaf.
Totally Hot Deaf Guy: Well, you don't look ignorant, but I guess you can't judge a book, right?

Bratz isn't done teaching valuable life lessons about how the deaf are just like you and me, only hotter, and way better DJs. In a remarkable sequence, the hot hearing-impaired athlete learns that being deaf and being def are not mutually exclusive when a sensitive Mr. Chips–type teaches him how to fuck shit up old school on the turntables by feeling the vibrations, Funky Bunch style.

He isn't just a brooding, telegenic deaf guy: He's a deaf jock who loves playing the piano and is also an awesome DJ. He's got five minutes of screen time and 18 different facets to his personality. I expect the deleted scenes will reveal that he's also an orphan, a Jehovah's Witness, a monarchist, double-jointed, telekinetic, and an illegal immigrant.

The four Bratz enter high school intent on ruling the school in their respective niches. "I'm owning the science!" enthuses the Asian science geek with rad cotton-candy-blue hair extensions. That line is followed by the record-skipping sound effect that serves as bad-movie shorthand for, "Oh snap, something zany just happened!"

This vexes the black cheerleader, who frets, "Okay! Work the IQ, girl, but please don't lose your passion for fashion!" The message is clear: Learning about science is all well and good, as long as it doesn't interfere with the superficial things that really matter.

In spite of their oft-repeated promises to remain BFF, the girls are pulled in opposite directions by their overriding passions. The jock abandons her friends to hang out with the jocks. The cheerleader kicks it with the cheerleaders, the geek blends in with the brains, and the girl with little discernible personality but a gift for making bitching clothes presumably hangs out with other girls with little discernible personality and a flair for sewing.

We then flash-forward two years. The girls' utopia of shared clothes and daily video-IM-ing chitchats has died at the hands of cliques and the narrow-minded tyranny of the school's most popular student. In a moment of haunting sadness, two of the Bratz reconnect briefly over their shared love of Peach Party lip gloss, only to watch their fragile bond dissipate just as quickly.

Then, with the help of shopping-and-trying-on-makeup montages, the Bratz resurrect their friendship. These montages contain the film's defining sequence, in which a gaggle of prepubescent girls gaze adoringly at the Bratz. In their infinite kindness, the Bratz decide to provide makeovers for these 8-year-old representatives of the target audience for the Bratz film and toy line. The moppets begin as ordinary girls, a little awkward and ungainly. Then the Bratz slather on the whore makeup and transform their pint-sized protégés into creepily sexualized Jon-Benét Ramsey doppelgängers. Oh, if only they could reach through the screen and do the same for all the 8-year-olds in the audience! In spite of such blatant pandering, *Bratz* mercifully bombed at the box office, thereby sparing the world an endless procession of theatrically released *Bratz* sequels and knockoffs.

The girls' bond and commitment to subverting the dominant paradigm threatens the school's most popular student, a pretty blond tyrant named Meredith that Chelsea Staub plays as a cross among Josef Stalin, Paris Hilton, and Tracy Flick from *Election*. Meredith's father, incidentally, is played by Jon Voight, though to be fair, he probably took the part only to pay back *Bratz* producer Steven Paul for giving Voight his career-making role in *Superbabies: Baby Geniuses 2*, as an ascot-wearing, smoking-jacket-and-Hitler-mustache-sporting German businessman engaged in a decades-long, multi-continent struggle with a superscamp who travels around in a flying car and never ages. Voight is nothing if not loyal. And insane.

To thwart the Bratz's sinister campaign to spread fashion, friendship, and montages set to peppy pop songs across clique divides, Meredith decides to throw herself a second sweet 16 party. The catch? In order to attend her chichi soiree, attendees are forced to agree to associate only with their cliques. Even worse, Meredith hires one of the Bratz's mothers to cater the affair. In *Bratz*'s fantasy world, even the girl without money has money. The film's idea of poverty is a mom who owns a catering business, and a computer-owning teenager who scoots around on a moped instead of in a sports car.

At said party, Meredith humiliates the singing, personality-devoid Brat by showing a video of her singing "La Cucaracha" with mom/all-purpose ethnic Lainie Kazan. Ha! That girl totally has a mother! And she doesn't always look like a runway model! Could she *be* any lamer? Tragedy turns to triumph, however, when a sympathetic DJ fucks up the mix, and soon everyone is boogying to a hip-hopified version of "La Cucaracha." But triumph soon morphs back into tragedy when a party elephant kicks Meredith into the pool. An enraged Meredith blames the Bratz for ruining her party, when we all know an unruly pachyderm was at fault. Must party elephants always spoil everything?

Suddenly, the same classmates who embraced the Bratz as liberators from the tyranny of cliques shun the fashion-forward foursome for costing them sweet 16 gift bags. Clearly, only a climactic performance of a song espousing the virtues of "Brattitude" at the big talent show can set things right and put Meredith in her place. Meredith and her nemeses are all about clothes, glamour, and performing forgettable synth-pop ditties. The crucial difference is that Meredith uses clothes and generic dance-pop to destroy; the Bratz use it to uplift and edutain.

Watching *Bratz* the first time around, I was filled with profound amusement, albeit not with the film so much as the culture that would produce such a shiny pink monstrosity. It's tempting to argue that the toy-pimping opus represents the evil of banality, but *Bratz* is far too stupid to be worthy of hate. I was less amused by *Bratz* the second time around, in part because the insane incongruity of watching such disposable pop-culture ephemera while surrounded by middle-aged men was gone. I was amused, however, by the DVD's coming attractions for animated adventures starring *Bratz: Kids* and *Bratz: Babies*. Can *Bratz: Fetuses* ("When your womb needs a makeover, these style-conscious prehumans take over!") and *Bratz: Spermatozoa* ("You will not believe how they accessorize their flagella!") be far behind?

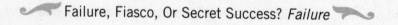 Failure, Fiasco, Or Secret Success? *Failure*

Chapter 7

The Floppiest Flops

Honestly Unpopular Case File #3: *Ishtar*
Originally Posted February 2, 2007

Comic genius Elaine May has led a schizophrenic existence as both an in-demand script doctor and a ferociously independent, obsessive überauteur who would rather feed her children to wolves than let a script doctor (or studio head) tinker with her vision.

May's control-freak tendencies are legendary. She made her directorial debut with 1971's *A New Leaf,* a dark screwball comedy about a deliciously sour misanthrope/professional ne'er-do-well (Walter Matthau, channeling W. C. Fields) who leads a pampered life happily devoid of substance until his inheritance runs out and he sets upon marrying, then murdering a daffy heiress (May) for her money.

In a troubling omen, producer Howard Koch Jr. tried unsuccessfully to get May fired. The film's budget more than doubled. After 10 months of editing, May still wouldn't let Paramount see the film. Paramount essentially had to wrestle the film away from her. *A New Leaf*'s paltry box office, coupled with Paramount's trials trying to wean the film from May's clutches, would be enough to kill the careers of most filmmakers. But May was too talented and strong willed to let that happen. *A New Leaf* was followed by May's sole box-office success: 1973's *The Heartbreak Kid*, a trenchant exploration of the perils of assimilation and the spiritual emptiness of the American dream.

An acidic companion piece to *The Graduate* (which was directed by May's former comedy partner, Mike Nichols), *Heartbreak* follows a directionless young schmuck (Charles Grodin) who dumps his sunburn-addled new wife (Jeannie Berlin, May's daughter) on their honeymoon to recklessly pursue shiksa goddess Cybill Shepherd. Where *The Graduate* ended on a famously ambiguous note, *Heartbreak*'s ending borders on emotionally apocalyptic. In a neat inversion of romantic comedy orthodoxy, pursuing an impossible dream girl turns out to be not just wrong, but immoral. *Heartbreak*'s bleakly ironic ending asks, "What does it profit a man to get the girl but lose his soul?" Grodin ends up with Shepherd, but it's a victory so empty it doubles as a crushing defeat.

May's follow-up, 1976's brilliant John Cassavetes homage *Mikey & Nicky*, found the enfant terrible once again inducing mass aneurysms in the Paramount executive suites. Her budget once again ballooned to more than twice its original size, and May again retreated to her bunker and steeled herself for another round of warfare with her corporate overlords. This cinematic David couldn't help picking fights with the Goliaths of her industry.

Lawsuits were filed and release dates missed by over a year. May was fired in postproduction, then rehired when she cunningly hid two reels of the film to ensure that it could not be completed without her. Paramount was not amused, and it buried the film.

By this point, May embodied "box-office poison." She should have been unemployable as a director. She was litigious. She was expensive. She was difficult. She viewed studios as enemies rather than collaborators or benefactors. From a commercial perspective, investing in an Elaine May film made only slightly more sense than purchasing magic beans or building a building a bonfire out of out of hundred-dollar bills.

Then in the mid-'80s, something inexplicable happened; Columbia gave Elaine May somewhere between $30 to $55 million to direct a comedy with two of the biggest movie stars in the world. If one of the marks of insanity involves doing the same thing repeatedly yet expecting a different outcome, then the studio executives should have been fitted en masse for straitjackets.

Where *A New Leaf* and *Mikey & Nicky* were small films that grew big and unwieldy, 1987's *Ishtar* was a big film that became the poster child for Hollywood excess. It embodies a phenomenon I call "the Curse of Bigness." The Bing Crosby/Bob Hope road movies that *Ishtar* riffs on reveled in cheapness and artifice, in rear projection and back-lot "deserts." So it seems perverse that *Ishtar* goes all David Lean with the production values, roping in the great Vittorio Storaro (*Apocalypse Now*) as cinematographer and filming on location in Morocco. *Ishtar*'s ballooning budget became the story instead of the film itself. The question became less, "Is it funny?" than "Does it provide $30 to $55 million worth of laughs?"

What could inspire studio suits to abandon their solemn fiduciary responsibilities to shareholders and re-up for another voyage onboard the Elaine May Express to Pauperville? The answer lies with the film's producer and star, Warren Beatty. If Hollywood is a status-obsessed high school, then Beatty is the valedictorian, class president, lead in the class play, and star quarterback in one shimmering package. And if the class president says his friend the weird girl who edits the yearbook should get Richard Avedon to shoot photos of the glee club, then who are we to doubt his wisdom?

According to a talk she gave with Mike Nichols after a sold-out screening of *Ishtar* at the Walter Reade Theater in 2006, May semi-seriously designed the film as a Trojan horse to smuggle a trenchant critique of American foreign policy inside a seemingly innocuous broad comedy. May was going to reach Ronald Reagan, no stranger to back lots himself, through a medium she was sure he understood—the Hope/Crosby road picture.

Since her pioneering days as half of Nichols & May, our intrepid heroine has struggled to rid comedy of its lazy reliance upon setups and punch lines, and invest it with the awkward, uncomfortable rhythms and painful silences of real life. She's spent her career doggedly chasing truth, so it's fitting that *Ishtar*, the pinnacle of her lifelong love affair with principled failure, opens with its sad-sack protagonists (Beatty and Dustin Hoffman) haplessly cocomposing a monstrous ditty about how "telling the truth can be dangerous business / honest and popular don't go hand in hand."

Hoffman and Beatty play best friends and songwriting partners leading lives unsullied by accomplishment. Beatty portrays a doe-eyed naïf too pure for a corrupt world; Hoffman plays a nebbishy hustler with a big mouth and a million doomed schemes. He's a cleaned-up Ratso Rizzo with a guitar and delusional dreams of becoming half of the next great songwriting team.

In composing songs for the film, Paul Williams, May, and Hoffman faced the unique challenge of writing tunes that aren't just bad, but painful. *Ishtar* walks a fine line between abusing audience eardrums and cleverly spoofing the clumsy wordplay and agonizing sincerity of clueless aspiring tunesmiths.

I adore *Ishtar*'s songs, though critics at the time probably wished the main characters had taken the advice of crusty, alcoholic agent Marty Freed (Jack Weston) to "sing songs people already know. That way, if they don't like it, they'll still have something to applaud."

Marty is understandably mortified by the duo's performance at an open-mike night but assures the boys he can book them in a Honduras hotel where, he confides casually, "the last act got nervous because of the death squads. But there's no danger if you don't drive into the countryside."

In flashbacks, we learn that Beatty's Lyle Rogers was once a humble ice-cream-truck driver, while Hoffman's Chuck Clarke tickled the ivories at a restaurant where the clatter of utensils and squawking diners drowned out his crooning. Separately, Lyle and Chuck aren't much. But when they join forces, they become even less than the sum of their negligible parts.

By the time Lyle is teetering along the ledge of an office building to try to keep Chuck from killing himself, *Ishtar* has become more than just a buddy comedy; it's a heterosexual romance, the sunshine flip side of *Mikey & Nicky*. Chuck and Lyle feed into each other's fantasies. They're miserable, but they aren't alone. That's tremendous comfort. When Chuck concedes that he lived with his parents until he was 32, Lyle tenderly tells him, "It takes a lot of nerve to have nothing at your age. Don't you understand that? Most guys would be ashamed! But you've got the guts to just say, 'The hell with it.' You'd rather have nothing than settle for less."

Ishtar smartly exploits the softness at the core of Beatty's persona. Without that dreamy vulnerability, it would be easy to hate Beatty for being too goddamned goodlooking, too goddamned successful, too goddamned perfect. But that cockeyed innocence renders Beatty human and allows him to fully inhabit the soul of a loser without irony.

Beatty and Hoffman decide to take their show on the road, high-tailing it to the fictional kingdom of Ishtar for a gig only slightly less fraught with danger than the death-squad-riddled booking they're passing up in Honduras. CIA agent Jim Harrison (a wonderfully deadpan Charles Grodin) recruits Chuck in Ishtar. Chuck's naïveté makes him an easy mark for Jim, who discusses the brutal pragmatism of Middle East realpolitik with the studied nonchalance of a grill salesman pontificating about propane. It's all just a game to the CIA veteran, who hides his relentless scheming behind a perfect poker face.

In the crazy world of *Ishtar*, the U.S. government and CIA prop up a brutal Middle Eastern dictator/torture proponent because he provides a bulwark against Communist expansion. Isabelle Adjani costars as Shirra, a mysterious left-wing operative whose brother left her a map with the power to destabilize Ishtar and throw the nation into chaos and civil war.

Ishtar offers a sly, *Duck Soup*–like take on the last days of the Cold War and a spy-vs.-spy milieu where KGB agents dress as Arabs, Arab agents dress like Texans, CIA operatives sport fezzes in addition to the regulation black shades and dark suits, and Turkish agents wear

Bermuda shorts. Oh, and the people in the Hawaiian shirts? Those are just tourists.

In a prescient scene, Jim meets with the emir of Ishtar, who demands that Lyle and Chuck be killed by next weekend, before they're hailed as saviors or martyrs. Jim responds with a droll, "The United States government will not be blackmailed. However, I see no difficulty in meeting your timetable." The CIA, as embodied by Jim, doesn't flinch at cosigning off on the deaths of two American citizens; it just doesn't want to get its hands dirty. Appearances are everything; reality is irrelevant.

Jim won't be blackmailed, just as George W. Bush wouldn't negotiate with the terrorists his dad and Ronald Reagan supplied with weapons throughout the '80s. The emir of Ishtar even utters the old aphorism, "The enemy of my enemy is my friend," recycling the logic that led the United States to arm Saddam Hussein in his war with Iran, and the Taliban during their righteous struggle against the Soviet Union.

Equal parts sly political satire, oddly poignant buddy comedy, road movie, and showbiz spoof, *Ishtar* runs into serious, if not fatal, third-act problems as it devolves into the movie its detractors accuse it of being, a borderline sadistic farce wherein Chuck and Lyle wander the desert for a seeming eternity after being led astray by both an angry, blind camel and the CIA. Also, it would have been nice if one of our most brilliant female filmmakers had written her female lead some funny lines. Or a character, really; Adjani is on hand exclusively to move the plot forward. Yet the film's exquisitely jaundiced take on the oily, malevolent pragmatism behind so much American foreign policy sustains it during its dry patches, as does Beatty and Hoffman's lived-in chemistry.

In her conversation at the Walter Reade Theater, May concedes that, in a fit of paranoia, she feared that the toxic buzz that sank *Ishtar* well before it opened to paltry box office and vicious reviews emanated not from enemies within Columbia but from the CIA. That's giving herself and the film entirely too much credit; nobody at the time seems to have noticed that the film was a sharp political satire, let alone a potentially dangerous one.

In its own strange way, *Ishtar* stumbles onto penetrating truths about American foreign policy and our willingness, even eagerness, to get in bed with murderous dictators when it suits our objectives. And it's fucking funny. As the protagonists warn us in the film's very first scene, telling the truth can be dangerous business; honest and popular don't go hand in hand. Amen.

Failure, Fiasco, Or Secret Success? *Secret Success*

How The West Was Sung Case File #50: *Paint Your Wagon*
Originally Posted July 17, 2007

An entire generation knows the 1969 musical *Paint Your Wagon* as the movie the Simpsons rent expecting a typical Clint Eastwood blood-bath, only to discover, to their shock and horror, a toe-tapping musical about the fun of painting wagons. Bart cheers up upon Lee Marvin's arrival, proclaiming, "Here comes Lee Marvin. He's always drunk and violent!" only to watch in disgust as Marvin begins singing about painting wagons as well.

The Simpsons' deliciously literal-minded spoof of *Paint Your Wagon* has usurped Joshua Logan's film in the public imagination, but it turns out the real *Paint Your Wagon* is far stranger than the *Simpsons* parody suggests, and it involves considerably less wagon painting.

Paint Your Wagon represents an odd marriage of convenience between the manliest cinematic genre (the Western) and the girliest one (the musical). It's a ragingly homoerotic film about a three-way marriage and two cowpokes who just can't quit each other, even after a fetching little lassie gets in the way of their partnership.

In a rambunctious lead performance, Lee Marvin plays drunken, lovable scoundrel Ben Rumson. Rumson teams up with Pardner, played by Clint Eastwood, after he discovers gold while burying Pard-ner's brother. Rumson makes it clear from the get-go that his concep-tion of partnership is as much emotional as financial. So he expects Pardner to "solace" him when he's feeling melancholy, pick him up when he's lying in the mud dead drunk, and lovingly caress his mut-tonchops while wearing a purty dress when the black dog of depres-sion is hot on his trail. Okay, that last part is an exaggeration, but the homoerotic subtext to Rumson and Pardner's friendship is so glaring it barely qualifies as subtext. In this relationship, Marvin is clearly the dominant one. Eastwood's nickname conveys his fragile state of dependency: It's as if he'd shrivel up and disappear if he didn't have a strong-willed friend to rely on.

In No-Name City, 400 lonely, horny men pine desperately for the civilizing touch of a woman's hand. So when a Mormon shows up with his two wives in tow, the entire town gathers to leer at them. A muscle-bound, shirtless brute offers to pay $50 worth of gold dust just to hold the traveler's baby, although it's unclear initially whether he wants to drink in its unspoiled innocence or devour it whole as an afternoon snack. Another lusty fellow gazes at Jean Seberg's Eliza-beth with a look that says, "Ain't you the filly what betrayed Jean-Paul Belmondo in *Breathless*? We don't see your likes much 'round here."

Four hundred men. Two women. That's a gender imbalance of Smurfian proportions. The fellas don't think it's right for one man to have two wives while they have none, so a surprisingly game Eliza-beth agrees to be auctioned off to the highest bidder. Rumson isn't too drunk to recognize the deal of a lifetime, so he purchases the rights to both Elizabeth and her "mineral resources" for $800.

Rumson then sets about transforming his podunk mining town into a dazzling mecca of sin and moral dissolution by kidnapping some French harlots for a two-story brothel, complete with moon-shine, card games, and vices of every imaginable stripe. The seeds of No-Name City's spiritual ruin are sewn when Rumson successfully completes his mission, only to learn that Pardner and Elizabeth have fallen hopelessly in love following a brisk getting-acquainted montage and a tender ballad that Eastwood croons through clenched teeth. Ah, the getting-acquainted montage, that deathless crutch of the lazy filmmaker. Why bother writing dialogue conveying characters' growing attraction when you can use a few soft-focus shots of leads gazing moonily into each other's eyes as glib shorthand for the complicated dance of courtship and consummation?

Rumson is angry at first, until it's decided that he and Pardner can *both* be Elizabeth's husbands, social conventions be damned. Why should Mormons have all the fun? *Paint Your Wagon* dramatizes how the West was civilized, then hopelessly corrupted. No-Name City becomes a boomtown Sodom and Gomorrah where bears fight bulls for the depraved enjoyment of the townfolk and whoring and gold dust thievery represent promising growth industries.

While No-Name City is devolving into a cesspool of depravity, Pardner and Elizabeth discover the joys of conventional morality when they play host to strangers hung up on the "one man, one woman" concept of matrimony. Like Sodom and Gomorrah, No-Name City ends up facing a profound reckoning when underground tunnels dug in part by Rumson and Pardner cause the entire city to collapse in on itself while Rumson stumbles obliviously, drunkenly through the wreckage like a muttonchops-sporting Buster Keaton.

Paint Your Wagon arrived at a time when musicals were rapidly losing favor with increasingly divided audiences. While the youth explosion that would soon transform Hollywood dug unconventional antiheroes like Marvin and Eastwood, they weren't eager to see them in antiquated musicals.

The *Paint Your Wagon* DVD thankfully includes an intermission, as if to say, "Sorry this movie is so fucking long. Here's five minutes for a quick smoke break." Beyond its elephantine running time, the film suffers from forgettable songs and a deathly vacuum at the center of its love triangle. Elizabeth is betrothed to Rumson because he paid $800 for her. Pardner and Elizabeth's bond, meanwhile, is cemented during the aforementioned getting-acquainted montage. Neither provides a solid foundation for either a love affair or a $20 million, 164-minute-long epic.

The fuzzy passivity of Eastwood's character proves equally problematic. Marvin gets to deliver a big, brawling, funny, cantankerous star turn, but Eastwood is stuck playing a wimpy role that Ricky Nelson could probably have played just as well. Audiences watch Clint Eastwood movies to see him kick ass or take brain-damaged female boxers off life support, not play house or defer to his more charismatic life partner.

Paint Your Wagon divided audiences and critics. With its central three-way marriage, debauchery, polygamy, and unconventional stars, it was too damn weird and adult for family audiences, and too old-fashioned for stoners. Nevertheless, I can imagine that at least a few acid freaks stumbled out of the theater wondering if they'd merely hallucinated seeing a three-hour-long movie where Clint Eastwood and Lee Marvin sang and danced and were married to the same woman yet seemed kind of into each other. I can also envision them freaking out hardcore when No-Name City began falling apart under the weight of its sins. It'd be enough to put them off the brown acid permanently.

Failure, Fiasco, Or Secret Success? *Fiasco*

Fucking Original Straight First Foremost Pimp Mack Fucking Hustler Original Gangster's Gangster Case File #52: *Gigli*
Originally Posted July 24, 2007

From the time the dashing male star of the 1901 silent film "Man Purchasing Hat" wooed the charming ingenue of "Lady Trying On Petticoats," we've been fascinated by movie-star couples. Clark Gable and Carole Lombard. Richard Burton and Elizabeth Taylor. Verne Troyer and the skank in his sex video. Their names are burned indelibly into our collective imagination. We live vicariously through their exploits, through sun-dappled vacations in tropical paradises and stormy on-set romances. We imagine what it would be like to be them, to breathe their rarefied air, to attend parties where everyone is someone. We coo at their newborns, recoil at their excesses, mourn their losses, and celebrate their triumphs.

Celebrity couples come and go. They bedazzle us with their new-ness, novelty, improbability, glamour, and sex appeal. Then we lose interest.

Why did the coupling of Ben Affleck and Jennifer Lopez fascinate and madden us so? Why did this particular celebrity romance shine so bright and burn out so spectacularly? Why was the media construct known as Bennifer a pop-culture phenomenon instead of the princi-pals' subsequent marriages?

Affleck and Lopez are certainly attractive and successful, but Hol-lywood is full of attractive, successful actors, many of whom have the decency to pair off with one another for our voyeuristic amusement. At the time of their doomed romance, Affleck and Lopez were both big stars, but they weren't Will Smith/Tom Cruise/Tom Hanks–level supernovas. So why did we care?

The answer, I suspect, is that the public is an angry god. We elevate stars to dizzying heights, then delight in destroying the false idols we've created. Affleck and Lopez won our hearts. Then they went too far. They abused our affection. They lingered in the spotlight too long. We gave them everything and still they wanted more. So we had to destroy them. As a warning. To send a message. To restore a sense of equilibrium to the universe.

But before we could tear Affleck and Lopez down, we had to build them up. Each exploded onto pop culture with a heartwarming tale of Triumph Over Adversity©. Affleck was the dreamer from Boston who wrote a screenplay with his buddy when he couldn't catch a break as an actor, won an Academy Award while still in his mid-20s, then became a ubiquitous movie star. Lopez was the 'round-the-way girl from the Bronx who danced on *In Living Color* and became a movie star playing tragic icon Selena Gomez in the 1997 biopic *Selena*. In an act of pop-cultural transubstantiation, Lopez gained Gomez's power by playing her, like a warrior devouring the heart of an enemy in order to acquire his strength.

Lopez was once a respected actress whose ruthless ambition hid an underlying softness. Steven Soderbergh brilliantly used this quality in 1998's *Out Of Sight*, but once Lopez decided to become a pop star, she seemingly lost interest in acting. Lopez apparently came to see acting as just one minor component of the J. Lo empire. Lopez stopped being a person and became a brand.

The newly minted pop star released a string of singles asserting her authenticity. She released a song called "I'm Real." On "Jenny From The Block," she simultaneously bragged about her glamorous lifestyle and patted herself on the back for remaining down-to-earth. The more Lopez sang about being real, the faker she seemed. People who are grounded and sincere don't generally feel the need to release songs asserting they possess those qualities.

In what astonishingly qualifies as only the third or fourth biggest miscalculation of her relationship with Affleck, Lopez decided to "spoof" the tabloid world's fixation with her torrid current romance by romping with her boyfriend in a series of glamorous locales in the video for "Jenny From The Block." The idea was to show that Affleck and Lopez had a sense of humor about themselves. But the video reeked of self-love rather than self-deprecation.

Lopez and Affleck seemed to be rubbing the public's face in the awesomeness of their lives. They were just like us, except for being stalked by the paparazzi and having mind-blowing celebrity sex on giant piles of thousand-dollar bills, then calling their famous friends on diamond-encrusted cell phones while riding cryogenically preserved woolly mammoths the non-famous know nothing about and guzzling an energy drink made from the tears of extinct animals.

We embraced Affleck and Lopez as underdogs. We rejected them when they became oppressively ubiquitous, when they peered out at us with smug smirks from newsstands and DVD boxes, engaging in the world's most visible and sustained PDA. Affleck had starred in too many terrible movies. Even worse, he starred in movies everyone saw but nobody liked, such as *Pearl Harbor* and *Armageddon*. Affleck and Lopez had reached a critical level of overexposure. Bennifer had aroused the Shiva the Destroyer within the general public. They were going down.

The 2003 flop *Gigli* proved the instrument of their destruction. But before I throw a little more dirt on *Gigli*'s casket, I'm going to praise it. Sort of. In its shaggy, digressive rhythms, focus on mismatched outsiders operating on society's fringes, and pop-culture riffing, it echoes funky '70s character studies and the early films of Quentin Tarantino the same way Kurt Cobain's feral howl survived his death and mutated into the goat-like bleating of an army of imitators. A film of sublime disharmony and staggering miscalculation, *Gigli* merits the consolation prize given out to movies with more ambition than brains; it ain't much, but at least it's going for something.

"You see, after all is said and done, the only thing you can be really sure of, the only thing you can really count on in this world, is that you just never fucking know," pontificates Affleck's protagonist, the eponymous Larry Gigli, in the opening voice-over. Watching *Gigli* for the second time, I found something soothingly familiar about Affleck's mini-monologue, in its fuzzy-headed philosophizing, excessive verbiage, and the way Affleck utters Each. Word. Slowly. And. Deliberately, as if giving audiences time to let the brilliance of the writing sink in. Where had I seen that combination before? Then it hit me: *Elizabethtown*.

Like *Elizabethtown*, *Gigli* is the story of a successful filmmaker's tragic love affair with himself and his voice. Like Cameron Crowe, *Gigli* writer-director Martin Brest is so in love with his words and ideas that he doesn't realize that the universe he's meticulously created bears only a passing resemblance to the real world.

In Brest's profane fantasy universe, for example, a low-level enforcer like Gigli exploits his captive audience—a gentleman he has tied up and stuck inside a dryer at a Laundromat—by subjecting him to a long-winded discourse on the nature of fate and the composition of the human body. After *Reservoir Dogs,* cinematic hoods everywhere morphed into strange combinations of Michel Foucault and Chuck Klosterman. Before, all a hit man needed was a gun and a menacing scowl. In a post-Tarantino realm, the price of entry rose to include novel ideas about popular culture and man's place in a godless universe and a gift for machine-gun banter.

Gigli is clearly talking to hear himself talk; even while "menacing" a duct-taped dude in a dryer, he poses no threat. He seems incapable of hurting people's feelings, let alone breaking their bones. He's a poodle masquerading as a pit bull, a hapless hood who can't even get weasel-faced boss Louis (Lenny Venito) to pronounce his last name correctly. (It rhymes with "really.")

The title character is so unthreatening—and invisible, apparently—that when he's assigned to kidnap Brian, the mentally challenged brother (Justin Bartha) of a powerful federal prosecutor intent on putting Louis' boss Starkman (Al Pacino) in prison, he's able to perambulate about Brian's special school without anyone paying him a second glance.

Gigli lures Brian into his car by promising to take him to "the Baywatch." Brian labors under the delusion that *Baywatch* is a real place. Louis and Starkman don't trust Gigli, so they dispatch a second "independent contractor" to look after him in the form of Ricki (Jennifer Lopez), a lesbian philosophy freak who speaks in the soothing, maternal tones of a patient kindergarten teacher, even when she's threatening a young punk with "digital orb extrusion" (that's *Gigli* fancy-speak for gouging someone's eyes out).

When Ricki disrespects Gigli's gangsta, he lays down the law, boasting, "I am the fucking sultan of slick, babe. I am the rule of fucking cool. You want to be a gangster? You want to be a thug? Just sit at my fucking feet. Gather the pearls that emanate forth from me. 'Cause I'm the fucking original straight first foremost pimp mack fucking hustler original gangster's gangster!"

Swearing is an art form. The more profanity a film uses, the less impact it has. By that standard, Brest should have had his swearing privileges rescinded during the film's first 20 minutes. Then he should have sat in a corner quietly and thought about what he'd done.

Ricki pays Gigli no nevermind. She sees him for what he is: a little boy throwing a temper tantrum. She's soon playing mommy to Brian and Gigli alike. Ricki is the contractor that mob types send for when they need kidnapping, intimidation, and other crimes executed with a woman's gentle touch.

Ricki herself hungers for a woman's gentle touch. When Gigli puts the moves on her, she tells him, "This might be a good time to suggest that you not allow the seeds of cruel hope to sprout in your soul," which is her way of saying she's a lesbian. Nobody in *Gigli* ever uses a simple, direct word when eight or nine flowery, polysyllabic ones will suffice.

Then Christopher Walken swoops in from Pluto as an enigmatic cop named Stanley and gives Brest's garbled, excessive, semi-undeliverable, comically wordy, and punishingly unnatural dialogue a lunatic bravado. It's like Miles Davis popping into a Holiday Inn lounge and jamming with the house band. Brest has written dialogue so doggedly strange and unnatural that only Walken can hack his way through it without looking like an amateur.

Walken delivers the lines, "Man, you know what I'd love to do, right now? Go down to Marie Callender's and get me a big bowl of *pie* with ice cream on it, mmmm, mmmm good, put some on *your head*! You'd probably slap your brains out trying to get to it! *Interested?*" in a conspiratorial purr that grows from creepily lascivious to insulting. The pregnant pauses, the unexpected emphases, the shifting eyes, and unnerving, rapacious sexuality—Walken puts on a master class in stealing scenes.

Then the genius soloist departs and Cinderella's coach turns back into a pumpkin. By the one-hour mark, almost nothing has happened in *Gigli*. Gigli nabs Brian and joins forces with Ricki. After that, it's all bickering and babysitting. Once upon a time, movies about criminals were full of action. In a post-Tarantino world, they're full of talk.

After an hour of jibber-jabbering, Gigli and Ricki are asked to cut off Brian's thumb so it can be sent to his father as a warning. They're horrified; when Ricki signed up to be a thug for hire, she never imagined she'd be asked to do something distasteful and, well, thuggish. So Gigli purloins a thumb from a corpse at the morgue, while Brian favors us with an a cappella rendition of Sir Mix-a-Lot's "Baby Got Back."

In *Gigli,* the gender roles are reversed; behind her soft, feminine exterior, Lopez plays a hunter and a warrior. Behind his ridiculous, transparent tough-guy façade, Affleck plays a vain, sensitive mama's boy who is happy to become Lopez's bitch. Gigli wins Ricki by exposing his vulnerable feminine side; it's only when he's willing to appear weak that he becomes attractive to her.

Ricki, Gigli, and Brian eventually form that hoary cliché: the trio of mismatched outsiders who come together to form an unlikely but loving surrogate family. Pacino's screaming enthusiast/mob boss is unmoved by the trio's familial bond, however, and he murders Louis, seemingly on a whim, just to prove how loco he is before climactically confronting Ricki and Gigli on their pathetic attempt to pass off the finger of a dead man as Brian's thumb.

Starkman vows to murder his underachieving flunkies until Ricki comes up with a better idea: Why doesn't he just let them go after they pinkie-promise to exterminate Brian with extreme prejudice? This makes no sense; if Ricki and Gigli couldn't bring themselves to cut off Brian's thumb, how could they kill him? Yet Starkman inexplicably acquiesces.

Gigli's tonal shifts grow increasingly violent as it races to the finish line. One moment, Starkman is waving around a gun and screaming at the top of his lungs (sadly, that now appears to be Pacino's normal speaking voice), the next Gigli and Ricki beam with parental pride as Brian wanders onto the set of a beach movie or television show where no one seems to notice the incongruity of a mentally challenged young man in a hoodie mixing it up with scantily clad hardbodies. For Brian has finally made it to "the Baywatch," a state of mind more than an actual location. Aren't we all, ultimately, just looking for our own Baywatch? *Gigli* ends on a preposterously upbeat note, as Gigli, bathed in a golden halo of light, watches Brian gyrate with a beach bunny while inspirational music soars in the background.

In the real world, Affleck, Lopez, and Brest never made it to their own personal Baywatch. There would be no happy ending for the film or for Bennifer. Lopez and Affleck broke up not long after the film flopped. Two-time Oscar nominee Brest, meanwhile, hasn't written or directed a film since, in spite of scoring successive hits in 1984's *Beverly Hills Cop*, 1988's *Midnight Run,* and 1992's staggeringly awful yet highly successful *Scent Of A Woman.* The world, it seems, no longer wants to sit at Brest's feet and gather forth the pearls that emanate from his laptop.

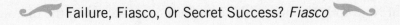 Failure, Fiasco, Or Secret Success? *Fiasco*

Bicurious, Hankie-Waving Case File #63: *Cruising*
Originally Posted August 30, 2007

Cruising arrived at a transitional time for gay culture. By 1980, the drug- and alcohol-fueled party that was gay sex in the '70s had been replaced by a punishing hangover of STDs and shattered idealism. AIDS lurked just around the corner, and with it a revitalized gay-rights movement blessed with a messianic sense of purpose. The American public hadn't yet had its consciousness raised by earnest message movies about how gays are just like you and me only with a more sophisticated understanding of musical theater and interior design. The world had yet to witness a deluge of reality shows in which gay men function as magical elves put on earth to help straight people eat better, dress better, and pick the perfect wine.

AIDS and the full flowering of the gay-rights movement pushed homosexuality out of the celluloid closet, but for much of the '70s and '80s, serious movies about gay life were so rare and weighed down with noble intentions that each was received as a major referendum on homosexuality. The emergence of AIDS made every television show, movie, or TV movie about gays an Important Cultural Event first and a work of art or entertainment a distinct second. Message movies were filled with noble, asexual Gay Martyrs who suffered for the audience's sins and showed us all how to withstand discrimination with quiet dignity.

Cruising functions as the moody antithesis of the Gay Martyr movie. In the time-honored tradition of its director, William Fried-kin (*The Exorcist, Sorceror, The French Connection*), it's a film devoid of good intentions or moral uplift, a sleazy wallow in the depths of human depravity. Friedkin set out to make a brutal murder mystery that just happened to take place in the underground gay S & M clubs of New York, but he couldn't have been surprised when the film was perceived, even before it finished shooting, as a movie about what senior citizens refer to as "the Gays." Friedkin, who also directed the landmark gay drama *The Boys In The Band,* certainly didn't intend for the film's glowering, muscle-bound leather boys to be representative of the rich and multifaceted gay community. But in the absence of more positive depictions of gays outside of Billy Crystal on *Soap,* it was perceived that way. Is it possible to remove politics from a movie as provocative as *Cruising?* Probably not. The film carried considerably more political and social baggage than it would if it were released today.

Loosely adapted from Gerald Walker's 1970 thriller *Cruising: A Shocking Novel Of Suspense* but updated for an era of leather bars and S & M clubs, the film casts Al Pacino as Steve Burns, a cop who goes undercover as a leather aficionado in New York's sleaziest underground sex clubs to track down a serial killer targeting the community. But first, Steve must prove himself up to the task. When trying to ascertain Burns' suitability for the job, his superior, Captain Edelson (Paul Sorvino), indelicately asks him, "Ever had a man smoke your pole?" (Strangely, that was also the first question in my job interview for *The A.V. Club*.)

Steve stumblingly learns the ins and outs of cruising for sex with anonymous leather-clad bruisers. Powers Boothe has a strange cameo as a "hankie salesman" who matter-of-factly informs neophyte Steve that he should wear his colored bandanna in one back pocket to indicate that he is in the market to receive a golden shower and/or blowjob, and the other pocket to show that he's eager to deliver the same. Apparently they don't cover that at the police academy.

As Steve plunges deeper into the subterranean realm of S & M, Friedkin cultivates a dread-choked atmosphere heavy with tension and menace, where every anonymous hook-up is charged with intimations of violence and brutality, as well as sad undertones of vulnerability and tenderness. But then a 6'5" black man clad only in a Stetson, necklace, and athletic supporter (an emissary, perhaps, of the NYPD's elite cowboy-hat-and-jockstrap division) comes out of nowhere to bitch-smack Steve for no discernible reason while he and a suspect are being hassled by cops, and I wondered, "What kind of motherfuckery is this?"

Also, Karen Allen is on hand to remind viewers that even though Steve spends all his time hanging with the leather daddies over at the Ramrod, this is the '80s and he's down with the ladies. Or is he?

In a bid to overturn stereotypes, Friedkin has the primary suspect write a thesis on the roots of musical theater between trips to the leather bars. To help offset the idea that all homosexuals are scowling sadists or masochists, Friedkin gives Steve an affable, mild-mannered sidekick named Ted (Don Scardino), whose sitcom perkiness clashes with the brooding intensity of the rest of the film.

Like many of Friedkin's films, especially *Bug, Cruising* flirts continuously with high camp, with purplish dialogue like, "I know this dude, too. Seen him on the Deuce. He gives the best beatings, like, six ways to Sunday." *Cruising* sometimes reads less like a missive from the front lines of sexual transgression than a bad pulp paperback come to life.

Much of *Cruising*'s ominous atmosphere comes from its sound design; Jack Nitzsche's score is unsettling, and Friedkin exploits the ominous clanging and jangle of zippers and buttons for maximum creepiness. In part because gay activists sabotaged *Cruising*'s sound on location, much of the film is post-dubbed. This can be frustratingly distancing for a film that prides itself on verisimilitude, but it can also be haunting, as when the same eerily disconnected voice comes out of several people's mouths.

The film's character arc traces the psychological damage that working deep undercover has on Burns' psyche, but since we never get to know Steve before the investigation, his psychological descent doesn't really register; he begins and ends the film an enigma. Part of that ambiguity is intentional: Friedkin wants the audience to suspect that Steve himself might be a murderer, so his character remains intentionally cryptic. The specter of AIDS casts a ghostly, funereal pall over the film. It's sobering to imagine how many of the film's extras—recruited from real S & M bars and directed to act as naturally as a hard-R rating would allow—wouldn't survive the decade *Cruising* ushered in on a singularly dark note.

Cruising explores seamy places Hollywood still fears to tread, delving deep into an ominous world redolent of sweat, fear, Vaseline, and sticky floors. In the three decades since its release, *Cruising* has come full circle and become a part of gay history, a strangely affecting time capsule of a subculture otherwise ignored by pop culture and the media. Today, it's compelling primarily as a sociological document of a dirty, dangerous New York where sex and death seemed inextricably linked even before AIDS. In its shameless excavation and exploitation of the killer-queen archetype—the gay man so riddled with self-loathing and guilt that he feels an insatiable urge to kill and punish others—the film is filled with bad politics and dodgy, flawed filmmaking, but it's weirdly resonant and haunting all the same.

Failure, Fiasco, Or Secret Success? *Fiasco*

Rat-Brained, Man-Animal-Friendly Case File #66: *Battlefield Earth*
Originally Posted September 11, 2007

I can't believe I somehow made it 66 entries into a feature about historic failures without writing about John Travolta, an actor who makes so many flops that when other actors fail, they have to pay him royalties. Yes, rat-brains and puny man-animals, I am finally writing about 2000's *Battlefield Earth*.

When *Battlefield Earth* was released, all the resentment toward Scientology that had been building up throughout the years exploded into a worldwide orgy of schadenfreude and Bronx cheers. A legendary disaster well before it was completed, the film hit theaters with a "Kick Me" sign on it so massive it could be seen from outer space.

The movie became a vessel through which people could vent their frustrations with Scientology without coming off as bigoted. I, of course, have nothing but respect and admiration for Scientology and the powerful Scientologists who control the world, but plenty of deluded souls who aren't my family, my co-workers, or myself inexplicably resent the wholly legitimate religious enterprise. They resent the way Scientology is as secretive, paranoid, and litigious as Disney, yet far more devoted to spreading fantasy and make-believe. They resent those obnoxious human-interest stories where Johnny CareerTrouble opens up to *People* about how Scientology helped cure him of his debilitating marijuana addiction. They resent the way Scientology seems to have made kissing up to celebrities the central component of the faith.

They resent those self-righteous press releases comparing the German government's treatment of Scientology to the Holocaust. They resent prominent Scientologists lecturing about the evils of psychology on television and condemning women who use psychoactive drugs to treat postpartum depression as weak-minded pawns of the pharmaceutical industry. They resent the idea that a hack science-fiction novelist could be a religious leader on par with Jesus.

Of course, if a preeminent figure in my faith had a sideline writing pulp fiction, I'd probably downplay that aspect of his life. If, for example, Moses used his downtime while writing the Torah to hastily compose fantasy novels exploring the adventures of Thoretta, She-Ogre, I'd probably steer clear of publicizing his side gig too aggressively. I wouldn't try to lure Brigitte Nielsen into starring in a feature-film adaptation of *Thoretta, She-Ogre* as a way of bringing converts to Judaism.

John Travolta doesn't feel the same way. For him, producing and starring in one of the great masterworks of L. Ron Hubbard (a book that reportedly sold more than a bazillion copies, including several to non-Scientologists) was primarily an act of religious devotion. I love John Travolta, but I love laughing at him even more. If you can't enjoy a laugh at Travolta's expense, then you aren't really living.

Battlefield Earth opens in a fanciful world where mankind has been defeated by a race of nine-foot-tall aliens from the planet Psychlo, whose gnarled appearance suggests what Klingons might look like if they took their fashion cues from the leather daddies in *Cruising*. Humanity has finally shaken off the highfalutin plague of book learning and stuff knowing and lingers in a caveman-like state of superstition and ignorance. Rather than invoke the wrath of demons and monsters, men hide in caves and eschew all but the faintest traces of civilization.

Travolta plays the head villain, a cackling dandy named Terl looking to maneuver his way out of an unwanted position as the head of security for an obscure mining planet called Earth. Where other, less visionary science-fiction movies waste their time with laser-gun battles, thrilling chases, and exotic worlds rich in spectacle, *Battlefield Earth* devotes much of its running time to corporate maneuvering among nine-foot-tall alien management types. This decision pays huge dividends when Terl's superior cackles that rather than giving Terl a reprieve from doin' time on Planet Earth, "We've decided to keep you here for another 50 cycles. With endless options for renewal!" Director Roger Christian repeats "With endless options for renewal" three times for effect. Who needs Wookies when you have characters talking about endless options for renewal? Sadly, *Battlefield Earth* really is all about Terl's plans to move up the Psychlo hierarchy through Machiavellian politicking, deceit, and blackmail.

Rather than wait out his 50 cycles and endless options for renewal, Terl concocts a harebrained scheme: He'll trick puny man-animals like Barry Pepper's intrepid hero Jonnie into mining gold for him, then use the rewards to fund a lavish life back on Planet Psychlo. But since no one believes a race as primitive as man-animals can operate complicated machinery, Terl hooks Jonnie up to a deus ex machina contraption that teaches him about flying and the Psychlo language and throws in the collective knowledge of the universe as a bonus. Jonnie quickly evolves from caveman simpleton to supergenius.

Who could have guessed that Terl's savvy plan to give Jonnie all the tools necessary to destroy him and Planet Psychlo and reclaim Earth would backfire? But that's just what happens: Johnnie decides to embiggen humanity by sharing his knowledge. Before long, the puny man-animals have hatched a plan to cast off their alien slave masters once and for all.

Any movie that relies on the presence of an all-the-knowledge-in-the-universe machine to advance its story isn't distinguished by brilliant plotting. So what is *Battlefield Earth*'s strength? It isn't dialogue. Here are some choice lines:

> *I am going to make you as happy as a baby Psychlo on a straight diet of Kerbango.*

> *Those corporate crapheads won't know we stole it.*

> *You are out of your skull-bone if you think I'm going to write on the report "shot by a man-animal" as the cause of death until I see it!*

Terl's bickering banter with Iago-like sidekick Ker (Forest Whitaker) is the stuff of middling sitcoms. ("After *Homeboys In Outer Space*, the out-of-this-world laughs continue with Terl and Ker in *Those Crazy Psychlos!*, only on UPN!")

It's a measure of the public's indomitable affection for the icon behind Vinnie Barbarino, Vincent Vega, Tony Manero, and Danny Zuko that our love affair with Travolta survived *Battlefield Earth*. And *Moment By Moment*. And *The Experts*. And *Perfect*. With *Battlefield Earth*, Travolta attained pop-culture immortality. He's proved that no film can destroy him, not even this one.

Failure, Fiasco, Or Secret Success? *Fiasco*

Animal-Abusing, Studio-Wrecking, Career-Killing Case File #81: *Heaven's Gate*
Originally Posted November 1, 2007

Steven Bach's fascinating, maddening book *Final Cut* chronicles the making and unmaking of the 1980 film *Heaven's Gate* from one of the least interesting possible perspectives: that of a United Artists executive despondent over spiraling costs and angry at an arrogant director who'd gone upriver and taken much of the studio's money with him. It's like reading an account of the sinking of the *Titanic* from the perspective of the guy who owned the company that made the boat.

Reading Bach's book, I felt powerfully conflicted. Critics almost invariably side with filmmakers in their battles with studio executives. For filmmakers are artists, and they don't need some Captain Bringdown in an expensive suit telling them what they can or can't do with the studio's money. And executives are supposed to be well-paid philistines with calculators for hearts.

But what happens when a filmmaker genuinely goes mad? Hollywood films don't exist in a vacuum. When a production like *Heaven's Gate* spirals out of control, companies go out of business (*Heaven's Gate* essentially killed its studio, United Artists, though MGM later revived it), ambitious filmmakers get rejected by executives terrified of green-lighting the next *Heaven's Gate,* and good, hardworking people lose jobs.

Some creatures lost more than just their jobs. The American Humane Association, which was barred from the set, accused Michael Cimino of slaughtering, maiming, or abusing animals during the production, primarily horses. You can indirectly thank Cimino for those "No animals were harmed in the making of this film" disclaimers at the end of films. The AHA's review of the film states, "The animal action in the film includes an actual cockfight, several horse trips, and a horse being blown up with a rider on its back. People who worked on the set verified more animal abuse, such as chickens being decapitated and steer being bled in order to use their blood to smear on the actors instead of using stage blood." It ends, "The controversy surrounding the animal action in *Heaven's Gate* prompted the Screen Actors Guild (SAG) and the Alliance Of Motion Picture & Television Producers (AMPTP) to contractually authorize AHA oversight of animals in filmed media."

Then again, has great art ever been produced that didn't involve staging cockfights, decapitating chickens, blowing up horses, and bleeding cows? I'm pretty sure all those things happened during the filming of the first three Muppet movies.

It's fitting that the original title of *Heaven's Gate* was *Johnson County Wars,* since the production resembled a war more than a typical movie set. Cimino kept an armed guard by the screening room to prevent executives from meddling with his vision, and he directed while wearing an admiral's cap and wielding a gun full of blanks. In the battle of *Heaven's Gate,* whom do you side with: the company man or the madman? Captain Willard or Colonel Kurtz? The man with the lunatic vision or the executive with shareholders to answer to?

Heaven's Gate helped kill the auteur-driven American cinema of the late '60s and '70s. It became the ultimate cautionary warning, a campfire tale senior executives tell junior executives to scare the bejeesus out of them during corporate retreats.

Watching *Heaven's Gate* today, it's easy to see why Cimino could look at dailies and think he had a masterpiece. It's equally easy to see how Bach could look at those same dailies and sense a looming financial disaster. From a creative standpoint, funding a movie like *Heaven's Gate* was risky. From a financial standpoint, it was insane.

With *Heaven's Gate,* Cimino went from being one of the hottest filmmakers alive to persona non grata. He went from auteur of the future to dead man walking. His career and reputation never recovered from the one-two punch of the film's legendarily troubled filming and box-office death. Cimino hasn't directed a film since 1996's barely released *The Sunchasers.* Rarely has a filmmaker fallen so far so fast. Cimino could have resurrected his career with 1984's *Footloose,* but he was fired after the shoot threatened to turn into *Heaven's Gate: The Musical.*

Yet today, *Heaven's Gate* stands as a stirring testament to Cimino's superlative gift as a cinematic stylist. It's a film of rare beauty and scope, a feast for the eyes and a harrowing, unflinching meditation on the cruelty of capitalism. It rivals William Friedkin's *Sorceror* in its bone-deep cynicism and eviscerating take on the free market's coal-black heart of darkness. In *Heaven's Gate,* being poor and an immigrant is a crime punishable by death, and the lives of the poor have less value than the cattle they steal to keep from starving.

The director's cut of *Heaven's Gate* begins with a series of stunning setpieces set at the Harvard graduation of James Averill (Kris Kristofferson) and his dissolute chum Billy Irvine (John Hurt), the booze-sodden class orator and class cutup. From the first frame, Cimino's roving camera goes anywhere and everywhere, panning endlessly and ecstatically across lushly orchestrated processions and a dance where the camera becomes a silent partner to the boozy, bleary graduates reveling in a hard-won sense of accomplishment. Cimino conveys in deliriously cinematic terms the pomp and grandeur of an Ivy League graduation. It's the benediction of the next generation of American aristocrats, filled with lawyers, senators, and other masters of the universe.

This luscious sustained glimpse of heaven makes the inevitable descent into hell all the more heartbreaking. The film then flashes forward 20 years to the wild frontier land of Wyoming, where James works as sheriff when not stealing drinks from his flask. To curb the theft of cattle, an association run by rich ranchers assembles a death list of suspected rustlers, anarchists, and ne'er-do-wells that essentially encompasses the entire county James serves. It's class war at its most vicious and overt, legalized murder to be carried out by an army of professional assassins while the powers that be look the other way. Christopher Walken costars as Nathan Champion, the ranchers' most brutally efficient enforcer and the third corner of a love triangle with James and French brothel keeper Ella (Isabelle Huppert). The cast is rounded out by a dazzling array of great character actors: Jeff Bridges, Brad Dourif, Joseph Cotten, Sam Waterston, Tom Noonan, Geoffrey Lewis, Richard Masur, Terry O'Quinn, and Mickey Rourke.

Walken's character receives a startlingly powerful introduction. At first, he's seen only in shadow, reflected through a sheet hanging in the wind, an image of civilizing sophistication in his hat and suit. Slowly, a rifle's outline emerges. Then Champion aims the rifle and blows a hole through the sheet and into the stomach of a knife-wielding immigrant, killing him instantly. It's only then that we realize that Champion is the one doing the killing. He's recognizable on-screen for only a split second, but that's all it takes to establish him as a figure of heartless authority, a cold-blooded killer in an untamed land.

For its first half, *Heaven's Gate* leaps from one gorgeous, sustained setpiece to another, driven by an exhilarating sense of possibilities. Why shoot an elaborately orchestrated hoedown with a full band and extras in period costume when you can shoot an elaborately orchestrated hoedown with a full band and extras in period costume as everyone glides about on roller skates?

Heaven's Gate is a film to get lost in. Any individual image from the film's first two hours could be isolated and hung on a wall at an art museum. It's that gorgeous. So far, so good. Until the intermission, I felt like I was watching a masterpiece.

The film's tone shifts from dark to unbearably grim once Huppert's Ella becomes the center of the action. Cimino excels at playing field general, a cinematic Patton commanding vast armies of extras, crew people, and animals soon to embark on trips to horse and chicken heaven. But that mastery abandons him when he's shooting interiors where people do nothing more kinetic than talk about their feelings. Cimino isn't helped by Huppert's strangely inert performance, with its perversely affectless line readings. When painting on a sprawling canvas, *Heaven's Gate* soars. When dealing with life-sized human emotions, it stumbles.

The love triangle among James, Champion, and Ella is supposed to be the film's emotional core, but within the context of an epic battle between warring historical forces, the problems of three little people don't amount to a hill of beans. As a killer, Walken is riveting. As a genial gentleman suitor, he's a stiff.

There are essentially two kinds of revisionist Westerns: those that forthrightly confront the harsh realities of life in the Old West, and those that sadistically rub the audience's collective face in the ugliest, most sordid aspects of Western life. For its oft-transcendent first two acts, *Heaven's Gate* is the first kind of revisionist epic. In its final act, it becomes the second.

In its remarkable opening sequences, *Heaven's Gate* immerses audiences in a world of startling vitality and richness. Then everyone rapes someone or gets raped, then dies a horrible death. The film's arc unwittingly echoes the arc of the New Hollywood of the '70s. At first, it radiates all the promise in the world. Then it devolves into a grim, ugly, overblown mess.

Though it was panned by critics and died at the box office, *Heaven's Gate*'s critical reputation took a huge upswing when Los Angeles' cinephile-friendly Z Channel played Cimino's 219-minute director's cut instead of the butchered two-and-a-half-hour version that bombed with audiences. The reviews were much more sympathetic, and people began to wonder if maybe Cimino was onto something all along.

Today, *Heaven's Gate* stands as a haunting, though profoundly flawed, elegy for a bloody and lost West, for a cinematic revolution on its last legs, and for one very talented, very troubled director whose untethered, uncontrollable ambition was both his greatest strength and his greatest weakness.

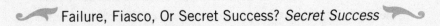 Failure, Fiasco, Or Secret Success? *Secret Success*

Tom Noonan On *Heaven's Gate*

Tom Noonan has led a dual existence as both a playwright/independent filmmaker (he won the Grand Jury Prize and the Waldo Salt screenwriting award at Sundance for his 1994 directorial debut, *What Happened Was . . .*) and as a popular character actor in genre fare, particularly horror films. The contrast between Noonan's hulking frame and underlying gentleness was used to terrifying effect in Michael Mann's *Manhunter,* which cast the towering thespian as a serial killer known as the Tooth Fairy. Noonan later played a goofy, lovable Frankenstein's monster in the cult horror-comedy *The Monster Squad* and a shadowy figure harboring dark secrets in *The House of the Devil.*

Tom Noonan: That was probably the worst experience I had in my adult life at that point. Michael Cimino's not a very nice person, at least he wasn't when he made that movie, and I had seen *Deer Hunter,* which I actually saw again recently for the first time in 30 years. It's such an amazing movie. I'd just started acting when I saw that, and I'd loved the movie so much. I thought, "Jeez, I would do anything to work with this guy." And so I auditioned, and the audition was sort of normal. But I was in this play, [Sam Shepard's] *Buried Child,* and they called me in May. I didn't think we were going to shoot the movie that soon, and they called up and said, "You have to go to Montana the next day." Or Wyoming, I can't remember where it was. I said, "I can't go tomorrow. There's no stand-in. This is a really intense part.

219

The play is a hit. I can't just leave. I don't want to do that." So basically I lost the part. A few months later, they called up again and said, "You remember that we called you in May, well now it's August, and Michael decided that he still wants to use you."

So he gave me a week, and I flew out there, and I went to the motel, and the three other guys that are in the scene with me had gone out in May and were sitting in the motel room for three months waiting to shoot the scene. He wouldn't let them go back to New York, even though he knew he wasn't going to shoot the scene. It was just crazy. He did that to all kinds of people. He kept sitting around in Kalispell, Wyoming, in these motels, people he knew he wasn't going to use for months. Just to create this craziness. And the set was really dangerous. He used to wear this sort of admiral's hat, like a navy admiral hat with the gold shit on it, and he would carry this huge blank gun, and he would fire it during scenes. He pointed a blank at my face once—which is really dangerous; you can kill somebody with a blank gun—like, threateningly. Like, "I want you to do this, and if you don't . . ." He was really crazy.

I mean, the best way to give you an idea of what the experience was like is that when I came back from shooting the film, six months later, I went to see *Apocalypse Now*. And the feeling you get watching that movie is what it felt like to be on the set of *Heaven's Gate*. Really dangerous.

Nathan Rabin: Reading *Final Cut,* Steven Bach's book about the making of *Heaven's Gate,* there's the sense that they were analogous experiences. Francis Ford Coppola basically wanted to re-create Vietnam for *Apocalypse Now,* and it seems like Michael Cimino wanted to create the violent, destructive epic world of *Heaven's Gate* on the set itself.

TN: I don't think there was any thought behind it at all. I think he was high and carried away with himself, and I don't even think he really directed *Deer Hunter.* I think the actors did. I mean, hard to say.

NR: Did you have a sense that he had a vision for *Heaven's Gate*? It's a beautiful film in many ways.

TN: I watched part of it once. It's sort of beautiful, it's like a European sort of Bertolucci Western. But personally, he was just really not a good person. I don't think he was really into making it anything more than just sort of serving his ego and this crazy vision he had of himself.

NR: Apparently at the height of his career, and his egomania, Peter Bogdanovich would direct from horseback. I think Raoul Walsh did it in the 1940s, so he thought, "That's what I'll do." Wearing an admiral's hat and wielding a blank gun sounds like a similar level of crazy.

TN: Well, you're in a little tiny room, too. I couldn't even stand up straight in the room, because the ceilings were really low, and it was this log cabin. He'd do crazy things, like apparently they built a whole cabin. I don't know if it was that cabin or another cabin, but he built this beautiful restored cabin, very authentic, and then they blew it up to see what it looked like when they blew it up, rather than waiting and filming it. Crazy things like that. Why would somebody possibly do that?

Trapped In A World It Never Made Case File #94: *Howard The Duck*
Originally Posted December 18, 2007

It all comes down to the rat tail. Nothing better symbolizes George Lucas' surreal disconnect from the world we live in, as opposed to the world inside his imagination, than the rat tail Hayden Christensen wears in *Attack Of The Clones*. But it could be worse. It's possible that a heroic unknown soul fought a fierce battle to convince Lucas that he shouldn't try to "update" the look of the *Star Wars* universe for its prequels and talked Lucas out of having the storm troopers rock acid-washed jeans or Zubaz track suits, but gave up on convincing him not to have the future Darth Vader don a hairstyle generally associated with insecure 11-year-olds circa 1983.

Lucas is deeply plugged in to the cultural zeitgeist. Unfortunately, it's the zeitgeist of 1937. While his peers were immersed in the sex, drugs, and rebellion of the '70s, Lucas thought, "Gee whiz! I'm gonna make the science-fiction serial to top all science-fiction serials! It'll make *Flash Gordon* look like yesterday's news! And I'll follow it up with a swashbuckling adventure about a daredevil archaeologist! Oh, it'll just be the bee's knees, I tell ya! And then maybe a murder mystery set in Radioland! Jumpin' gee willikers, will it ever be swell!"

By the time *Attack Of The Clones* went into production, Lucas probably hadn't interacted with a human being not in his employ for decades. He undoubtedly now surrounds himself with an army of servant droids who carry out his every whim and protect him from interacting with the unpredictable creatures known as "humans."

It wasn't always that way. Back in the early '70s, Lucas teamed up with the husband-and-wife screenwriting team of Gloria Katz and Willard Huyck, who seemed to have an inside line on how these mysterious "humans" talk and behave. Together, they wrote the script for *American Graffiti*. In appreciation, Lucas employed Katz and Huyck long after the rest of the world had forgotten them: He commissioned them to write a sequel to *Indiana Jones*. When the two couldn't come up with a halfway decent script, he went ahead and had Steven Spielberg film what they'd written anyway.

But it was all just a warm-up to 1986's Lucas-produced *Howard The Duck,* the feature-film adaptation of Steve Gerber's cult comic book. Gerber's creation had serious underground cred before Lucas, Katz, and Huyck had their way with it. Howard ran for president in 1976, popped up in the fiction of Philip K. Dick and Stephen King, and was referenced in an early Pretenders song. He'd even been the subject of legal threats from Disney, which is the ultimate badge of underground respectability. Disney complained that Howard T. Duck infringed on Donald Duck's copyright. As part of the settlement, Howard was forced to wear pants. For reasons I can't get into, a lawsuit by Disney also forced me to wear pants. Fucking Disney.

Gerber's *Howard* comics knowingly played with comic-book conventions. But the character's self-awareness of his medium appealed less to Lucas than the prospect of turning out a special-effects-heavy creature feature about a lovable anthropomorphic misfit along the lines of Steven Spielberg's *E.T.*

The Huyck-directed *Howard The Duck* begins by introducing its eponymous hero in his own world. Against a backdrop of smoky jazz, the camera moves deliberately around Howard's apartment, lingering on posters advertising Mae Nest and W. C. Fowl in *My Little Chickadee* and *Breeders of The Lost Stork,* before panning to magazines like *Rolling Egg* and *Playduck.* A mere three minutes into being introduced to *Howard The Duck*'s comic-book universe, I was looking for a way out. See, Howard's a three-foot-tall wisecracking duck who acts just like a person! That's joke number one: the artless juxtaposition of man- and duckkind. For the next 112 interminable minutes, I waited patiently for joke number two. It never arrived.

Howard is then sucked from his universe, past some disturbing anthropomorphic duck-women posing topless, and into ours via an interdimensional ray that drops him somewhere in the grungy depths of Cleveland. A narrator explains, "The cosmos: countless worlds upon worlds. Worlds without end. In these galaxies, every possible reality exists. But what is reality on any one world is mere fantasy on all others. Here all is real and all is illusion. What is, what was, and what will be start here with the words, 'In the beginning there was Howard The Duck.'"

In rapid succession, Howard is kidnapped by menacing new-wavers, gets thrown out of a club, and finds a friend in Lea Thompson's Beverly. Thompson's role was originally offered to a struggling hair-metal vocalist named Tori Amos, then of Y Kant Tori Read, but the offer was rescinded when Lea Thompson became available.

Thompson's role provides unique acting challenges, like the queasy-making scene where Howard begins (jokingly) hitting on Beverly and she "pretends" to reciprocate his affection. But before Howard can pummel away at a scantily clad, flirtatious Beverly with his sweaty, engorged, feather-encrusted member, she backs down and insists she was only kidding, thereby sparing filmgoers a sex scene of interest only to a handful of deeply disturbed fetishists.

Howard The Duck has more on its mind than generating sexual tension between a three-foot-tall anthropomorphic duck and a rock vixen so dense she regularly transgresses the thin line separating spacey from mentally challenged. For it seems the ray that brought Howard to Earth has unwittingly unleashed one of the Dark Overlords of the Universe. In its bid for world domination, this Dark Overlord takes control of the body and mind of Jeffrey Jones, transforming him into a fiendish beastie with a sinister rasp that suggests he has also been invaded by the demon Pazuzu of *The Exorcist II: The Heretic*.

The Dark Overlord subplot provides the film's lone moment of glory. In its true form, the Dark Overlord ranks as a triumph of old-fashioned moviemaking magic, a nifty monster that looks like a fearsome cross between a Tyrannosaurus rex and a scorpion. In this lonely island of awesomeness in a sea of bad ideas, *Howard The Duck* briefly redeems Lucas' regressive vision of a cinema rooted inextricably in the sugar-rush highs of his early years as a movie-mad kid. But no film should subject audiences to two hours of labored duck jokes for the sake of a cool-looking monster.

Universal president Frank Price was asked to resign following *Howard The Duck*'s failure. In a noble act of executive seppuku, he acquiesced. Price got off easy: In many cultures, a man would be tarred and feathered for professionally midwifing such a film. If, as its narrator suggests, there are galaxies in which "every possible reality exists," then in some alternate universe, *Howard The Duck* qualifies as a Secret Success instead of a Failure.

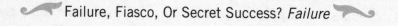 Failure, Fiasco, Or Secret Success? *Failure*

Pointlessly Postmodern Case File #103: *Psycho*
Originally Posted January 20, 2008

The triumph and tragedy of Anthony Perkins' career is that he could never stop being Norman Bates. When you're famous for playing a crazy baseball player (1957's *Fear Strikes Out*), a crazy motel proprietor (1960's *Psycho*), and a crazy crazy person (1968's *Pretty Poison*), romantic leading-man roles are out of the question. The *Tiger Beat* demographic was forever out of his reach.

The unexpected triumph of Vince Vaughn, meanwhile, is that he couldn't convincingly be Norman Bates even for 105 minutes.

For Perkins, Bates was a cross to bear, an identity he couldn't shed, a blessing and a curse. For Vaughn, the role was but a bump in the road, a part he played and discarded on his way to big paychecks for playing variations on his finely honed persona as the charmingly obnoxious overgrown frat boy who fucked your girlfriend.

Bates haunts Perkins even in death. Watching Gus Van Sant's interesting-in-theory, painful-in-practice remake of *Psycho*, I was struck by a strange notion: Why didn't they have Perkins play Mama Bates' skeleton? It would have been a big improvement over the skeleton they ended up using, which looks like it was stolen from a low-rent haunted house.

All Van Sant would have to do is get some production assistants drunk, then offer to read their screenplays, and possibly even show them to his close personal friend Ben Affleck, on the condition that the PAs dig up Anthony Perkins' corpse, slip a dress on his skeleton, and deliver it to the prop department. Some folks have no commitment.

Van Sant's perversely faithful yet strangely disrespectful remake of *Psycho* engages in a less elegant form of cinematic grave robbery. Van Sant famously vowed to make a shot-by-shot remake of *Psycho* that would be *exactly* like the original, except for the parts that would be different. It would be entirely the same, only not.

Though the scripts and shots they chose are essentially identical, Hitchcock and Van Sant approached the material from antithetical places. When he made *Psycho*, Hitchcock was a classy filmmaker happily slumming with a nasty shocker shot on the cheap in black and white using the low-budget crew of *Alfred Hitchcock Presents*. The brown paper bag of a title says it all: This was pure pulp, a cinematic gut punch from a filmmaker who generally opted for a more sophisticated brand of suspense.

Hitchcock's *Psycho* provided a master class in misdirection. The predatory antiheroine who steals a small fortune becomes the prey, while the meek victim of an innkeeper is revealed to be a deranged murderer. A white-knuckle, hard-boiled noir about a scheming woman on the run morphs unexpectedly into a psychological horror film. The protagonist never even makes it to the halfway point, and a seemingly key supporting character—the innkeeper's demented, hectoring mother—is revealed to have died a decade earlier.

Van Sant, in sharp contrast, was making the film as an art school lark, a self-indulgent postmodern experiment made possible by the unexpected success of *Good Will Hunting*. Indie film darling Van Sant suddenly had Hollywood cooing into his ear, "You're the man now, dog!"

Van Sant's artsy debacle asks intriguing, easily answerable questions about the nature of art and genius. Can genius be replicated? Can it be cloned using the creative DNA of an earlier masterpiece? Or is true genius ineffable, tricky and elusive, as difficult to pin down as a whirlwind? The answers, respectively, are no, no, and yes.

Van Sant's miscalculations begin with casting Anne Heche as a woman with a dark secret at a time when Heche was notorious for not being able to keep anything about herself secret. I could be misremembering, but I vaguely recall Heche and Ellen DeGeneres unexpectedly showing up at my apartment in Madison sometime in the late '90s to deliver an hour-long presentation on their sex life. It was all part of Heche's campaign to educate America about what was going on with her vagina.

Heche plays Marion, a bored career gal who impulsively decides to make off with $400,000 from her employer. While hotfooting it out of town, Marion stops for the night at creepy old Bates Motel, where she and fidgety proprietor Norman Bates share a drink they call loneliness because it's better than drinking alone. Vast universes divide these two lost characters, yet they're united by isolation. Marion's loneliness is temporary, however; it's the alienation of having done something criminal that she can't possibly share with the world. For Bates, that loneliness is permanent. It defines him.

This scene marks the pinnacle of Vaughn's otherwise misfiring performance. Part of the problem is physical. Much of what made Perkins such an effective and surprising killer is that he's unassuming physically. He looks like someone who wouldn't harm a fly. Though tall, he's slight and creepily androgynous, whereas Vaughn looks like a college wrestler. There's an underlying vulnerability and sadness to Perkins' performance that Vaughn recaptures only during his scenes with Heche, and then only fitfully. Vaughn can't get inside the character's tormented psyche; his laugh, a sort of trilling, high-pitched, nervous giggle that gets stuck in the throat, feels theatrical and forced. It's a jock's feeble attempt to channel what it must be like to be the weird kid at the lunch table, the one whose mom writes Bible verses on his lunch bag. Once Heche exits the film, Vaughn's Bates seems less tragic and tormented than pissy and unpleasant.

Also, there is masturbation. And bare asses. Lots and lots of bare asses—male and female. In the film's biggest detour from the original—other than being in color and sucking—Bates gazes at Marion through a peephole and engages in feral, simian masturbation. In what universe does artlessly spelling everything out qualify as an improvement over subtext and intimation? It'd be like remaking *Citizen Kane* but changing the protagonist's last words to "Rosebud . . . which incidentally was the name of my childhood sled, which represents a lost childhood Eden of innocence and purity that throws the materialist emptiness of my adulthood into even sharper relief. Alas, I've said too much and now I must die, mysteriously. Or not."

Then comes a riotously anticlimactic shower sequence. Arguably the most famous bloody scene of all time is rendered paradoxically bloodless and lifeless. In Van Sant's retelling, it feels like a bad cover song; the notes are the same, but the soul is sorely lacking. The shower scene highlights another of the film's fatal flaws: The novelty and surprise of the original are gone. Audiences were understandably shocked to see a heroine get brutally murdered halfway through a film back in 1960. Audiences in 1998 were waiting patiently to see how Van Sant would handle one of film's most iconic sequences.

After Marion's disappearance, sharp-witted shamus Milton Arbogast (William H. Macy) goes looking for her, as does Heche's sister, Lila (Julianne Moore), and Heche's lover, Sam (Viggo Mortensen). In a 2001 interview with *The A.V. Club*, Macy argued that his primary job as an actor is bending other actors to his will. In his only scene with Vaughn, he bulldozes over the innkeeper's evasions and stonewalling. Yet even here, Macy's perspicacity works against him; he's such a smart cookie, I half expected him to haul Bates off to the police station minutes into grilling him for the first time.

When Bates murders Arbogast, Van Sant indulges in a pair of shock cuts from Macy's character plunging backward as Bates stabs him to jarring, brief images of a masked, nearly naked woman in a sordid erotic tableau and a cow in the middle of the road, footage apparently left over from Van Sant's first student film or a Marilyn Manson music video. It's an addition that adds nothing. The part where Moore's Lila says, "Let me get my Walkman," however, came close to single-handedly redeeming the film; I can't imagine why there weren't more references to Walkmans in the original.

From there, it's simply a matter of biding time until the big reveal about the true nature of Momma Bates and her loving son, and Dr. Fred Simon (Robert Forster) explaining to the audience that poor old Norman Bates went a little nuts after killing his mom and her lover.

Gus Van Sant's *Psycho* never feels like anything other than a dry academic exercise. Van Sant's much-maligned folly ultimately belongs not in a movie theater or a drive-in but in a conceptual art museum in a wing devoted to pretentious experiments in pointlessness, where it could join a real 1993 museum project called *24 Hour Psycho*, an installation that slowed the film down over 24 hours and provides a major setpiece in Don DeLillo's *Point Omega*.

 Failure, Fiasco, Or Secret Success? *Fiasco*

Epic, Extravagant, Excruciating Book-Exclusive Case File: *Cleopatra*

There is a sequence in 1963's notorious *Cleopatra* that encapsulates the film in miniature. In it, Cleopatra, the Great Seducer, sets her sights on bewitching an entire city. Having won the heart of Caesar, Cleopatra dazzles the people of Rome with a spectacular entrance.

The procession begins with wave upon wave of trumpeters on horseback, followed by chariots, archers shooting brightly colored scarves into the air, a buxom, nearly naked dancer gyrating seductively while scantily clad women twirl scarves, Africans in tribal garb unleashing great plumes of canary-yellow smoke and then dancing to pounding drums, dancers in animal costumes, sexy women dressed as birds flapping their golden wings in unison, a flurry of doves soaring skyward, and more fanfare before the main event: Cleopatra entering the city on what appears to be a pyramid on wheels pulled by a battalion of slaves.

At first, it's exhilarating. Such color! Such spectacle! Such unabashed sexuality! Such a cavalcade of Technicolor delights! Then it gets a little old. Then it grows tedious, and I began to wonder if it would ever end. I thought perhaps my body and mind would decay, I'd grow ancient and develop an interest in *Reader's Digest* and the soccer games of my grandchildren, and then die, while Cleopatra's procession was still only half finished. I wound up asking myself that question an awful lot while watching *Cleopatra*: "Will it ever end?"

Since the cut of the film I saw runs 248 minutes, the answer comes painfully close to no. Astonishingly, both the film and the procession were initially much longer; according to Martin Landau's audio commentary, the procession was originally twice as long, and writer-director Joseph L. Mankiewicz conceived of the film as a two-part six-hour epic, with the first half devoted to Cleopatra's dalliance with Caesar and the second to her stormy fling with Marc Antony.

Fox, which was hemorrhaging money as the budget skyrocketed with no release date in sight, would have none of it. Studio head Darryl F. Zanuck demanded that three hours be shorn from the film. (The video and DVD release runs a little over four hours, as did the première and road-show version.) Even in truncated form, the film seems to last several eternities. The six-hour cut of *Cleopatra* remains one of film's great what-ifs. Would the director's cut have validated Mankiewicz's bold vision? We may never know.

Mankiewicz, the slashing wit behind *All About Eve,* set out to make an "intimate epic." The resulting film is epic but the intimacy apparently ended up on the cutting-room floor, along with much of Mankiewicz's most sophisticated dialogue. What's the point in marshaling 10,000 extras, a fleet of ships only slightly smaller than the U.S. Navy's, and a $44 million budget (adjusted for inflation, that'd be about $300 million today) if you're just going to fill the screen with bons mots?

Job had it easy compared to Mankiewicz, who must have felt cursed by the gods. Mankiewicz inherited an already-troubled production when original director Rouben Mamoulian quit early in the process after a headache-inducing litany of disasters, including leading lady Elizabeth Taylor contracting meningitis, which shut down filming for months, and a change in location from Italy to England.

The troubles picked up speed once Mankiewicz took over; the fragile Taylor developed a life-threatening case of pneumonia, and terrible English weather necessitated another change in location, this time back to Italy. When shooting resumed, the script was only half completed; according to the *Cleopatra* DVD booklet, Mankiewicz shot all day, wrote all night, and staved off exhaustion with Dexedrine in the morning, a shot of uppers after lunch, another after dinner, and then finally a downer at night so he could grab three or four hours of sleep before repeating the whole process the next day.

Oh, and Mankiewicz's very married leads (Taylor and her future ex-husband Richard Burton) began a steamy extramarital affair en route to becoming a tabloid couple for the ages. Bad press abounded. But the biggest heartbreak was yet to come: Mankiewicz saw his baby cut almost in half and had to shoot additional footage to paper over the plot holes left by the giant sections of his film that had been mercilessly excised.

So when Rex Harrison's Caesar begins the film dispirited and exhausted, his air of resignation seems to belong equally to a leader who has just won a bloody, dispiriting war against Pompey and a veteran actor in the midst of a hellish shoot. Caesar understands that there is no glory in war, only survival. He seems much older than his 52 years; war will do that to a man.

Caesar rediscovers his lust for life when he travels to Egypt and is irritated and then bewitched by its glamorous queen Cleopatra (Elizabeth Taylor). Cleopatra's bona fides as a world-class seductress are clumsily established when Caesar's right-hand man Rufio (Martin Landau) reports soberly, "In attaining her objectives, Cleopatra has been known to employ torture, poison, even her own sexual talents, which are said to be considerable."

At first, Caesar treats Cleopatra like a petulant child, bratty and mischievous but dangerously smart and seductive. Cleopatra oozes sex. Caesar radiates propriety. He's a very English Roman: droll, literate, and adult. Cleopatra uses her sexuality as a weapon. One might even argue that in attaining her objectives, Cleopatra has been known to employ her sexual talents, which are said to be considerable.

Caesar soon discovers for himself the full extent of those talents. Hatred, barbed insults, and sultry glares soon give way to passionate kisses, lust, and then love. Cleopatra reawakens Caesar's world-conquering ambition in addition to his libido and joie de vivre. She's a Lady Macbeth of the Nile who encourages her lover to pursue a position grander than his current title as Dictator For Life. (You know you're ambitious when Dictator For Life isn't good enough.)

This terrifies the Roman Senate, so on the ides of March, they decide to employ stabbingcentric means of curbing Caesar's reckless ambition. Just as Great Caesar's Ghost haunts the film's lesser second half, Shakespeare's ghost haunts the proceedings. Mankiewicz earlier directed the 1953 adaptation of *Julius Caesar* featuring Marlon Brando's mumbly, marble-mouthed Marc Antony, so he couldn't have been surprised when audiences half expected Caesar to utter a heartbroken, "Et tu, Brute?" upon receiving the unkindest cut of all, or for Marc Antony to beckon friends, Romans, and countrymen to lend him their ears.

It's unfair to compare Mankiewicz to Shakespeare, but in light of the film's subject matter, such comparisons are unavoidable. Perhaps that's why Mankiewicz films Caesar's murder like a Roger Corman B-movie, with Cleopatra "watching" the proceedings through what Mankiewicz describes as "the flames of a temple ritual." Since we can't hear Caesar as he gets stabbed, we can imagine he's saying, "What the fuck? I thought you were my bro, Brutus," just as easily as "Et tu, Brute?"

Burton's Marc Antony slides into Cleopatra's bed, conquers her heart, and takes over the film's second half. Where Caesar's relationship with Cleopatra was paternal in nature, Marc Antony matched her fire with his own. *Cleopatra* morphs into another film altogether in its second half, as the tart banter of its Caesar sequences devolves into overheated romantic melodrama.

Marc Antony lives forever in the shadow of Caesar, haunted by the knowledge that he'll never measure up to a man deified in his death. Underneath his hot-blooded passion, he's fundamentally pragmatic, so he marries Caesar's dull sister for political reasons. Mankiewicz designed *Cleopatra* as a two-part epic, but it feels more like a trilogy with its superior first third devoted to Cleopatra and Caesar, the second to Cleopatra and Marc Antony, and a deadly dull final third concerning Antony's betrayal of Cleopatra via his marriage of political convenience and his subsequent war with Roddy McDowall's scheming Octavian.

Where Mankiewicz seems conflicted about the gaudy spectacle favored by his bosses at Fox, he seems downright apathetic about the film's battle scenes. By this point, I too suffered from the exhaustion plaguing the film's characters. By the time Mankiewicz's epic ended, I was ready to crawl into Cleopatra's tomb and be put out of my misery alongside the good queen and Marc Antony.

Yet traces of Mankiewicz's brilliance remain. Upon hearing of Marc Antony's death, McDowall has a wonderful monologue in which he upbraids an underling for his dispassionate way of conveying the news about the demise of such a worthy foe. Surely an event of this magnitude deserves pomp and circumstance. It takes death for Octavian to show his respect for a very worthy adversary.

Cleopatra was the top-grossing film of 1963, and it scored seven Oscar nominations, yet the stakes were so high that it's still considered one of the all-time flops. Much of the blame deservedly went to Taylor, who doesn't inhabit the soul of a legendary seductress so much as she pouts, strikes poses, models comically elaborate outfits and headdresses, and spits out her lines. Granted, Mankiewicz doesn't make it easy for Taylor with purple dialogue like, "My breasts are full of love and life. My hips are round and well apart. Such women, they say, have sons." But Taylor's Cleopatra is less a tragic heroine than a precursor to Julie Newmar's campy vixen Catwoman on the '60s TV incarnation of *Batman*.

Ironically, given the film's emphasis on eye candy and bleary excess, *Cleopatra*'s best scene eschews spectacle. Immediately following Cleopatra's endless procession, Caesar schools his apple-cheeked son in the fine art of leadership. Caesar teaches him all the basics: cultivating an angry glance to shoot in the direction of someone who displeases him, how to make a crowd tremble, how to pardon a prisoner dragged before him, and how to treat a duplicitous former friend. The moppet is a quick study, though he needs to be counseled not to smile adorably while making his subjects tremble in fear of his wrath.

Extravagant costumes, giant sets, oceans of extras, a budget equivalent to the gross national product of a small country, and voluminous star power are no match, it seems, for the timeless appeal of a cute kid.

Failure, Fiasco, Or Secret Success? *Fiasco*

~✲ Chapter 8 ✲~

A Fairy-Tale Ending, Or, Manic Pixie Dream Girls I Have Known

Constant, Total Amazement Case File #40: *Joe Versus The Volcano*
Originally Posted June 12, 2007

I was at a greasy spoon recently when I overheard a smartly dressed, seemingly sane woman in her 50s gush to her companion, "Have you ever heard of a movie called *The Other Sister?* It is just delightful. Just a wonderful, wonderful film. Diane Keaton plays a very strict mother whose daughter is disabled. Now this disabled daughter—I don't know whether she is really disabled in real life—is just about the biggest free spirit you would ever want to meet! It is just a wonderful, wonderful lighthearted comedy, and it's just about my favorite film."

The woman's passionate endorsement of *The Other Sister* served as a poignant reminder that just about every film has a cult, even if it's a cult of one. The world could have *Citizen Kane* and *Casablanca*, but *The Other Sister* belonged to her.

When I laid down the ground rules for My Year Of Flops, I stipulated that I wouldn't cover films with substantial cult followings.

But I've learned from readers and commenters that I am far from alone in my passion for some of the films I've written about. I would venture to say *Joe Versus The Volcano* boasts an even bigger cult than *The Other Sister.* That's one of the great gifts of the Internet: It affords us the opportunity to simultaneously assert our individuality, stray from the pack, and find like-minded communities that share our passion for Pogs or *Mr. Belvedere* or the lesser films of Paul Mazursky. It reminds us that we are not alone, even if our favorite film is *The Other Sister.*

Joe Versus The Volcano has proved especially popular in self-help circles, where its message of self-actualization through letting go of the fears and anxieties that hold us back has found an appreciative audience. *Volcano* has the unusual quality of being simultaneously frothy and quietly profound. As my *A.V. Club* colleague Scott Tobias wrote, the film is about "nothing less than the joy of being alive." It's an incandescent trifle that nevertheless speaks to deep spiritual questions. What does it mean to be alive? Is it a gift wasted on the living? Does impending death inherently give life greater meaning?

Writer-director John Patrick Shanley—the successful screenwriter and playwright behind *Moonstruck,* who didn't direct another film until his 2008 adaptation of his play *Doubt*—establishes a storybook tone with an opening scrawl reading, "Once upon a time there was a man named Joe who had a very lousy job." This introduces us to our hero (Tom Hanks), a miserable sad sack with a ghostly pallor who joins an army of the damned as they trudge zombie-like to work each day at American Panascope, a gothic factory out of Charles Addams' morbid imagination. Hanks works for Mr. Waturi (the eternally Nixonian Dan Hedaya) at a company that manufactures both frightening-looking medical implements and human misery. It leaves its employees soul sick from buzzing fluorescent lights and deadening routines, stuck in a corporate hellhole that cheerfully trumpets dubious distinctions like "Home of the Rectal Probe," "50 Years of Petroleum Jelly," and the particularly suspicious "712765 Satisfied Customers."

Waturi essentially repeats endless minor variations on the same bit of dialogue—"But can he do the job? I know he can *get* the job, but can he *do* the job? I'm *not* arguing that with you. I'm not arguing that with *you*. I'm not *arguing* that with you. I'm not *arguing* that with you"—in a hellish loop. The effect is twofold: The repetition develops a hypnotic rhythm, and it conveys that Waturi has been having this same circular, meaningless conversation for years, if not decades. He's locked in the poisonous machine from which Joe is about to extricate himself permanently. When Joe complains that he doesn't feel well, Waturi responds with words that sum up the gray universe Joe currently inhabits: "You think I feel good? Nobody feels good. After childhood, it's a fact of life. I feel rotten. So what? I don't let it bother me."

So it's almost a relief when raging hypochondriac Joe learns from Dr. Ellison (Robert Stack) that he's contracted a mysterious condition called a "brain cloud" and has six months to live. Joe has been dying a long, slow, painful death since quitting the fire department years earlier. His impending departure from this world liberates him from the grim concerns of day-to-day life, especially after beetle-browed Manic Pixie Gazillionaire industrialist Samuel Harvey Graynamore (Lloyd Bridges) offers to let him "live like a king and die like a man" by sailing to the tropical island of Waponi Wu to appease its inhabitants by ritualistically sacrificing himself, jumping into a volcano so Graynamore can seize their natural resources as a reward.

Joe is a man reborn. He quits his job in a flurry of righteous indignation and asks out mousy coworker DeDe (Meg Ryan), who is turned on and a little terrified by Joe's newfound ferocity and lust for life. On their date, a skyline that loomed lifeless and dour as a lump of coal during the American Panascope sequences now seems lit from within by all the colors of the rainbow. Like Joe, it was once dead but now seems gloriously alive.

After scaring away DeDe with news of his imminent death via brain cloud, Joe learns about style from debonair limo driver Marshall (Ossie Davis, that sonorous-voiced exemplar of dignity and grace), who admonishes his slovenly protégé to do the right thing and splurge on dapper duds. It's a tricky role that borders on Magical Negro territory, but Davis pulls it off with such understated finesse that he makes materialism seem incongruously spiritual, as if getting the right clothes, accessories, and hairstyle are matters of profound moral importance.

Joe then ventures deep into Manic Pixie Dream Girl territory. In Los Angeles, Joe meets Graynamore's eccentric daughter Angelica (Ryan again, in a sparkly bustier and a halo of red curls), a pill-popping, deeply troubled poet/painter/flibbertigibbet with a breathless trill of a voice. Under her bubbly façade, she's broken and sad; she's less someone who can save Joe than a wounded creature in need of saving.

Existential ennui runs in the family. Angelica's more practical half-sister, Patricia (Ryan, yet again, now liberated from mousy wigs and hair dye, and almost oppressively adorable), retrieves Joe from Angelica and travels with him via a yacht headed to Waponi Wu, and explains, "We're on a little boat for a while and I'm soul sick. You're going to see that."

As with Joe, it takes a brush with death to re-ignite Patricia's lust for life. When their yacht capsizes during a typhoon, Patricia lingers unconscious, hovering somewhere between life and death for days. Joe occupies himself by cranking up a transistor radio playing "Come Go With Me" and launching into a gloriously geeky dance. His exuberance is infectious, his charm undeniable.

In *Joe Versus The Volcano*, Shanley smartly allowed songs to play long enough to brood, sulk, bleed, and develop a life of their own. After Joe learns of his brain cloud, Shanley lets Ray Charles' majestic take on "Ol' Man River" linger long enough for its broken-down grace to shine through and illuminate Hanks' miserable existence. A soundtrack that segues from the pessimism of "Sixteen Tons" to the infectious ebullience of "Good Loving" reflects Joe's dramatic evolution from suicidal despair to rapturous joy.

Before a death sentence allowed him to finally live, Joe couldn't imagine a world beyond his all-encompassing sadness; to him, history was destiny and life a long, joyless slog to the grave. He couldn't see the big, beautiful world beyond the fluorescent lights and ominous smokestacks belching out black clouds of toxic smoke at the factory where he sold his soul for $300 a week. Now Joe sees and feels everything: the majesty of a moon that dwarfs and consoles him, the beautiful melancholy of Patricia, the whole transcendent, aching wonder of the world.

Joe embraces his destiny, but he's come too far in too short a time to end it all. Joe and Patricia, having proclaimed their love for each other and gotten the quickest of quickie weddings, leap into the volcano together. But, as if sensing their newfound vitality, it spits them out into an ocean that sparkles like diamonds.

Oh, and that brain cloud? It's not a real medical condition but rather a sinister scheme to trick Joe into sacrificing himself. Joe and Patricia's future is uncertain; their world is now ripe with potential as they sail on to their next big adventure.

While gazing at Joe in the moonlight, Patricia earlier reflected, "My father says that almost the whole world is asleep. Everybody. Everybody you know, everybody you see, everybody you talk to. He says that only a few people are awake, and they live in a state of constant, total amazement." For 102 minutes, Shanley gives us a glimpse of what that must feel like.

It's easy to see why a cult has embraced a film considered a big disappointment upon its original release. In traveling an elegantly simple line from fatalism to optimism, *Joe Versus The Volcano* appeals to our sense that the world can be whatever we want it to be, that we are the masters of our own destiny. It's a film of bold, unabashed sincerity, a life-affirming fable about how failure can become success as long as we don't abandon hope. That's a lesson equally applicable to Joe and to many of the Case Files in this book, orphans just waiting for people to look at them with fresh eyes and recognize the beauty and truth in films haphazardly tossed into the dustbin of history by folks unwilling to look beyond their initial failure.

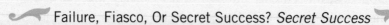 Failure, Fiasco, Or Secret Success? *Secret Success*

John Patrick Shanley On *Joe Versus The Volcano*

John Patrick Shanley has written 24 plays, including *Doubt* (2004), which won a Pulitzer Prize, and Tony, Obie, and Golden Globe awards. In addition to his playwriting, Shanley has written the screenplay for the movies *Five Corners, January Man, Alive, Congo,* and the romantic comedy *Moonstruck* (1987), for which he won an Academy Award for Best Original Screenplay. His experience directing *Joe Versus The Volcano* scarred him to the point where he didn't direct another film until the Oscar-nominated adaptation of *Doubt* in 2008.

John Patrick Shanley: *Joe Versus The Volcano* was actually an autobiographical film. I worked for a medical supply company that had terrifying medical instruments and artificial testicles and all that stuff, and I was very depressed [Laughs.] at the time that I was there. And then, by dint of writing movies, I ended up on a yacht off of L.A., going to Catalina, in just complete shock that I had come from the Bronx and ended up in this completely different environment because I wrote movies. The film was kind of an exploration of that strange path. It wasn't so much a movie about other movies as it was a movie about my perception of the things I was experiencing.

Nathan Rabin: When did you start working on the screenplay for *Joe Versus The Volcano,* and how did the story evolve?

JPS: What happened was, I wrote *Joe* as a spec screenplay, and I said to my agent, I've never said this before, "I think Steven Spielberg might like this." She sent it off to him, and then the Writers Guild strike hit. When I won the Academy Award for *Moonstruck,* I was on strike, so that was in 1987. While I was out there, Spielberg called me and said, "I read this screenplay. I really like it. I want to make it, and I think you should direct it." And I said, "Okay." And he said, "We should meet." And I said, "I can't, I'm on strike." And he said, "You can meet me as a director. The directors aren't on strike." And I said, "Oh, okay."

So I went over, and we talked, and we hit it off. We ended up working together for the better part of five years. *Joe* was one of the things we did, but we hung out and did a lot of stuff until I couldn't take the whole thing anymore and went back to New York. Actually, I worked with him from New York for a while too, but I just had to move on into other stuff.

So then when the strike was over, we went into pre-production and did the film, but it was a big, drawn-out preproduction. It was five months of pre-production, and then like a 70-something-day shoot, and then six months of postproduction. It was endless. So by the time it was over, I felt like my whole life had dried up and blown away. Then when the movie got this bad reception, I just thought, "Man, I've sacrificed everything to do this. I've been away from home for so long that I don't have any friends anymore, and I never want to go through this again." So that's what sort of drove me away from directing movies for a few years.

NR: I've read that you had trouble with Warner Bros. making the film.

JPS: It was a very basic thing. In pre-production, I storyboarded the entire movie. I brought in Mark Canton, who was one of the heads of Warner Bros. at that time, and I think Terry Semel. Terry Semel and Bob Daly were the heads of Warner Bros., and then Mark Canton was under them, him and Lucy Fisher. I went through this certainly with Mark Canton, Lucy Fisher, and I basically showed them the entire film, and they loved it. They said, "This is great, fantastic." Then I started shooting the movie, and they were like, "What's this?" And I said, "This is the movie." I shot exactly what I said I was going to shoot.

They were astonished and frightened of this at every step of the way, and I felt like I was in some sort of surreal conversation. I was like, "How can they be surprised?" I was so forthcoming with this information. They began to send voluminous notes to me about things that I should cut, things I should do differently, and I would have none of it. I offered to leave. I said, "Look, I'll go home," and this was in the middle of shooting. It happened three different times. One time, I called the car to take me to the airport, and each time they would back down. And they would say, "No, no." [Indistinct grumbling.]

Then the line producer came to me and said they weren't going to release the money to build the volcano, and this is—I don't know exactly how far, but it was way into the shoot. And I said, "What are they gonna call it, *Joe Versus The*? [Laughs.] What are you talking about? What do you mean they're not going to build the volcano?" They tried to hold this over my head, that they weren't going to build the volcano, and I said, "Of course we're going to build the volcano. What the hell are you talking about?" In the end, they had to release the money, and we built the volcano, but it was that kind of thing all through the movie. So it was very wearying, because all I was getting back was complete non-enthusiasm and negative comments and threats, and I was like, "I don't need this shit, let me go home."

NR: It seems like one of the reasons people responded to *Joe Versus The Volcano* was that it had a very clear, unique vision. That seems to scare studios.

JPS: It didn't connect with the broad audience. People went and saw it. It sold some tickets and it had its fans, but it was just a different time, you know? I just did a play, and there was some joke in the play, and before Barack Obama was elected, people laughed at the joke, but after he was elected they stopped, because it was a cynical joke.

And suddenly everybody was a true believer again, and that's how fast the culture changes sometimes. When I did *Joe*, I said to the cameraman, "I want you to treat the camera like it weighs 5,000 pounds and is difficult to move." Because I was just desperately tired of the highly mobile camera that was just doing these circular shots around round tables for no reason in movie after movie that I was seeing. I wanted to make a movie that was shot differently, that was edited differently, and that left significant time for the audience to have thoughts and feelings. So if an audience didn't want that time, they thought the movie was slow. I was saying, "No, spend some time within this frame, there's some stuff going on in this frame. Give yourself a second to pick up what it is." And they were not there. They were someplace else. Though, you know, *Joe Versus The Volcano* wasn't a financial failure. It cost $39 million, including Tom, and made $40 million.

NR: Why do you think it was perceived as a failure?

JPS: I think these things just sort of take over in a culture, and it came out of New York, because the *New York Times* hated the film and gave it a very bad review. It was a film that wasn't in sync at all with the times. A lot of audiences just didn't seem to have that music in them. They were in a different place. The rhythm of the film was very different for them. In the intervening years, it seems as though quite a lot of people have found that rhythm.

Full Circle Case File #1, Take 2: *Elizabethtown*
Originally Posted January 25, 2007; Revised

I'd like to end with a return to the beginning. Three years ago, I began a long, strange trip through cinematic failure with an essay about 2005's *Elizabethtown,* the first My Year Of Flops Case File, and one of the primary inspirations for the series. When we first contemplated turning My Year Of Flops into a book, my editor Keith proposed that I revisit *Elizabethtown* at the end of the process. I've now seen the film three times; the first before it came out, the second for the first My Year Of Flops entry, and now for the very last Case File of the book.

The idea was to look at the film that began it all with fresh eyes, to see how, or if, the journey changed me. Had I, in the parlance of lobbyists, gone native? Had I spent so much time trying to see the good in films generally considered unambiguously bad that I was capable of appreciating anything, no matter how wretched? So I decided to rewatch *Elizabethtown* shortly before turning in the book, and I was shocked, horrified, and strangely delighted to discover just how radically my take on it had shifted. This journey has changed me. I'm in a better place emotionally. For example, I no longer consider joy and happiness my enemies. So I'm a much more receptive audience for Cameron Crowe when he evangelizes for community, kindness, and common decency. Three years of My Year Of Flops have instilled in me an eagerness to see the good in everything.

Elizabethtown is a remarkable specimen in the history of cinematic failure, in that it is both a flop and a meta-meditation on failure. So when its characters deliver aphorisms about the secret glory of failure ("Those who risk, win." "No fiasco ever began as a quest for mere adequacy." "You have five minutes to wallow in the delicious misery. Enjoy it, embrace it, discard it. And proceed."), they seem to be commenting on the film and preemptively consoling its creator.

When I first saw *Elizabethtown,* it rattled my soul. I was apoplectic. I came close to stopping random strangers on the street and complaining about it. Though I had been primed by months of bad buzz, I could not believe that a man as talented as Crowe could create a film this singularly, devastatingly bad.

Elizabethtown is incredibly ballsy in a girly-man sort of way. If, as the Smiths proposed, it's easy to laugh and hate but takes strength to be gentle and kind, then Crowe is the world's strongest man and *Elizabethtown* is his masterpiece, a film of hardcore niceness and explicit sensitivity.

The film is an auteurial endeavor in the truest sense: Crowe lurks proudly behind every unnecessarily verbose wisecrack, every lovingly handcrafted bit of homemade philosophy, every cutesy exchange. And that bugged the hell out of me the first time around. And the second time around. I resented that the film was populated less by human beings than magical sprites whose lives seemingly revolved around teaching a sad young man that it's a wonderful world even if you're responsible for the athletic-shoe design equivalent of the *Hindenburg.* Rewatching it I found this vision of the universe as infinitely kind oddly touching. In the past few years my defenses have become less formidable, perhaps because the world has been very kind to me as well; I have a wonderful girlfriend, a great job, have put out some books, and inexplicably have a semi-indulgent audience for my foolishness.

After watching *Elizabethtown* three times, I became a cultist by default. I have spent 369 minutes in Elizabethtown. I came to know the geography awfully well. I discovered that I was looking at *Elizabethtown* all wrong. As a film about human beings residing in the American South, it's preposterous, overwritten, mannered, and precious. But as a big-hearted fairy tale populated by enchanted creatures that takes place in a Kentucky that exists only in Crowe's imagination, it's strangely irresistible as well as preposterous, overwritten, mannered, and precious. I checked my cynicism at the door and gave myself over to the beguiling tenderness of Crowe's vision. (And to the music in his iPod. *Elizabethtown* is ragingly imperfect, but its soundtrack is a thing of beauty.)

Our maddeningly blank hero Drew (Orlando Bloom) begins the film as the man behind the most disastrous product launch since New Coke: Mercury Shoes' Spasmotica. Drew's boss, Phil Devoss (Alec Baldwin), runs Mercury Shoes as a cross between a dot-com start-up at the height of the Internet bubble and a benign cult. Its employees aren't just worker bees, they're "denizens of greatness." At Mercury, success is a secular religion and failure is heresy. So when Drew is flown to company headquarters to face a grim reckoning, the employees regard him with looks of pity mixed with scorn.

It's the closest Drew will ever come to attending his own funeral. This invites the question, "Why would a successful company like Mercury invest nearly a billion dollars in a shoe without testing it extensively?"

In moments like this, it's important to remember that *Elizabethtown* is an American fairy tale. Fairy tales play by a different set of rules. No child has ever demanded to know the scientific basis for Snow White being woken from an endless slumber by her true love's kiss. Crowe plays everything big. So it's fitting that Drew's boondoggle should be world-class and unprecedented. Any fool can accomplish failure. It takes a special kind of dreamer to lose a company a billion dollars.

Drew decides to commit suicide, but before he can head to the great corporate retreat in the sky, he receives a call from his sister, Heather (Judy Greer), informing him of their father's death. Suddenly he has a reason to live. He'll head down to the titular locale, drop off his beloved father's blue suit, then head straight back home and commit suicide. Here's what his lifetime checklist looks like:

1. Drop off blue suit in Kentucky
2. Kill myself

Little does he suspect that the entire world is conspiring on a massive plot to turn his frown upside down and restore his lost faith in humanity and himself. The conspiracy of joy's chief agent is an almost psychotically perky stewardess/Manic Pixie Dream Girl named Claire, played by Kirsten Dunst. Claire decides she's going to fill his soul with sunshine even if she has to kill him in the process. While bidding Drew good-bye, possibly for the last time, she leaves him with the parting words, "Look, I know I may never see you again, but we are intrepid. We carry on."

When Drew finally hits Elizabethtown, every front lawn becomes a Norman Rockwell painting: children bouncing ecstatically on a trampoline, a shaggy-haired kid mowing a lawn, American flags waving happily in the breeze. Everyone shoots him a smile and a wave that implicitly says, "You seem to be suffering from a crippling, perhaps failed-shoe-related suicidal depression. That's nothing a few enchanted days in our magical town won't cure."

That night, Drew's girlfriend (Jessica Biel) dumps him by phone as he juggles calls from her, his sister, and Claire. In Crowe's benevolent world, when Jessica Biel dumps you, you literally have your next gorgeous love interest on the other line. That night, Drew and Claire fall in love over the phone in a thrilling sequence that captures the butterflies and manic energy of fresh infatuation. Suddenly, the breathless bigness of Crowe's dialogue seems perfect. What is flirtation, if not an attempt to make ourselves seem cooler, smarter, and infinitely more clever than we actually are? Drew and Claire are trying to impress each other with their wit, wisdom, and verbal dexterity just as thoroughly as Crowe is trying to dazzle us.

Drew reconnects with his family at a potluck where cousin Jessie Baylor (Paul Schneider) announces theatrically, "This loss will be met with a hurricane of love." I nearly groaned when I first heard that line; by the third time, it struck me as equally cringe-inducing and heartwarming, in large part due to Schneider's laid-back charm. If anyone can sell that line, it's Schneider. Jessie epitomizes everything I love about Crowe. He easily could have come off as a cartoon redneck, but when Schneider's character tells his father (Loudon Wainwright III), "I teach [my son] about Abraham Lincoln *and* Ronnie Van Zant, because in my house, they are both of equal importance," it's ridiculous, but also glorious. As someone who venerates music, former teen rock journalist Crowe is not one to cast judgment on, well, anything. So if Jessie is disproportionately proud of the time his old group Ruckus almost opened for Lynyrd Skynyrd, there's something sweet and endearing about that as well.

A revitalized Drew ends the film by embarking on a road trip Claire has organized seemingly down to the second, accompanied by a mixtape of songs beloved by either spacey twentysomething stewardesses or former rock journalists in their late 40s.

The road trip might be the quintessential sequence in Crowe's career; it's nothing but sound, image, music, history, and the world outside exploding with life, color, and vitality through the windshield and the rearview mirror. It's Crowe's love letter to the South, to road trips, to mixtapes, to music, to God's own United States. Claire, of course, is the pot of gold at the end of this rainbow. Twenty thousand roads Drew goes down, down, down, and they all lead straight back home to Claire.

Elizabethtown is blessed and cursed with an incredible generosity of spirit. Crowe loves everyone and everything. Crowe shows us not who we are, but who we could conceivably become. His films are aspirational rather than realistic. Like Frank Capra, Crowe wants to show us what life could be like if we were all just kinder, more hopeful, and had better taste in music. So it would be churlish of me not to match Crowe's tremendous generosity of spirit with my own.

As one of her many life lessons, Claire tells Drew, "You want to be really great? Then fail big and have the courage to stick around and make 'em wonder why you're still smiling. That's true greatness to me." Accordingly, I hope the two-and-a-half-hour-long cut of *Elizabethtown* makes it to DVD someday. Crowe hasn't made a film since *Elizabethtown*. Nevertheless, I have faith in Crowe. He is intrepid. He will carry on. So will we all.

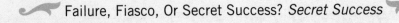 Failure, Fiasco, Or Secret Success? *Secret Success*

Death Is Not The End: An Afterword

As *Joe Versus The Volcano* indelibly conveys, death sentences can sometimes be illusory. Being diagnosed with a fatal brain cloud can become an invitation to embrace life. Dying at the box office is not the end. Devastating reviews are not the end. There is always hope. A film's reputation is not static; it evolves over time. Critics and audiences rendered harsh, even cruel verdicts on the films in this book. Hell, I often rendered harsh, even cruel verdicts on the films in this book. But history can be kinder. Yesterday's failures sometimes become tomorrow's masterpieces.

Hope springs eternal every time someone pops in a DVD or the lights go down in a movie theater. At this very moment, there is a brave soul out there deciding that maybe *Waterworld* isn't so bad. There's a weird kid who's discovered that *Freddy Got Fingered* is his all-time favorite movie. Every day, we're afforded the opportunity to rebel against the tyranny of mass opinion.

As a troubled youth, movies provided me with a means of escaping the world. As an adult, they're a way of engaging with the world. My Year Of Flops began as one man's journey deep into the heart of cinematic failure, but it quickly became a communal experience. The Internet is often a powerful incubator for cynicism and spite, but it can also be a glorious conduit for love, so it has been deeply satisfying to see how many people share my passion for movies like *Heaven's Gate, Ishtar, The Apple, Pennies From Heaven,* and dozens of other Secret Successes that didn't make it into this book.

I began My Year Of Flops not to bury cinematic failures but to praise them. I have strayed early and often from that mission, yet I've tried my damnedest to live up to the good intentions I laid out in my introduction. I love the idea of watching, thinking about, and writing about movies *because* of their resounding failure with critics and audiences, not in spite of it.

My alliteration- and malapropism-prone father sometimes accidentally refers to My Year Of Flops as "My Decade Of Disasters" or "My Century Of Calamities." Could documenting cinematic failures be my life's work? Have I found my true calling? I don't know. So I encourage you to embark on your own Year Of Flops. Don't let a cultural consensus scare you away from these films. This may be the end of the book, but it isn't the end of this journey, for you or for me.

Appendix: *Waterworld*: Director's Cut, Minute-By-Minute

In *You'll Never Make Love In This Town Again,* a transcendentally trashy tell-all by an all-star aggregation of dirty, dirty whores, a high-priced call girl recounts a memorable encounter with James Caan. Caan, it seems, loves oral sex. (And you thought this book wouldn't be educational!) When it comes to oral pleasure, Caan is a believer in the aphorism, "'Tis better to give than to receive." So he spent three or four hours performing cunnilingus on the prostitute.

At first, it was exciting. Sonny Corleone was feasting lustily on her honeypot! Then her legs started to cramp and mild enthusiasm turned to annoyance and frustration. By the two-hour mark, her mind had probably left her body and she was reduced to thinking random thoughts like, "Why did we reject the metric system? It was good enough for the rest of the world. Why must we always be so god-damned different? Why do we always have to be the lone wolf?" By the three-hour mark, she was probably ready to give Caan his money back if only he would stop.

I share this anecdote not to pollute your mind with the horrifying image of Caan's leathery visage covered in vaginal secretions and pubic hair, but rather to illustrate that even something widely considered pleasurable—receiving oral sex from a *Godfather* cast member—can become tedious and even excruciating if done for too long. Everything wears out its welcome eventually.

But what happens when you devote three endless hours to something you've found borderline unbearable even in a much shorter version? To find out, I decided to watch the 177-minute director's cut of the 1995 boondoggle *Waterworld* and record my observations on a minute-by-minute basis. Why? So you wouldn't have to. (Oh, and if you're looking for a correlation between the preceding paragraphs and what you're about to read, Caan reportedly turned down the villain role in *Waterworld*, which eventually went to Dennis Hopper.)

1:03—*Waterworld* opens with the Universal globe logo losing its landmass and devolving into some sort of world of water, accompanied by the mellifluous sounds of Hal Douglas, a prolific trailer voice-over artist, doing a mild variation on his "In a world where . . ." shtick. When Douglas melodramatically intones, "The future—the polar ice caps have melted, covering the Earth with water. Those who survive have adapted to a new *world*," I'm reminded of Criswell's *Plan 9 From Outer Space* narration, which includes the line, "We are all interested in the future, for that is where you and I are going to spend the rest of our lives." That's probably not what the filmmakers intended.

1:34—*Waterworld* opens with a tight close-up of Kevin Costner's ass in striped leather pants, followed by . . .

2:06—Urine filtration/guzzling!

3:57—Costner's character, Mariner, is pruning his bonsai tree. He may guzzle urine, but he's no philistine.

5:32—Popular sartorial statements in a Dry Land–free hellscape: soggy leather and camouflage vests, chokers, fingerless gloves, and loincloths.

11:18—Mariner's lowly drifter has some dirt. This makes him King Shit of Fuck Mountain in his World of Water, and the atoll where he comes to pimp his wares.

20:26—An old woman requests Mariner's "seed," then pushes a teen girl in front of him as an old man pleads, "We can look to our own for impregnation, but too much of that sort of thing, it's *undesirable*." Pimping a relative to Kevin Costner = better than inbreeding?

24:35—While Mariner rots in a cage, atoll dwellers go through his belongings as part of a makeshift justice system, singling out, for example, a grimy ThighMaster as "what appears to be a torturing device!" (It sure is, am I right or am I right, ladies?)

25:31—Theoretically sexy store-proprietor/atoll dweller Helen (Jeanne Tripplehorn) proposes that Mariner's dirt may have come from a mysterious utopia known as Dry Land. This earns indignant snickers. That's about as far fetched as a man-animal learning how to read, use weapons, or operate a vehicle!

31:38—An imprisoned Mariner tries to hit crazy Old Gregor (Michael Jeter) for asking whether his gills are vestigial or functional. In spite of his rage, Mariner is still just a pee-drinking man-fish in a cage.

34:26—For being a threat to the atoll, Mariner is sentenced "to be recycled in the customary fashion," that is, killed. Looks like the movie is going to end two hours and 26 minutes early. Sweet!

37:49—Or not. A group of malevolent, cigarette enthusiasts/pirates known as the Smokers pick a narratively convenient time to attack the atoll. Don't blink, or you'll miss Jack Black's star-making turn as Pilot.

38:31—Stuff is blowing up good.

39:20—Finally, a post-apocalyptic movie with Jet Skis and waterskiing! It's like a cross between summer fun in Cape Cod and Al Gore's worst nightmare.

40:41—A dude water-skis up a ramp and crash-lands on Mariner's cage, freeing him.

41:04—If you're following along at home with the *Waterworld: Director's Cut* DVD, please stop. I get paid to do this. You have no excuse, and hopefully more productive uses for your time and energy. Have you considered reading to blind orphans? Deaf orphans? Orphans too lazy to read?

45:00—Dear God, I'm only a quarter of the way through this.

48:02—Mariner triumphantly reunites with his bonsai tree!

49:03—Why is Smoker leader Deacon (Dennis Hopper) wearing a codpiece over his pants? Isn't that redundant? He must *really* need to protect his junk. And what's with Deacon's medal-festooned post-apocalyptic Sgt. Pepper look?

54:03—Hopper's performance in a nutshell: He removes a handkerchief covering his mutilated eye and quips, "We better keep an *eye* out for that icky freak!" Apparently Mr. Freeze ghostwrote Hopper's dialogue.

56:11—I may have misjudged Mariner, as he just offered to take Helen to the fabled Dry Land. He's less indulgent toward Enola (Tina Majorino), an orphan with a mysterious tattoo rumored to be a map to Dry Land on her back. Mariner grouses of his prepubescent charge, "The kid, we gotta pitch over the side!"

56:37—More lovable banter from our hero: "It's better that one of you dies now than both of you die slow."

57:30—Helen offers to have sex with Mariner if he agrees not to murder Enola. What a fun scene to re-create with Hasbro's line of *Waterworld* action figures!

59:00—Mariner has difficulty trusting the motives of those without gills and webbed feet. Don't we all?

59:12—Our intrepid mutant antihero rejects Helen with a cold, "You got nothing I need." He seems like he'd be more into dolphins anyway.

59:44—Mariner is awfully butch for a man-fish wearing a choker, leather vest with no shirt, and seashell earring.

1:05:04—But he isn't entirely heartless: When Helen asks for some of his filtered piss water for Enola, he glares at her, chugs some, waters his bonsai, then gives Enola the last few drops.

1:06:07—Enola repays Mariner's generosity by chirping, "Thanks for not killing us!"

1:07:37—The uneasy peace is broken when Mariner loses his shit upon discovering Enola using his green crayon. Don't touch his fucking crayon, little girl. He's killed people for less. Much less.

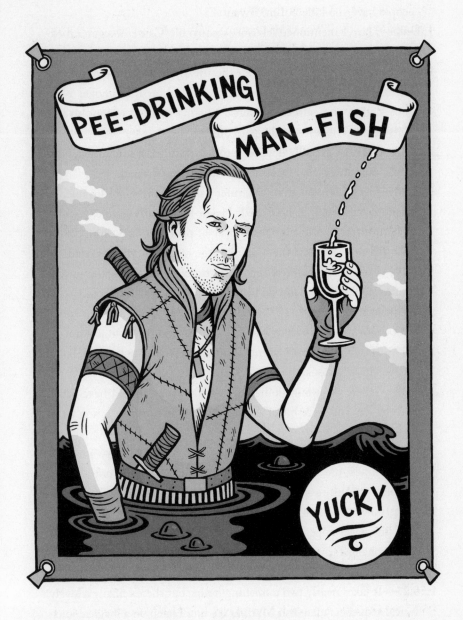

1:08:50—More adorable banter from Enola to Mariner: "How many people have you killed? Ten? Twenty?"

1:09:00—Have I mentioned Mariner's ponytail? 'Cause he's got a fucking ponytail. Oh, and he just threw Enola overboard in a fit of anger.

1:16:49—A key difference between the theatrical and director's cut of *Waterworld*: more screen time for Jack Black as the Smoker pilot. Those letters and calls to Universal begging them to restore his role to its original majesty finally paid off.

1:18:30—Mariner greedily devours a tomato while the sunburned, half-mad Enola and Helen look on with naked desperation.

1:22:40—Just when you think Mariner can't get any more lovable, he offers to trade half an hour with Helen to a clearly insane, possibly violent drifter in exchange for a piece of paper but kicks him off the boat before he can seal the deal. The Age of Chivalry is not dead.

1:42:10—I wondered, before I began this experiment, if Stockholm syndrome would kick in and I'd begin sympathizing with my cinematic tormentor. Otherwise, 177 minutes is an awful long time to spend with a movie you don't like. Nope. It's still fucking terrible, just longer.

1:45:00—If this were a normal movie, it would be over by now. Hell, it'd be over 15 minutes ago.

1:46:09—"There's nothing human about you! They should have killed you the day you were born!" Helen screams at Mariner, acting as an audience surrogate.

1:46:30—In a weird bit of flop meta-textual motherfuckery, in *Cable Guy*'s climax, the title character screams, "Dry Land is not a myth! I've seen it!" before saying he can't see what all the fuss is about: He's seen *Waterworld* nine times and thinks it rules. It's worth noting that that line never appears in *Waterworld*. Like "Play it again, Sam," it's apocryphal. Mariner says Dry Land is a myth, and Helen says, "I've seen it," but that's as close as the film gets.

1:50:21—It takes nearly two punishing hours, but there's finally a lovely, lyrical sequence: man-fish Mariner leading Helen on a magical journey under the sea to the abandoned ruins of a long-lost civilization. It also explains where Mariner gets all that magnificent dirt; he's a fish, so of course he can treat the ocean's bottom like an all-you-can-scoop dirt buffet.

1:53:17—Here come the Smokers, and the ugliness returns. In their first scene together, Deacon (who was so voracious in chewing scenery that he apparently devoured Earth's entire landmass) calls Mariner "sperm of the devil" instead of "spawn of the devil." Mistake? Tweaking of a cliché? Who the hell cares?

2:01:56—Mariner and Helen reach the stage in every relationship where the woman asks the man why he didn't accept her earlier offer of sexual favors in exchange for passage on his vessel. This leads to a clammy, awkward kiss. I haven't seen sexual chemistry this explosive since Justin Guarini wooed Kelly Clarkson in *From Justin To Kelly* with text messages like, "Kelly, I O U A BRGR. U GAME? JUSTIN." Tripplehorn must be glad she wasn't typecast as a fish-fucker after *Waterworld*. That nearly ruined Deanna Durbin *and* Troy McClure's careers.

2:03:48—Mariner has grown less emotionally and physically abusive over the last 20 minutes. This, friends, is what screenwriters call a "redemptive arc."

2:04:12—"I am what I am. I may not be human, but I don't quit, never have," Mariner boasts, proving that humans do not have a monopoly on being 2 legit 2 quit. Or ripping off Popeye.

2:05:46—Crazy Old Gregor returns in a homemade hot-air balloon not unlike the one Austin Pendleton and Jackie Gleason use to escape prison in *Skidoo*. It's funny how flops tend to echo one another, as if they're all one misbegotten organism with a collective consciousness.

2:05:49—Gregor tells Mariner that it's "mighty human" of him to save Helen from certain death. As an action adventure, *Waterworld* is grim and endless, but as an elaborate allegory for racism and the challenges faced by the multiracial, it's also fucking terrible.

2:13:41—The Smokers, having absconded with Enola, propose cutting the tattoo off her back, stretching it, and mounting it. Enola doesn't seem pleased with this idea. Deacon talks to a picture of his hero, "Saint Joe," disgraced *Exxon Valdez* captain Joseph Hazelwood.

Hazelwood got a bad rap: Who hasn't gotten drunk and crashed an oil tanker? It's a rite of passage in many small towns.

2:20:00—Enola brags of Mariner, "He even kills little girls," to which her Smoker tormentor replies, "Haven't we all?"

2:20:59—Deacon waxes poetic, enthusing, "If there's a river, we'll dam it. If there's a tree, we'll ram it. Because I'm talking progress here! I'm talking development. We shall *suck* and *savor* the sweet *flavor* of Dry Land!" Unlike Joyce Kilmer, Hopper shall never see / a poem as shitty as a tree.

2:21:08—Now a Smoker is threatening to put out a lit cigarette in Enola's eye after she sasses him once too often.

2:25:26—Deacon, upon Mariner showing up on his turf, the rusty remains of the *Exxon Valdez*: "Well, I'll be damned. It's the Gentleman Guppie. He's like a toilet that won't flush." Great bad dialogue, or just bad? I spent many a happy hour at the Gentleman Guppie back in college. Good times.

2:25:53—Deacon calls Mariner a "total slime-o." Really, that's the best you can do?

2:26:43—Mariner says he's come for Enola because "she's my friend." My response is the same as Deacon's, a witheringly sarcastic, "Golly gee, a single tear rolls down my cheek!"

2:27:37—The *Exxon Valdez* blows up good.

2:28:00—It's safe to assume the words "Gee, Dennis, you might want to rein it in a little" were never uttered on the *Waterworld* set.

2:28:05—When Enola tauntingly asks, "Was this your big vision?" as the *Valdez* burns, she could be addressing director Kevin Reynolds and Costner as easily as Hopper.

2:30:30—The hero is finally behaving heroically, racing around the oil tanker killing baddies and trying to save Enola. How deliciously out of character.

2:32:02—To give the sperm of the devil its due, the climax to *Waterworld* qualifies as moderately rousing.

2:32:50—More stuff blowing up good. It's a recurring visual motif.

2:33:15—After the *Exxon Valdez* goes down, Deacon emerges from the wreckage to fire a single shot at Gregor's hot-air balloon that causes Enola to tumble gracelessly out of the dirigible and into the water below. I am beginning to question the film's commitment to verisimilitude.

2:34:08—Mariner bungee-jumps into the water to retrieve Enola, then soars back into the hot-air balloon just in time to escape the fiery aftermath of three Smoker Jet Skis colliding as, yet again, shit blows up good. *Waterworld* is again starting to strain credibility.

2:37:03—It's taken 157 minutes, but they finally reach Dry Land! It's not just a myth! I've now seen it with my own eyes!

2:38:29—Dry Land is even more of a green paradise than I could ever have imagined! Enola finds a music box, plays it, and dreamily announces, "I'm home," thereby satisfying the film's government-mandated quota of treacle.

2:40:25—Dry Land has horsies! Majestic, majestic horsies. But does it have kittens? And rainbows? And lollipops?

2:44:37—Alas, Mariner must return to the sea whence he came. It's all very *Shane*; I half expect Enola to call out to him as he leaves, "Surly Pee-Drinking Man-Fish! Come back!"

2:47:31—Helen dusts off a plaque commemorating Edmund Hillary's trek up Mount Everest. *That's* your big reveal?

2:57:00—It's over! It's finally over! The long national nightmare of me watching/writing up the nearly three-hour-long director's cut of *Waterworld* is over! I feel liberated. And exhausted. And hungry. And relieved that soon I will never have to watch, think, or write about *Waterworld* ever again.

Acknowledgments

I would like to thank my agent, Daniel Greenberg, and editor, Brant Rumble, for making this book happen, and my colleagues and friends Keith Phipps, Scott Tobias, and Tasha Robinson for their invaluable input, editing, and all-around awesomeness. Danny Hellman, thank you for your amazing illustrations. I have been blessed with an amazing team over at Scribner, including Anna deVries, Christina Mamangakis, Kate Bittman, and Amber Husbands, and the greatest group of co-workers anyone could ever want here at *The A.V. Club*: Stephen Thompson, who took a chance on me as a green college kid; Donna Bowman; Josh Modell; Kyle Ryan; Amelie Gillette; Noel Murray; Sam Adams; Sean O'Neal; Steve Hyden; Steve Heisler; Genevieve Koski; Claire Zulkey; Emily Withrow; Jesse Woghan; Leonard Pierce; Andy Battaglia; and Todd VanDerwerff. I'd also like to thank all *The Onion* comedy writers past and present, especially the folks I knew back from my Madison days: Rob Siegel, Todd Hanson, Carol Kolb, Chris Karwowski, Maria Schneider, Joe Garden, Mike Loew, Jim Anchower, Jean Teasdale, and Ben Karlin. Also, Steve Hannah and all the bookstores who were kind enough to host me during my *Big Rewind* tour.

Other people who have improved my life immeasurably through their presence: my beloved Danya and the Maloons, Mary Lou Coyle, Lori Rush, Dr. Eisenberg, Dr. Bloom, Aaron Perna, Steve Delahoyde, Michelle Welch, Monika Verma, Chuck Klosterman, Jennifer Cohn, everyone I interviewed here, Josh Kendall, Squirt, Maggie May, Sweetie Pie, Bandit, Paul DeGrassi, Matthew Lurie, Amy Allen Schleicher, my dad, Anna, Shari Lisa, Louis, Judy, Benjamin, Seth, Ephrem, Mary and Beth Rabin, everyone who purchased *The Big Rewind,* the Sackses, the Gerbers, Stephanie Kuenn, Allison Tobias, Isabelle Tobias, Bob, Mark Bazer, Joseph Gibson, ZODIAC MOTHERFUCKER, Roger Ebert, Mike Sacks, Cameron Crowe, everyone at *Movie Club with John Ridley* and *Switch,* Edgar Wright and Patton Oswalt for supporting the column and generally being great.

Thank you, world, for allowing me to do what I love for a living. I will forever be grateful.